BIG
BABIES

BIG BABIES

Or: Why Can't We
Just Grow Up?

MICHAEL BYWATER

Granta Books
London

Granta Publications, 2/3 Hanover Yard,
Noel Road, London N1 8BE

First published in Great Britain by Granta Books 2006

A CIP catalogue record for this book
is available from the British Library.

1 3 5 7 9 10 8 6 4 2

ISBN-13: 978-1-86207-883-3
ISBN-10: 1-86207-883-1

Typeset by M Rules
Printed and bound in Great Britain by
William Clowes Ltd, Beccles, Suffolk

For my daughter Ditta, a grown-up

Acknowledgements

As always, I owe a debt of gratitude to all those whose conversation, suggestions and help I have shamelessly exploited, and who have put up with my infantile tantrums over the composition of this book.

I should explicitly like to thank the Master and Fellows of Magdalene College Cambridge for electing me as Writer-in-Residence, a post whose duties seemed largely to consist of (a) writing and (b) residing, leavened by evenings at the College's table which exemplified that happiest of all the grown-up virtues, commensality. As Dr Donne wrote:

> *The University is a Paradise: Rivers of Knowledge are there, Arts and Sciences flow from thence. Counsell Tables are Horti conclusi, (as it is said in the Canticles) Gardens that are walled in, and they are Fontes signati, Wells that are sealed up; bottomless depths of unsearchable Counsels there.*

I wish I had been able to make a more fitting tribute to their hospitality but gratitude will have to supply where accomplishment falls short.

For the rest: you well know who you are: *concede ut tibi debitum obseqium praestare valeo.*

Contents

CHAPTER 1

What on Earth Is Going On Here?

Something Has Gone Wrong

Something has gone wrong.

We all know it. Of course we do. Even if we haven't seen it for ourselves, we know something has gone wrong.

Perhaps we are among the fortunate ones who look at the world and see nothing but improvements. Perhaps we are rational: when things seem black, we may make little lists of how things are getting better.

But it doesn't really help. We still know that something has gone wrong.

We know that something has gone wrong from the media, from its shrill infatuation with yobs and chavs, sodomitical politicians and drug-fried popsters, lurching nouveaux and dumbed-down telly, paedophiles and mullahs, black men and pension funds, carcinoma and speed cameras, disintegrating railways and diabolist rappers, skimped maintenance and dodgy travel companies and a terrible, overarching conspiracy against something called (though seldom directly referred to as) 'decency', defined only by its absence.

We know that something has gone wrong from walking round our towns, with their dead hearts and street furniture, chain stores and electronic goods, slouching youths and inarticulate ape-cries – 'Ooooouurrggggh! Oooooourrrghaaaooo!' – in the early hours, their gum-flecked pavements, their concrete-hangar malls, their parking schemes and invisible cops, their 'city rangers' with bulging utility-belts, their grilles and burger-joints, their litter and their obese, sportswear-clad, snarling, crop-haired families yoked in greed and hatred, their slashed prices, their ugliness, their interest-free deals with the hint of bulky bailiffs and Tums-scoffing repo men behind the sharking grin of the Pay-Nothing-for-a-Year sales staff.

We know something has gone wrong from the television, with its endless multiplexing death-dance of desperate, pointless and uncelebrated celebrities, its Roman entertainments predicated on humiliation, sadism and contempt, its grotesque sentimentalising of an imaginary, florid and sumptuous past.

We know something has gone wrong from the glossy magazines, populous with Eurotrash and really, really exciting designers with no actual mention of what they actually design, actually ('Tamasin Leuchtentrager d'Isigny Cholmondely-Knobbe invites us into the elegant Provençal holiday home she shares with her husband, Russian extortionist and former KGB hit-man energy billionaire Evgeny Tolstoyevsky') and desperate greed, anorexia, commodification and flat-eyed emptiness.

We know something has gone wrong from books. The *I-Was-a-Victim* books, the *Why-Your-Doctor-Hates-You-and-Wants-You-to-Die* books, the *How-I-Was-Terribly-Terribly-Abused-but-Survived-to-Write-This-Book* books, the *Whatever-You-Do-You-Will-Never-be-Acceptable* books, the *Read-This-Book-if-You-Want-a-Hope-in-Hell-of-Keeping-Your-Job* books, the executive bullshit books and the life-coaching books and the phoney instant spirituality books and the angel books and, of course, the *Why-Does-Everyone-Hate-America?* books and the *Why-Does-America-Hate-Everyone-Else?* books and the *How-Did-We-Get-Stuck-with-George-Bush/Tony-Blair?* books and, of course, the *Everything-Is-Shit* books . . . And if some enterprising publisher were to come up with a series of little something-has-gone-wrong-but-there's-worse-to-come books, they would make a fortune. *Chant Your Way to Cancer. Eat what You Like and Remain Horribly Fat. Heart Disease: Nothing You Can do About It. Fifty Reasons Nobody Will Ever Love You Again. Yes, Your Mother Hated You and You Know What? She Was Right.* Oh, there's a market there all right.

There is.

Because something has gone wrong.

The Odd Thing

The odd thing, though, is that it has gone so far undiagnosed. There was a time when doctors knew little and could cure less, and instead of diagnosis they did translation. You would go to the doctor with a sore tongue and throat and he would make you say 'Ahhh' and push your tongue down with a little spatula and then he would say 'Ah' and you would say 'Ahhh?' and he would say 'You have glossopharyngitis' and charge you a guinea. But all he had done was describe back to you what you had already described to him, except he described it back in Greek, which was worth a guinea of anyone's money.

This is what the media do now. We know that something has gone wrong, and the media describe it back to us. We know that Donald Rumsfeld is as slippery as hell, so we buy books and newspapers telling us so. We know that our civil liberties are being carefully and maliciously eroded under the guise of 'Homeland Security', so we buy books and newspapers which inform us that our civil liberties are being carefully and maliciously eroded under the guise of 'Homeland Security' . . . and somehow we feel we have got our money's worth.

The mechanism is venerable. It used to be called 'religion' and worked on a very simple cycle:

1. Acquire a set of unshakeable but ill-founded prejudices, whether by culture, birth, conversion or coercion.
2. Pay to have those prejudices confirmed.
3. Repeat step (2).

This may sound absurdly simplistic, but think about it. Suppose (to take a most improbable example) you decided, or were told and chose to believe, that the world was created by an invisible person who, despite all the evidence that he occasionally disliked us but was mostly indifferent, actually loved us and thought about us all the time. Suppose, piling absurdity upon improbability, you also decided, or were told, and chose to believe, that this same person decided to split himself in two and turn one part of himself into an ordinary person like you or me, and pay a visit to a desert tribe and get himself executed for treason; at which point he performed a conjuring trick, came back from the dead, vanished mysteriously but planned to return and punish all the bad people and make everything nice (though in the meantime, the bad people could go on getting away with it and the good people could go on getting buggered up by the bad people – that is, when they weren't getting cancer, or run over, or bankrupt, or tortured, or flogged or worked like beasts or raped or killed in power struggles which were nothing to do with them).

Suppose you were misguided enough to believe that lot. What would you do?

Would you devote all your spare hours to finding someone who would disabuse you of these intensely peculiar delusions, so that you could finally sleep at night? Or would you go, once a week or more, to listen to someone telling you that you were quite right, and everything you believed was true, and, what's more, if you ever stopped believing it, terrible things would happen to you even *after* you had died?

4

The Answer Is Obvious

You would want to be comforted; to be told that you were right. And that's what the media do. It's what advertising and marketing and PR do, and executives mouthing nonsense at press conferences, and computerised voices at railway stations saying 'I am very sorry for the delay'. It is what the talking gas-flames in the gas advertisements ('Oh, I say, let's use up some gas!') do, and the little 'badges' you get for writing reviews on Amazon, and what Todd Stitzer, CEO of Cadbury Schweppes, does when he says, 'It's one of the funnest jobs to be responsible for a company that provides so much fun.' It is what Microsoft does when your computer offers you the talking paperclip or the cute doggy that wags its tail to show that it's doing a searchy-wearchy for a docky-wocky . . .

They are all doing one essential thing. They are drawing you – drawing us – into the circle of reinforced false beliefs.

⚠ 'The customer can count on us to synergistically administrate world-class resources and assertively revolutionize effective leadership skills while promoting personal employee growth.'

- 'Our mission is in combining infrastructure solutions, technology leadership and business insight to achieve business goals.'
- 'It is our mission to globally maintain value-added meta-services while promoting personal employee growth.'
- 'We exist to interactively facilitate unique sources.'

Three of these mission statements are from the Dilbert Mission Statement Generator (<http://www.dilbert.com/comics/dilbert/games/career/bin/ms.cgi>). One is from a real company. Can *you* tell?

We could trade examples endlessly: call centres and yellow 'Wet Floor' bollards and dancing food and personal development, old guys on Harley Davidsons and Homeland Security and 'respect'; *Modern & Mature* magazine and hair products and beauty products and iPods and PlayStations and WordsRunTogether. We could go on about mission statements and bonding weekends, name bloat, cancer and acronyms, moist toilet tissue and Pret A Manger, Woolworths and Botox and bukkake and warnings and street furniture and gym bunnies and Google and porridge and Cheese Whizz and date rape and soft-shelled-crab bibs . . . and it would get us nowhere.

Not until we realise what is actually happening. What all these things mean. Why we have this sense that something has gone wrong. Why we have a curious feeling of insubstantiality, as though we are somehow gaseous and our lives untethered, although, in reality, this is (materially at least) perhaps the best time in human history to be alive.

So let us have a diagnosis.

Here Are the Results. Perhaps You Should Take a Seat

What is wrong is this: you are a Big Baby.

Or, to put it more kindly, you are being *treated* like a big baby.

You are surrounded by an ocean of voices speaking to you in baby-talk, and here is a small and random sample of what they think of you; of *all* of us:

- We have no discrimination
- We are unable to control your appetites
- We cannot postpone gratification
- We have little sense of self, and what we do have is deformed

6

- We have no social sensibilities beyond the tribal
- We have no articulable inner life
- We are pre- or sub-literate and use words as a railwayman uses flags
- We have no impulse control
- We are solipsistic
- We are potentially, if not actually, violent
- We are easily habituated
- We do not have the ability to exercise responsible autonomy
- We are driven by the desires of our reptilian hindbrain
- We require constant surveillance and constant admonition
- Our wishes are not to be considered, though they may, just for appearances, be consulted
- We cannot meet our own needs but instead must have them met by others
- We cannot tell that we are regarded in this way

Welcome to the world of Big Babies.

Here Is the Proof

In a moment, close this book and go out for a walk or potter round the house, office or wherever else you may be. Look carefully – perhaps for the first time in a long while – at what surrounds you. Look at the architecture, the packaging, the products, their exhortations. Look at the notices ticking you off for things you haven't done yet, perhaps for things you weren't considering doing; perhaps even for things you didn't know were possible. Look how many little rhymes and jingles are thrust at you. Count the anthropomorphic animals; count how many unverifiable assertions are made to you (anything that would, when you were little, be backed up only with 'Because Mummy says so, damn it' counts as unverifiable). See how many times you are warned about things that anyone with the intellect of a fern would know are dangerous. See how many times you are warned about things which aren't particularly dangerous but simply very improbable. See (this will be a low number) how many things you can identify which treat you with dignity.

See yourself treated as a Big Baby.

Now read on.

Why? Because I say so. Just do it. I know someone who is asking for a smack.

What to Do if You Are Not Asking for a Smack

If someone is *not* asking for a smack, the best thing someone can do is as they are told.

If someone is still reading this in the bookshop, then the best thing someone can do is buy the book and walk slowly away from the store. Or run quickly away. Or, gosh, someone can even leave the store and leap on the back of a powerful motorcycle, providing all someone's documents are in order and someone is wearing an approved crash-helmet . . . and someone's motorcycle is not emitting any untoward emissions, and someone observes the speed limits currently in force and shows Respect (which is terribly important to the Government* and to the traffic enforcement official who may well have a different set of personal beliefs to which HE OR SHE is ENTITLED and which he or she has CHOSEN and which, having been chosen, are deserving of someone's Respect because they are the choice of a FELLOW HUMAN BEING).

A fellow human being who is *also* being watched.

---

* Perhaps on the basis that if we show respect to each other, regardless of whether it is earned or not, the government can go on showing *no respect at all* to the electorate.

> ⚠ An American whistleblower, Mark Klein, has alleged that the giant US telecoms company AT&T has been helping the National Security Agency spy on more or less everyone, constructing a special 'secret room' in a facility near San Francisco so that it can tap Americans' communications without a warrant. (Source: *Wired News*, May 2006.) But surely spying on everybody, all the time, is no more than good parenting on the part of the US Government?

Of course he (or she) is being watched. We are all being watched, like babies on a baby monitor. So it doesn't matter if you stroll, walk, run or roar like a Hell's Angel, an oil-stained outcast who probably has staphylococci in his beard and an unhealthy diet lacking the five recommended daily portions of fruit or vegetables . . . and who is probably exceeding the recommended MAXIMUM WEEKLY UNITS of ALCOHOL and (you want to know the sort of people we are dealing with?) in all probability SMOKES . . . It doesn't matter, because this book has a little chip in it, and the little chip sends data and will transmit your whereabouts and what you are doing and how you paid for it and They will know.

Who Is This 'They' Who Will Know?

Oh come on. *They. They* will know.* They have the right to know, just as they have the right to tell us what to – pay attention – do,

---

* We know where They lives: Branson, Missouri. In September 2004, Andrew Wilson (who invented a system for making the underneath of your pimped ride ('car') emit an eerie glow, as well as sunglasses with little visors on so you don't have to wear a hat) legally changed his name to 'They', on the grounds, They said, that 'somebody had to take responsibility'.

even in our private lives. They have these rights because they know what we really are.

You know what they think of us, but you may not yet have realised that you know. The secret is the Billy Connolly test. Some years ago, in Australia, Connolly was doing one of his remarkable extempore riffs on a politician with a comb-over. The terrible thing was not (said Connolly) that the man thought he looked good. Nor was it that he assumed we would think he looked good. The terrible thing was the second-level assumption: that we would look at him and think, 'That bloke's not bald.' As Connolly put it: 'That's what he thinks we're like. That's how stupid he thinks we are.'

Those of us who are not entirely obsessed with commercial or political advantage spend a lot of our time complaining about the metaphorical comb-overs. There is an entire small industry devoted to writing books describing comb-overs: books that tell us how the advertising industry is manipulating us, how the media are telling us what to think, how globalisation is making fools of us all, how politicians are nakedly abusing democratic principles, how the food industry is making us fat, how educational standards are collapsing into a welter of imbecility founded on the silliest principles of ethical relativism, how everything is going to hell in a handcart.

Handcart?

We will identify the handcart in due course. But the first thing to say is this: everything is not going to hell.

There's no mileage in that, of course. Every now and then – the last famous example in the UK being the television reporter Martin Bell, who later put on a white suit and went into Parliament – someone says 'Why can't we concentrate on the good news?' The simple answer is 'Because nobody cares.' We enjoy hearing good news about people we know; good things happening to people we've never heard of at best bores us, at worst leaves us furious. Just as the *Daily Mail* dream headline would be 'Underage Gay Sex with Asylum-Seekers Causes Cancer of the Housing Market', so the ultimate non-starter would be 'Nothing Untoward Happens to Man, 51'. We just do not want to know.

But nothing untoward is happening to most of us, most of the time; this might even be the most prolifically non-untoward period in human history. If it seems terribly untoward, much of the time, perhaps that is simply in contrast to the thirty years between the invention of the contraceptive pill in 1951 and the first identification of AIDS in 1981, which now seems like a brief golden age. No wonder that, for those born between 1946 and 1964 – the Baby Boomers, who are now running the world, and are now turning sixty – that magical trentennial was a world of grace from which we are now – seemingly inexplicably – falling; no wonder that, like our ancient forebears enacting their apotropaic rituals and placating the gods, they are now almost frantic with the need to turn back the hand of time, to find out what our collective sin was and to expiate it so that, once again, the good times may roll.

And they were, by all accounts,* good times. No wars to speak of (none noticeable anyway, except for Vietnam, which seemed, back home, more an excuse for rebellion and counter-culture than an actual war), easy sex which meant life, not possible death, an innovative form of tribal youth music which had not yet saturated every fold of our culture nor reached the terrible exhaustion of the 1990s, no infectious diseases that antibiotics could not cure, a seemingly stable planet, neither warming up nor cooling down, and, best of all,

---

* I was alive then; but too young for the Sixties, too shy and ill-at-ease to have enjoyed them anyway (organ music, evolutionary biology and Latin poetry did not make for a happening sex life), and, by the late Seventies, married.

no computers:* this, it seemed, was the future of the world. Humanity had triumphed; and if it danced in the monstrously glamorous shadow of the H-bomb, it danced all the same, bugs and bowler hats both on the losing side and youth and freedom winning through. Surely it would go on like this. Surely it would.

And now we believe ourselves to be back where we began, where humanity has spent most of its time: under threat from drought and infection, small wars erupting all over the planet, torture commonplace, democracies falsified, the principles of social welfare eroded under the ineluctable demands of the marketplace, the old facing poverty as their pension funds are depredated . . . and, on top of that, anomie and alienation in the societies of the west, a Balkanisation of ethnicities, a tidal wave of privacy-invasions both legal and illegal, a sense (justified or not) of violence in the air, a terrible loss of cultural confidence beneath the yoke of triumphant relativism, religious fundamentalism on the march again with crusades both figurative and literal, a descent into superstition and mumbo-jumbo, the collapse of intelligent public discourse, a seemingly unstoppable erosion of personal freedoms, the increasing legalisation and medicalisation of our lives, the repositioning of the individual human being not as a member of society but as an economic unit – specifically, as a consumer whose duty it is to go shopping – and, beneath it all, and beneath the fine words of governments, the sense of a collective loss of faith in the ability of people to manage their own lives.

---

* Except for those used by the Gas Board, which charged elderly ladies living alone in bedsits £2,100,399 2s.3d. for their gas, and those used by the *Reader's Digest* which sent endless ineptly-personalised letters to people saying 'Dear 376 ACACIA AVENUE, imagine the look of envy on the faces of your neighbours in MISTER GRAEME <SURNAME> when they see that *you*, MISTER<MISTER<MISTER>>> have won . . .' etc. Subsequently, the Gas Board bought a new computer. The *Reader's Digest*, on the other hand, is still in business. (The serious point, however, being that they didn't know the things that computers could do, then, and so they didn't know that they wanted to do them.)

No wonder the Baby Boomers are desperate; more surprising, perhaps, that they have, in so many ways, triumphed.

How the Baby Boomers Made Infants of Us All

Let us go back to the beginning. I imagine myself to be a grown-up, as, presumably, do you.

And now let's make a few more assumptions:

You think that because you negotiated puberty and developed secondary sexual characteristics, and got qualifications and opened a bank account and subjected yourself to the scrutiny of anti-terrorism laws and anti-money-laundering laws* and learned to drive and got a job and perhaps a spouse and maybe even children, and quite possibly even pay your taxes – quite possibly even SMOKE[†]– you are a grown-up.

And, believing yourself to be a grown-up, you take some interest in the world around you.

Sometimes, things strike you as a bit odd. Some things (it seems to you) are out of kilter, even though you do not know what kilter means.[‡]

It strikes you, for example, as out of kilter that between getting off the plane and reaching the outside world at London Heathrow** there were, at the last count, ninety-three notices

---

* In March 2006, a retired schoolteacher, Walter Soehnge, paid off his J C Penney credit-card bill in full – $6,522 – and found the payment blocked by the US Department of Homeland Security. It was over $5,000, and Soehnge and his wife were therefore, according to the Bank Secrecy Act (1970) immediately under suspicion of laundering money for organised crime or terrorism.

† Not for long. Not even in your own home. But once nobody is smoking any more, where will the law turn next?

‡ And I can't help you. Find another sucker.

** It really *is* the outside world; it just doesn't seem like it.

telling you off for things you hadn't done or which hadn't even occurred to you to do.

It strikes you as out of kilter that Merseyside firefighters have been banned from running or doing circuit-training after one of them fell over and hurt himself and sued and got £100,000 in damages and the fire service spokesman said: 'We hope we will be able to issue good-practice guidelines soon.'

⚠ 'A **Labour member of the Scottish Parliament, Duncan McNeil, has called for contraception to be added to methadone to prevent addicts having children . . . A Scottish Drugs Forum spokeswoman said: "Methadone is known to actually increase fertility and therefore people on this prescription need to be advised of such."**

'Rosemary Burnett, of Amnesty International Scotland, said the move could never be implemented as it would contravene Article 8 of the Human Rights Act, which guarantees people's right to a private and family life . . . A Liberty spokesman said the organisation had grave concerns about Mr McNeil's comments. He said: "It's completely outrageous . . . it would be a gross interference with people's reproductive rights."' (BBC News, 11 May 2006)

It strikes you as out of kilter that there's a notice at London Paddington station which says 'Please be ready to move away with your luggage when you reach the top of the escalator' because it implies that otherwise you *wouldn't* be ready to move away with your luggage but, instead, would stand there like a moron with other morons piling up against you so that eventually something has to give and you all tumble back down the escalator in a mêlée of morons and get sucked into the mechanism and ground to hamburger and they'd hose the blood down and scrub the gobbets of stupid flesh out of the machinery and start it up again and the same thing would happen again . . . or, if not, why the need for the notice?

It strikes you as out of kilter that the sad and flat-eyed people working in McDonald's are made to wear shirts that say 'I'm lovin' it' when (a) they obviously aren't and (b) nobody could be expected to and (c) there is a 'g' on the end of 'loving'.

It strikes you as out-of-kilter that federal regulators in the USA fined the CBS network $550,000 for televising one of Janet Jackson's breasts during the 2004 Super Bowl, but doesn't fine anyone anything for the 10,000 acts of violence (including 8,000 murders) the average American child – in a nation where the average household watches seven and a half hours of television a day – will have seen on TV by the time he or she is eleven years old.[*]

So many other things strike you as out-of-kilter. Call centres where people can do nothing but read from scripts on a computer screen. The Halifax advertisements featuring one of their bank clerks in a space suit, holding up a credit card under the slogan 'Why wait? Treat yourself today!'[†] The Moto service station on the M4 at Reading which will not sell petrol between 10.30 and 11.00 p.m. because of 'shift change' and 'paperwork' and 'company policy'.[‡] The rise of 'addiction culture' and the apparently innocuous Serenity Prayer[**] which, on closer examination, turns out to be a sort of divine go-ahead for anyone who wants to impose their will on others, with the sole, pragmatic and amoral, test being 'Can I pull it off?'

---

[*] Statistics cited in Chen, Milton, 'Television as a Tool' available at <http://snipurl.com/lrk0> and in Thomas H. Davenport and John C. Beck, *The Attention Economy: Understanding the New Currency of Business* (Cambridge, MA: Harvard Business School Press, 2001), 101.

[†] Which translates, as all bank advertising translates, as 'Give us the money. Now fuck off.'

[‡] And which translates as 'You can keep your money. Now fuck off.'

[**] 'God grant me the serenity to accept the things I cannot change; courage to change the things I can; and wisdom to know the difference.' Reinhold Niebuhr (1892–1971)

The pictograms on roads (the man opening an umbrella, the thing which is only recognisable as a camera if you were born before 1920), which are frequently so obscure that they have to have the explanation beneath them. In English. But the point of pictograms is that they transcend any particular language, so a pictogram that has to be explained is pointless.

The railway announcements which are made by a computer, escalating its self-abasement according to the delay, starting with 'I am sorry for the delay . . .' and moving via 'I am very sorry for the delay' to 'I am extremely sorry for the severe delay to your journey' (and the 'obvious inconvenience this will cause' – obvious to whom?), which would be all very well except we know it's a computer and so we also know that there is no 'I' to be sorry: it is just a form of empty words, of acting, a pacifier for baby.

And the list goes on . . .

The way in which airline cabin crew stress all the wrong syllables in their announcements. The way in which airline cabin crew speak of what to do 'in the unlikely event of an emergency' because surely if it were not unlikely, it wouldn't be an emergency.

The Holt Primary School in Skellingthorpe, Lincolnshire, which cancelled a Harry Potter day because a local vicar said it would 'lead our children into areas of evil', demonstrating that children (who know perfectly well that Harry Potter is a story and is made up and therefore not true) are rather more grown-up than the vicar.

The advertisement for Andrex lavatory paper which shows a pretty female backside in yellow underpants on which is emblazoned a cartoon monkey holding its nose with an expression of disgust and, underneath, the words: 'Could you be cleaner?' (And how long will it be before the advertisers add 'Are you sure?' and, in due course, 'Show me'?)

The way in which all human activity is becoming a branch of television, to be ratified by television; the way in which people on televison are more real than people who are *not* on television; the way in which other media acknowledge it; the way in which we collude with it.

Our obsession with actors, and what actors think, and who actors are having sex with, and where actors live, and what actors like to eat, and what actors like to eat while they are thinking about having sex, and actors' troubles and their brave battles on the way to their multi-million-dollar mansions which, it is never mentioned, are acquired for doing what Peter O'Toole described as 'farting about in disguises'.

The way in which media (whether television or otherwise) assume their readers suffer from some borderline psychosis which makes them potentially incapable of distinguishing actor from character or diegesis from reality.

The way in which this is quite possibly (unless you are a literary critic or academic) the first time you have seen the word 'diegesis' even though this is surely the most over-entertained age in all of human history, 'ordinary people' (another term of contempt masquerading as egalitarianism, deployed by television people and politicians*) now being diverted more determinedly, and probably at greater cost, than the most despotic of emperors.†

The way in which anything which could seem difficult, or complex, or a matter of 'high culture', is either denied, by television, to be so, or required, by television, to be presented by a comedian.

The prevalence of comedians.

Paul Auster's observation, in *The Book of Illusions*, that

> [Hector] was a grown-up, and the very presence of such
> a person seemed to run counter to the established rules
> of comedy. Funny men were supposed to be small,
> misshapen, or fat. They were imps and buffoons, dunces

---

* And the alignment of television people and politicians here should tell you something nasty, too.

† Diegesis is the formal term for everything that takes place within a play, film or whatever. If we had our wits about us, it would be one of the key terms of our times.

17

and outcasts, children masquerading as adults or adults with the minds of children. [. . .] They are all misfits, and because these characters can neither threaten us nor make us envy them, we root for them to triumph over their enemies and win the girl's heart.

Government proposals that bad parents 'should be punished', matched with other proposals that children should *not* be punished.

⚠ The once-great perfumer Guerlain is now owned by the 'luxury goods' company LVMH. Terrified of . . . *something*, Guerlain is now removing three major ingredients from its perfumes – coumarin, oakmoss and birch tar – on the grounds that these *might* cause allergies. The industry body IFRA has made no ruling on these ingredients, and in any case adopts the sane principle that it is perfectly all right to put a little label on the bottle, just as menus now do not serve Egg Custard, but, instead, serve Egg Custard (E) to show that Egg Custard has Egg in it.

This will not do for Guerlain, and their actions mean the end of three of the greatest perfumes in history: Jicky, Mitsouko and Shalimar. Will Guerlain go on selling them? Yes. Will it relabel them 'Jicky: Not', 'Mitsouko: Different from How You Remember It' and 'Something Called Shalimar But Don't Be Misled by the Name'? We do not know, any more than we can predict what Laphroaig might do if they decided peat smoke was no good and had to be replaced with Uncle Dougie's BBQ Sauce. We do, however, know what Guerlain are looking for in a 'technical perfumer': someone between 25 and 28 years of age who is good with computers and fluent in English.

The prevailing obsession with death: as something to be avoided and evaded, as the ultimate evil, as God or Nature's way of telling you that you've done something wrong, when you might feel, as Robert Pogue Harrison claims, that

> Adult societies – human societies – are in dialogue with death. The infantile society pretends death does not exist, or is someone else's fault, or a punishment for doing something wrong. But the infantile society is paradoxically mired deeper in dialogue with death than any other.

. . . and that our current dialogue with death seems that of a petulant child, *schrei*-ing against the inevitable.

The insistence by governments that we should all be engaged in this infantile, scaredy-cat dialogue with death by only being allowed to go to hell in – I promised we would come back to it – a handcart officially designated as fit for purpose and embodying best-practice design standards complying to standards set out in Consultation Notice OG/OTHG 21,* while our own personal handcarts – unsafe sex, cigarettes, drinking like a fish, over-eating, having a long sit-down, too much coffee, too much cake, too few vitamins, taking drugs, dangerous sports, Mount Everest hypoxia holidays, not wearing a crash helmet and so forth – are gradually legislated out of existence (simultaneously legislating *into* existence a whole new NCO class of grit-faced enforcers, narks and pettifoggers). There is no shortage of denunciation to help them along. The yelping rant, froth at its lips, is all around us. There is, in Great Britain, an entire newspaper (the *Daily Mail*) devoted to ranting, and, in America, an entire industry (the media). But declaring that things are not what they were, and that change means worse, is as old as the hills. The older people get, the

---

* No such thing, but *we* aren't to know that, are we?

more they are ready to hear it. At eighteen, the world may be mystifying or perplexing, but it is full of hope. By eighty, it offers the same prospects but has deteriorated and collapsed to the same degree as the ageing body. In between, we approach disillusion and dissolution equally. The twenty-year-old who swears 'I will never say "I don't know what the world is coming to"' is the same sixty-year-old who no longer *cares* what the world is coming to because it has already gone wholly to pieces (and, in between, has been the same parent who was astonished to find himself saying 'My father would never have stood for it').

An amorphous sense of despair at the ways of the world. This is inescapable. It's barely worth commenting on unless there's something new. Children not respecting their elders? Businessmen out to cheat their customers? The old intolerant of the young? The music of the young (not 'music' at all, of course) offensive to the ears of the old? No; these are all the stock characters. The list of dramatis personae is extensive. Politician: corrupt. Clergyman: adulterous. Actor: vain. Schoolmaster: pederastical. Doctor: addicted. Footballer: cunt-struck. Newspaper columnist: pompous. Newspaper columnist: vapid. Newspaper columnist: spluttering. Newspaper columnist: hypocritical. The list goes on, this dreary cast of the old play *Mundus Senescit*, reflecting the deterioration, not of the world, but of ourselves. The wonder is that the characters still populate the pages of the newspapers, which profess surprise or outrage. *Soap Star in Three-in-a-Bed Sex Romp*, they yell, expecting us to be appalled; but while Mr and Mrs Normal are intimating disgust to each other, the subtext of titillation runs strong and true. 'Disgusting,' she says (but wishes she'd married a soap star). 'Disgusting,' he says, wishing he *were* a soap star. The numbers in the bed, the drugs and liberties taken, the twelve-megapixel blast of the paparazzo flashgun, the limos, the lap-dancers, the bungs and pay-offs and fortified houses, the designer schwag and luxury bling, the swagger and endorsements and the whole damned *meshuggos* . . . these are all new metonyms for old indulgences: liberty, conspicuity, a life sanctified by the glare of observation, a fine and sun-drenched vista of an infinity of transgressions which cannot be called out.

The life of an Emperor.

And are things . . . *getting worse*, because the imperial life is being democratised, seeping down, settling upon the unworthy shoulders of Mick and Posh and Becks and Wayne and all those people who (like an Emperor) are referred to by a single, discon-nected, god-like name;* people who we think we know because (like the Emperor Augustus) their images are before us all the time? Is it *getting worse* that you can now live like that by singing bad songs or kicking a ball, when once you could only live like that if you had killed and betrayed, and betrayed and killed again? Is this really 'getting worse'?

It is not. *Things* are not. Things may appear to be deteriorat-ing, but, measured by some absolute standard (and excluding the brief golden age of 1951–1981) there has probably, for those of us in the developed world, never been a better time to be alive.

There is, on the other hand, something wrong. Not the lots of things wrong that papers and pundits and scaremongers and misery-gutses endlessly trickle out, but one, quite big, thing which is the cause of all the little things. We may not be going to hell, but, because of the one thing, we are in a handcart. Or, to be precise, a perambulator. A stroller. A baby-buggy. For god's sake: a *pram*.

---

* You will never hear this conversation: 'Do you believe in God?' 'God who?' (Though one might be comforted by the fact that Jesus had a surname. Perhaps it should be used, out of respect, to distinguish him from Dido or Bill. 'I acknowledge Mr Christ as my personal saviour.')

Not a Handcart but a Pram

As we said at the beginning: you are being treated like a baby. A big baby, it is true, but a baby all the same.

You, I, all of us – particularly in the United Kingdom and the USA – are on the receiving end of a sustained campaign to infantilise us: our tastes, our responses, our behaviour, our private thoughts, our decisions, our buying habits, our philosophies, our political sensibilities. We are told what to think. We are talked down to. We are distracted with colour and movement, patronised, spoon-fed, our responses pre-empted and our autonomy eroded with a fine, rich, heavily funded contempt. We are surrounded by a sea of faces: a roaring ocean of voices, speaking to us in baby talk.

And we don't quite notice it.

We walk around the edges, talking – with that cheerful gloom which characterises our times – of the empowering nature of popular culture and the dumbing-down effect of that same popular culture, of the wonderful *politesse* of PC and the hideously patronising nature of PC, of the *importance* of language and of the *debasement* of language, of the rising gullibility of the young and the wonderful liberation of relativism, of the decay of cultures and the delights of multiculturalism, of the bad old days of nationalism and the bad new days of globalisation. But we seldom, if ever, ask of any phenomenon or product or law or political utterance: 'Is this a proper way to treat grown-ups?' – perhaps because we don't feel grown-up, perhaps because we have no exemplar of adulthood. The old Jewish concept of the *mensch* has almost entirely vanished. Find one in British or American public or commercial life. Find one.

No. That won't do.

Homer Simpson is a cartoon.

Find a *real* one.

There aren't any real ones? Of course there aren't, because one of the defining prerequisites of the *mensch* is his solidity. The *mensch* has a substance which is not merely to do with his autonomy, his morality, his crucial ability to discriminate and to judge (both of which, though fundamental to adulthood, have become inexplicably cognate with two fundamental failings of infantilism: bigotry and prejudice).

The solidity of the *mensch* is in strange contrast to the figures of contemporary public or media life, who are notable above all for a strange and disturbing insubstantiality. It is impossible, when considering the records of Tony Blair or George W. Bush – let alone any of the interchangeable media confections of the moment – to imagine anyone actually *being there* when the cameras cease to roll and the lights go out. One imagines them peculiarly emptied; deflated, perhaps, hanging limply on a hanger in a closet until morning; and when they make their protestations of religious belief* we find it oddly unpersuasive, and only in part because we doubt their sincerity.

For a man to recite his credo – 'I believe in God' – God himself is not necessary. God may be there, or may not be there; either way, God is not brought into being because a man – even Tony Blair or George W. Bush – declares his belief. The prerequisite of the utterance, if it is to mean anything, is not 'God' or 'believe', but 'I'. And somehow we find it hard to quite believe in so many of our political leaders; Tony and Dubya are human Californias; as Gertrude Stein said of her childhood home town, Oakland, 'There is no there there.'

But where are the exemplars of how to be grown-up? Was there ever a *there* there . . . or do we just feel that there was, because we were little and they were big? The director Chris Webb and I planned to make a movie which we will never now see, called *Grown-Ups, Incorporated*, based on the premise that when we were little, there were always grown-ups around when things went badly wrong. They might tell you off, but they would sort it out. And then we grew up – or, at any rate, got bigger – and where were the

---

* cf. Tony Blair: 'I only know what I believe.'

grown-ups? Our idea (Mr Webb's idea, actually; I was just the screenwriter) was that some entrepreneur would start up a company – Grown-Ups, Inc. – to make good that lack. You would be able to call them up and say 'Help – I need a grown-up', and they would send one round. Grown-ups for grown-ups: a beguiling idea. What actually happened, of course, was close, but very, very different: entrepreneurs did indeed set up companies, but what the companies did (and we will deal with them as we go along) was simply tell us that it was all right to be childish, and, if we gave them our money and our details and our date of birth and our address (previous address if resident less than three years) and our allegiance, we wouldn't have to grow up at all, not ever.

> ⚠ One of the things grown-ups learn is not to try to use kid-speak, because the point of kid-speak is to mutate so fast that no grown-up can understand, let alone deploy, it. Paradoxically, then, nothing seems more childish than a grown-up trying to use the language of the kids on the street. Merciful heavens, even clergymen don't do it any more, not since the guitars-on-the-sanctuary debacle of the 1980s which turned the solemn and dignified worship of the ineffable Divine into, like, whatever. (Jesus digs a groovy hot beat combo, man.)

And we bought it.

So What's in It for Us?

We are being treated like big babies, infantilised at every turn, but what's in it for us? Why do we go along with it? What do we get out of the deal that makes us accept it?

There are plenty of possible answers, but the most worrying came in the course of a casual conversation, when a friend said: 'You've got the question the wrong way round. Perhaps being infantilised is the reward? Perhaps we put up with the indignity, the surveillance, the patronising, the tickings-off and all the rest of it so that, in the end, we can be infantilised.'

And perhaps he is right; though it summons all sorts of dreadful images of those men – one imagines them as porky, blotchy-legged, wet-lipped – who will pay hundreds of pounds an hour to be put in nappies in giant cots and allowed to soil themselves.

⚠ Seen on a carton of orange juice: 'New & Improved'. This is nonsense. How can orange juice be new? How improved? We are considered too stupid for our belief to be beggared; so infantile that we retain a terrible hunger for novelty – a hunger vital for children, who must acquire new information in order to survive, but one we should grow out of when we grow out of wearing short trousers with our shirts hanging out. (But we don't grow out of that, either.)

They are us; just more honest. We soil ourselves (or are soiled) all the time. When Tesco despoils another town with another supermarket. When the government suggests a 'traffic light' system for marking healthy foods because we are fat fools. When Tesco refuses to implement the 'traffic light' system for marking healthy foods because we are fat fools with credit cards. When we are told about vegetables and exercise and threatened with compulsory fat tests. When people are dismissed for flirting at work. When men are told to obtain consent for sex at every stage lest they be prosecuted for rape by a woman (women, too, in this scenario are less than adult) too drunk to remember what happened. When library books are labelled 'GOO' as short for GOOD READ. When *Zoo* magazine holds a 'bag a new set of rib lamps for your girlfriend' contest.* When the BBC website 'Have Your Say' section (itself horribly *de haut en bas*: 'all right, little man, you have your say') asks for 'Toronto Air Crash: Your Reaction' ('Great! Loved it!'). When the US government bans grandmothers from flying because their name is the same as someone else with the same name, so don't tell the US government that *that's* a coincidence, or when the British government proposes a bill to enable it to do almost anything, without consent of Parliament, insults us by calling it the Legislative and Regulatory Reform Bill, and asks us to trust them to use its powers wisely.† When a once-great newspaper is reduced to 'reviewing' a £35 lip balm as 'the Rolls-Royce of lip balms, this lives up to all the Crème de la Mer hype. It's packed with nutrient-rich ingredients including a marine antifreeze protein, which soothes, protects and comforts . . .' When a power station has a sign outside it saying 'Producing Power for Millions of Customers. Innogy. nPower'.‡ When Tony Blair lectures the electorate on 'respect' and appoints a 'Respect Czar' as if respect is an absolute, not a reward. When a divorcing husband called Alan Miller claims, through his paid mouthpiece,

---

* 'All they had to do,' reported Jemima Lewis in the *Independent*, 'was send in a picture of their partner's inadequate breasts and the name of the celebrity pair they would like substituted, and a surgeon would take care of the rest. As well as getting some "new playthings", the lucky winner – yet to be announced – will get £1,000 and the chance to "show just how much they love their girlfriend".'

† Powers which will permit it to 'Curtail or abolish jury trial, permit the Home Secretary to place citizens under house arrest, allow the Prime Minister to sack judges, rewrite the law on nationality and immigration, "reform" Magna Carta (or what remains of it).' – Letter from Professors Spencer, Baker, Feldman, Forsyth, Ibbetson and Williams from the Law Faculty at Cambridge (*The Times*, 16 February 2006, 18)

‡ We may wonder what else a power station would be doing (fishing? Sudoku?) and at the depravity of minds which could think that 'Innogy' and 'nPower' are the sort of imbecilic neologisms which will somehow impress us . . . and perhaps it will encourage us to write our own mission statements. *Writing This Book Because I Signed a Contract to Do It When It Still Seemed a Good Idea*. mBywater. There; can I have the £500,000 branding fee now, please?

that if he 'had knocked [his wife] down with his motor car, and she had suffered severe injuries – brain damage and losing the ability to have children – at most the damages would be £2m' instead of the £5m she had been awarded after he ran off with another woman. When we see advertisements for a 30-inch Jesus, 'a beautiful Full body, Half body [*sic*], rod arm puppet. This big Mouth puppet is 30" tall and has removable legs, mouth straps, 1.5 inch neck movement, same fabric through out and comes with one puppet rod. This religious puppet is an excellent choice for puppet ministry'.* When the elderly Rolling Stones have their lyrics censored at the Super Bowl concert in case some Americans (or possibly Jesus) are appalled at the word 'come' even when the founding principle of the Christian faith is that of the Second Coming. When store chains offer 'loyalty' cards, as though a giant corporation run by megalo-maniacs is worthy of 'loyalty' (merciful heavens, what sort of arse is loyal to Tesco?). When we go into a train lavatory (or a motorway service-station lavatory, or any lavatory except per-haps those in London gentlemen's clubs) and see lavatory paper and piss all over the floor, and the lavatory itself unflushed. When we read advertisements for the iMusic Brain Enhancer. When we read that cirrhosis is on the increase as teenage girls drink themselves into unconsciousness (and there's a photo-graph, one sprawled on the pavement in a wet pool, skirt ridden up over chicken-skin thighs and surrounded by the accessories of modern life: strappy shoes, denim jacket, kebab and chips, carrier bag, lurching mate, mobile phone). When . . .

But enough. We could extend the list *ad infinitum* but the evi-dence for every assertion which follows is available at the end of your own nose. Just look around you and ask: Is this a grown-up world? Or, in its thoughtless embracing of change, its endless fiddling and quibbling and law-making and nose-poking, is it a

---

* <http://www.puppetrevelation.com> Hurry while stocks last.

world of Big Babies, in which we abandon autonomy and dignity for the guilty pleasure of wearing nappies and sucking our thumbs till we fall, sniggering, into the grave?

We are already balanced on its edge, the dug turf rocking beneath our feet; our balance itself is precarious, as we smile at our perpetual present, seduced by the terror of death which hides behind our obsession with youth, novelty, image, consumption and eternal vigour into abandoning our connections with our shared past. Cicero identified it some two millennia ago: *to be ignorant of what occurred before you were born is to remain always a child.* For what is the worth of human life, unless it be woven into the life of our ancestors by the records of history?

But how do we step back onto firmer ground?

CHAPTER 2

Who Do You Think You Are?

There once was a series of children's books called *I-Spy*. They had pictures of things in, and you ticked them off as you saw them. They came in handy on car trips, and in some mysterious way were supposed to prevent car-sickness. Although they were quintessentially English, the effect must have percolated across the Atlantic somehow, because anyone hearing Homer Simpson's majestic line – 'That guy impressed me. And I am not easily impressed . . . Wow! A blue car!' – would immediately remember the *I-Spy* series and be catapulted back to a golden age (smelling of car-sick and soggy tomato sandwiches and petrol fumes and hot upholstery and irritation) in which the world could be tabulated by exemplars and categories: *I-Spy Cars. I-Spy On the Pavement. I-Spy On a Train Journey. I-Spy Churches. I-Spy Recherché Sexual Positions* was not published; nor was *I-Spy Drive-By Shootings, I-Spy Paedophiles, I-Spy a Kid Being Mugged for His Trainers* or *I-Spy Bailiffs Harassing Single Mothers*. It was a kinder, gentler, infinitely more absurd world, the *I-Spy* books being ostensibly published by Big Chief I-Spy, operating from Wigwam-by-the-Water, Bouverie Street, London EC. He wrote to you when you sent in a completed *I-Spy* book, and sent you a feather and a badge.

The first Big Chief I-Spy was a man called Mr Worrell, who

eventually died aged 106. His spirit lives on; and in better times might have provided the inspiration for this book. For all that really need be done to make the case is a simple quest for the reader: keep your eyes open and decide for yourself whether you are being infantilised.

But these are harsher times, and the reader may need further persuasion: reasoned argument, a litany of offences against taste and decency, and the erosion of his status as an ostensibly autonomous, fully grown adult.*

The thesis is simple: that the Boom Generation, cosseted beneficiaries of both post-war idealism and the sexual and cultural revolution of the Sixties, have no mechanism for coping with adulthood, let alone with ageing, and every inclination not only to remain perpetually infantilised themselves but (now that they are running the show) to infantilise the rest of us.

Among the many ways of dividing the world into two sorts of people, we may divide it into those who want everyone to be like them, and those who don't mind. The former group is the one that causes all the trouble. Ideologues are there, and chartered accountants; officials of all sorts, the worse kind of doctors, political bullies, authoritarians, monogamous heterosexuals, the more unevolved (or reborn) Christians and Muslims, stroppy vegans, animal rights activists, businessmen, health-and-safety obsessives, and all the rest who believe they have the answer, whether the answer is that a dead Judean has told us all what to do and will come back and *get us* if we don't do it, or that the only model for any sort of human endeavour is the one which involves giving as little as possible for as much as you can get (also known as 'sound business principles'), or that the worst possible thing that can happen to us is that we can die.

But of all those who want everyone to be like them, the Baby Boomers are the oddest. Given their (apparent) embracing of freedom, individualism, self-expression, relativism, equality and

___

* Please do not complain about gendered pronouns. 'His' includes 'her'.

diversity, one might have expected the Boomers to fall firmly into the second camp: those who know what they want to be like, and accord others the same freedom. Alas, this is not how the Boomers operate. The Boomers want everyone to embrace their values, bow down to the lifestyle (which endlessly changes, as the Boomers struggle to cope with tricky realities like responsibility, power and ageing) and, as dedicated non-conformists, to conform.

> ⚠ There was a time when children wanted to get the hell out of the family home just as soon as they could. Now they are staying at home for longer and longer – not to mention the relatively new phenomenon of the 'boomerang generation': those who leave home *and then come back*, often staying until their late twenties or early thirties. These are not the dutiful children looking after ageing parents; they are enjoying a sort of frat-house life with parents who are themselves – hey – *just big kids at heart*, albeit big kids with washing machines, food and comfortable furniture.
>
> 'How do you raise your children to be normal when you're not? I wouldn't trade most of my memories of growing up for anything in the world . . . Since becoming a dad I have to come to grips with the fact that I'll never be the man I wanted to be. So, instead I want to raise my boys to be the man I wanted to be . . . that's a huge burden . . . I wish I could have been an action hero . . .' – An *Indiana Jones* fan at <http://www.theindyexperience.com/columns/raiders_connection_2004_raising_boys.php>

The reason seems to be that the apparent liberalism of the Boomers is nothing more than a stunt or a misconception; or, perhaps more accurately, the poison-seed at the very roots of their philosophy. For, far from being the first generation to think things through for themselves, the Boomers are utterly bogged down in the mire of that most dangerous and badly articulated political and moral philosophy, Modernity.

It's Never Too Late

To be Modern is to be trapped. Modernity constructs a beautifully crafted logical trap from which it is hard to escape without a strenuous process of reasoning for which the Boomers show little stomach.

The Modernity trap (as implacable and inescapable as any Victorian morality) is described by philosopher Mark Rowlands as having four components.

The first component is **individualism**, which puts the individual human being, and the individual's duty to fully realise his life, at the centre of the moral stage. As 'life-coaches' – an occasionally useful but generally nightmarish, selfish and self-indulgent pseudo-profession which epitomises and exploits all that is depressing and prescriptive about Modernity – are fond of declaring, 'It is never too late to be what you might have been.' The quote is usually attributed to George Eliot, but while Eliot may have had her longueurs, she was no more known for writing nonsense than life coaches are known for scholarly rigour; and nonsense this certainly is. Although I cannot find it anywhere in Eliot, something very similar is to be found at the end of chapter 36 of the lamentable *John Halifax, Gentleman* (1897) by 'Miss Mulock'. It is worth quoting in context:

> A gleam, bright as a boy's hope, wild as a boy's daring, flashed from those listless eyes – then faded.
> 'You mean, Mr. Halifax, what I might have been. Now it is too late.'

'There is no such word as "too late," in the wide world – nay, not in the universe. What! shall we, whose atom of time is but a fragment out of an ever-present eternity – shall we, so long as we live, or even at our life's ending, dare to cry out to the Eternal One, "It is too late!"'

In so far as it is possible to make head or tail of this ecstatic gibberish (moments later, as you will have guessed, Mr Halifax is seized by 'a sudden flush or rather spasm of color [which] flushed his face, then faded away, leaving him pallid to the very lips'), the never-too-lateness requires a belief in post-mortem self-actualisation which may undercut the promise of earthly reward offered by life-coaches, but nevertheless is perhaps the apotheosis of Modernity: *becoming what you ought to be* is the main purpose of every life, and even the Universe is designed to make it possible.

It is, of course, unspeakable balls. It is certainly too late, in many (if not most) of our lives, to be what we ought to be, if what we ought to be is something which we, rather than others, have the right to decide. I may now arrive at the opinion that I ought to be the Artistic Director of the Royal National Theatre,* that I ought to be Senior Captain of the British Airways 747 fleet, that I ought to be an Internet billionaire, that I ought to be a world-renowned conductor. But that counts for nothing. *It is too late*, and one might bear in mind the general (and wise) observation that if you want to find out what someone wants, look at what they get.

The first stage of the Modernity trap, as Rowlands declares, will have none of this, as it bites shut around your unsuspecting leg. 'This above all, to thine own self be true,' adherents are

---

* In place of the current incumbent, Nicholas Hytner, whom I once spent a few pleasant weeks lying beneath in a different city every night. (It was an undergraduate production of *The Tempest*. He was Trinculo, I, Caliban.) Who would have foreseen how things would turn out?

prone to announce, as though it were an unassailable moral principle rather than a line given to the pompous and ineffectual Polonius in *Hamlet*. Polonius ends up dying like a rat behind an arras, but his sententious line (which would have failed to persuade the audience, more concerned, in the first years of the seventeenth century, with saving their bacon and possibly their souls) has lived on as a founding tenet of those who assert that our primary duty, overriding all others, is self-realisation. Which would be fine were it not for the possibility – all those children who want to be celebrities, all those porky men who want flat stomachs – that the self to which one must be true may, for its own part, be telling us lies; and that we may therefore be acting on self-delusion . . . or delusions inflicted upon us by someone else.

Hard on the heels of individualism comes **relativism**, pinioning your arms to your sides. If the greatest moral good is self-realisation, then that's as true for you as it is for me. Which in turn means that I have no right to judge your life or your choice of what you want to be, unless I am prepared to indulge in some very slippery moral conjuring. I could, perhaps, say that my own self-realisation lies in becoming the sort of person who is morally inconsistent. I might therefore claim that, while I am bound by a moral absolute to become (or to indulge in the process of becoming) the 'me' I feel I must become, you, conversely, have no such duty and no such right. Curiously, this has become a crucial symptom of the Boomers' moral sickness, and we shall be seeing a lot of it as we go along. All the same, if I want to be consistent, and if I allow that self-realisation is the ultimate moral good, I have to be a relativist and refrain from judging your choices.

Immobilised and pinioned, we are now ready to be tranquillised, and here comes the silver needle, droplet gleaming at its tip: if I have no right to judge your actions, and you have no right to judge mine, then how can you prove that yours are valid? And how I, mine? The answer is **voluntarism**, the principle that what validates any given choice is *the very fact that it has been made*. The act of choosing is what makes the choice a valid one.

Finally – *snick* – the noose drops down and circles your throat, choking any protest: **instrumentalism**, the principle that our social intercourse is primarily limited to (or at least defined by) what you can do to help me along the road to my own self-realisation; and, of course, what I can do for you.

Put them all together and they all spell . . . well, they spell 'Modernity', true, but let's think for a moment of the string of declaratives they prompt:

'I want to do it.'

'You can't stop me.'

'Who are you to judge me?'

'I'm as good as you are.'

'You don't understand me.'

'I've got a right to.'

'Do it for me now.'

'You've got to.'

'What have you ever done for me?'

Yes . . . the unmistakable infantile voice. Modernity and infantilism are eager bedfellows, and the moral conjuring of the Boomers – Modern to the last man, while insisting that we must be like them – can only result in their making (or trying to make) infants of the lot of us.

On Being Infantile

Being infantile is, however, easy, and can be rather nice, and indeed – with the taking-off of all the brakes which constrain adult behaviour – relaxing. The infantile need no impulse control, nor can they muster it. They want it now, whatever it is: sex, a Rolex, food (watch the middle-manager cram that McDonald's into the onion-reeking mouth, grease slicking the commuter chin), sugar, a holiday, going too fast, *get out my fuckin' way*, credit, the illusion of comprehension, the quick fix, the adrenaline zing, the beer, the punch in the face, the dividend, the deal, the menu, whatever it is, but *now*. *NOW*

The infantile have no discrimination. They believe or reject what they are told, not by the application of reason, but according to whim: how they feel, how well or badly disposed they are to their interlocutor, how persuasively or excitingly the proposition is put, the extent to which the pill is sugared, the social consequences of acceptance or rejection (torn, always, between a tense but vaporous individualism and a sheepish yearning to belong).

The infantile cannot absorb language. Any argument is instantly deconstructed and mined for advantage or (almost as good) the opportunity for grievance. Don't like what someone says? *Hate* them! They are saying it to annoy or impede or diminish: *hate* them!

⚠ **Big Babies seek approval. Big Babies are terrified of assertion of anything other than the most infantile desires. Everything else must be appeasing and contingent. So for Big Babies things are never *so*. Things are, like, whatever. And nothing is ever a statement, which may meet with disapproval; everything must be a question? An opinion, tentatively expressed? With a, like, rising intonation? *Whatever*.**

The infantile cannot defer gratification; they lack the ability to extrapolate from the present into the future, and the authority to command themselves and their impulses. They want it now, and they want it delivered. If they can't have it now, they'll have it now anyway; and if they can't get it anyway . . . well, it's *unfair*, and someone's being *mean* to me, and that's, like, *not right*, see?

The infantile are not collaborative; they are not commensal, nor are they collegiate. They can be none of these things because they do not converse. Instead, they assert, tattle or reminisce. Someone else had a bigger one, they deserved a bigger one, they'll tell on someone who claims to have a bigger one, they knew someone who had a bigger one, did, didn't, did, didn't, 'tis, 'tisn't, 'tis. They have an excuse: they are in constant negotiation with a still-unfamiliar world with its apparently capricious rules and quirks of fate, subject to mighty powers, but nothing yet making sense.

The infantile yearn for novelty, possessing only a tiny attention span, so that everything is constantly new to them.

The infantile are ill at ease with ambiguity or complexity and, by some brute instinct, loathe those who aren't in the same boat.

The infantile are torn apart by the opposing forces of a monstrous egocentrism and a terrible, almost sacrificial, need to belong: an inherent duality of nature which reaches its zenith in the conflagrations of adolescence.

The infantile are reckless. They can't estimate danger, don't even recognise it, can't be trusted to keep themselves safe, need to be checked, supervised, cracked down on, kept in their place on a short lead with an eye on them, stamped out.

The infantile are emotionally labile and need to be palliated in case they *go off on one*, which will simply annoy everyone else . . . and the thing is, you can never tell what will set them *off on one* so the best thing to do is palliate them all the time, except when checking, supervising, cracking down on or stamping out.

If we had never seen a child or an adolescent, we might all the same be able to get a pretty shrewd idea of what they might be like, simply by reverse-engineering from the evidence. If we look at the advertisements on television, on hoardings, in the newspapers;* if we look at the newspapers themselves (particularly the

---

* Or indeed petrol pumps, milk bottles, in Post Office queues and anywhere people might be exposed to them; we would be advised not to linger too long over our lovemaking, in case an advertiser sneaks in through the window and glues an ad to our arse.

Sunday ones) or the magazines, or browse through the horrors of our onscreen satellite TV programme guide; if we walk about the streets and look into the shop windows, at the clothes people are wearing, at the things they are buying or being exhorted to buy, at the stuff they are eating and how they are eating it and what they do with the remains; if we walk around the streets later on at night and watch (and listen) to people as they come out of the bars and restaurants; if we go to the movies and watch whatever is being done to us, from up there on the screen; if we look at the warnings and admonitions, whether on road signs or notices or leaking perpetually from the sodden, smirking or scowling mouths of politicians; if we pay even a little attention to these things, we can deduce what the infantile are like.

The infantile are what *They* think we are like. Or what we *should* be like. Or what we *are*, secretly, like.

Are they right? *Is* that what we are like? Is that what we *want* to be like?

On Being a Grown-Up

Or would we rather be – and be thought of as, and treated as – grown-ups?

It's tricky, being grown-up. The great thing about being a Big Baby is it's so easy and so rewarding, and everybody else can just bugger off. Once one has embraced Modernity's Big Four – individualism, relativism, voluntarism, instrumentalism – and lapsed into the hooting, crooning self-validating babyhood which inevitably follows, then one is beyond criticism. Anyone who says otherwise just doesn't understand us and, what is more, is just plain wrong; and can bugger off. It's lovely.

Being grown-up is not nearly as comfortable. Let's, just for a moment, beg the question and say that one of the qualities of being a grown-up is what the Romans called *discrimen* and what we would perhaps call 'discrimination', though that doesn't quite cover it, and, anyway, under the strictures of Modernity, discrimination, far from being a cardinal virtue of adulthood, has become a – if not *the* – deadly sin. So *discrimen* it is.

Discrimen is the ability to judge a situation and to take right action without being confused or sidetracked or derailed by peripheral considerations. Sailors would call it 'seamanship'. Pilots refer to 'command authority'. Surgeons speak of 'decisiveness'. In all cases, *discrimen* is about knowing what to do in the circumstances, even if there is no guarantee (there is never a guarantee) of pulling it off.

But if *discrimen* is a cardinal virtue of adulthood, the tenets of infantilism work against it. *Discrimen* requires right judgement; but the idea of something, even judgment, being 'right', is in profound conflict with individualism (which says I can only claim my judgement as being right *for me*). It is in conflict with relativism (which says others may have different ideas which are right for them) and with voluntarism (which says that those different ideas are just as valid as mine, because they, too, have been chosen). And if it is not in conflict with instrumentalism (I can, of course, use other people in pursuit of my own self-realisation – in this case, the exercise of *discrimen*) then that is because it reveals the internal contradictions of Modernity.

Discrimen, in short, is emasculated. The appeal to some external absolute, whether expediency or morality, is disallowed. Instead, we are left with what we can get away with, what we can sell to others, under the guise of the sort of watered-down Utilitarianism which presents itself in the more glutinous song lyrics ('All men are brothers', when we most palpably are nothing of the sort) or the more fatuous lies of both the British Labour Party ('Equality for everyone unless Tony Blair doesn't want them to have it') or the American Republicans ('Homeland Security').

Without *discrimen* (and without a number of other things, which we shall encounter as we go along), not only is it impossible to be grown-up, but we also find ourselves making foolish remarks which we are unable to rescind, about everything, as we shall see, from cigarettes to religion.

But there are worse things than foolishness; and perhaps it is easier to live surrounded by relativism and silly remarks – and adding our own contributions to the tide-wash of idiocy – than to confront the difficulties of being a grown-up in the post-Darwinian era. If we remain infantile, childlike, perpetually adolescent until we die, then we may be taken by surprise (and, increasingly, outraged) by our own morbidity and mortality, but at least until then we can persuade ourselves that we are holding death at bay. Infantility, indefinitely prolonged, is also the indefinite prolongation of (false) promise. It's never too late . . . Never too late to stomp, cadaverous, around the stage singing 'Can't get no satisfaction'. Never too late to cast off the old wife and find a new one. Never too late to make the big killing, to score the goal, to find the perfect shoes, to acquire the perfect six-pack, rack, complexion, butt, pecs or thighs. Never too late (hell, *someone* must be answering the spam) to get the perfect dick, pumped up with a scoopful of mail-order Viagra; never too late to give her the perfect orgasm, get the perfect house, fill it with the perfect furniture, take the perfect vacation, drive the perfect car . . .

As the body ineluctably decays (the mind's long gone, of course; who needs it?) perpetual infantility glosses over the rheum, the presbyopia, the pains and creaks and flaccidities. As the opportunities dwindle (we are all piloting our lives into thick fog and no safe landing, as the escape route closes in behind us) perpetual infantility offers us illusion on easy terms with pick-'n'-mix spirituality, self-improvement, angels and goddesses, diversion and aspiration. As time slides past, doling out its irreversible quanta, perpetual infantility offers us . . . the perfect wristwatch: shockproof, waterproof, antimagnetic, a perpetual movement which says everything about us except the single intolerable truth: that we have had it and are headed for oblivion, tick by tick.

Once, we were immortal. Immortal no longer, abandoning infantility for adulthood can seem intolerably sombre. What

40

good is *discrimen* when the lights are going to go out? We might as well enjoy ourselves, because this is all there is. And who, after all, enjoy themselves more than Big Babies? Let the politicians patronise us, the broadcasters diminish us, the columnists patronise us with their own belittled lives; let the advertisers treat us like infants; let our freedoms be curtailed and our intellects clouded. As long as the burden of responsibility is lifted, we can divert ourselves with delusions and fun, and someone will be there to blot the dribble from the corners of our mouths.

Please Sir, May I Be Autonomous?

But if we strike the neo-Faustian pact – not power, not knowledge, but a sort of childish, impotent fun – we should at least be aware of the other side of the bargain: *The stars move still, time runs, the clock will strike. The devil will come, and Faustus must be damned.* 'Must be'? But he was damned all along. The terror was in the ironic gap, that it took him so long to realise it.

Our damnation (if it is damnation) is that we so happily trade our *discrimen* – our autonomy – for the illusion of perpetual promise. Our democratic institutions, as well as our adulthood, are based on the assumption that we not only are entitled to be, but in reality are, autonomous: literally, 'self-governing'.

Of course there's a continuum. At one end is the pure self-ruling individual, answerable to nobody but with nobody to offer help, support, protection or approval. At the other lies the self-subsuming of communism, approaching the condition of insects – ants, bees – or of the coral reef, where only the collective can possess any individuality. It's always a trade; but the discriminating grown-up acknowledges the necessity of rational consensus as a condition of autonomy in a practical sense: if we comply with a reasonable set of consensual laws, we are, the rest of the time, free to govern ourselves.

> ⚠ 'Residents of Shoreditch are to receive live CCTV and an on-screen rogues' gallery of local recipients of anti-social behaviour orders [...] Viewers will then be able to use an anonymous e-mail tip-off system to report to the police anyone they see breaching an Asbo or committing a crime.' (*Sunday Times*, 8 January 2006)

Infantility makes a different bargain. Free-thinking, self-actuating, self-indulging, Modern people that we are, we delude ourselves that we have an absolute autonomy when, in reality, we submit, inch by inch, to a busybody tyranny which controls, restricts, surveys and admonishes. Any autonomy we have within such a system, we have under sufferance. The admonishing state deludes us into believing that we have permitted – no, *petitioned* – it to watch us and manipulate us; that the watching and manipulation are for our own good, for our own safety, for our freedom of choice. The admonishing state, as always, lies. We are watched, manipulated and controlled (whether, as Juvenal had it, with bread or with circuses) because it is the instinct of the state to do so, and because the technology exists to make it possible.

When Americans have to show identification to travel in their own country; when Britons are forced to carry a biometric identity card to give account of themselves to the authorities: then we know the balance of power has been shifted through 180 degrees. The West has spent many centuries establishing the principle that the state is accountable to the citizenry. With the twin catastrophes of Modernity and information technology, the principle is being reversed. The citizenry are once again becoming accountable to the state. And we are sitting back, grizzling, gurgling, and amusing ourselves to death.

On Just Being Yourself

But (we might say) isn't it splendid that we have come to embrace such diversity, such self-realization, so that nobody now need skulk in a corner, dodging blows, because of their personal circumstances, nature or predilections? Isn't it marvellous that people can listen to the music they want, be the colour they were born, have sex with whom they wish, believe in whatever god they choose or none at all, escape the circumstances of their birth, retain the accents of their origins, dress as they wish, and all these things without being despised or beaten in the street?

Of course it is. But we are not here to roll back hard-won freedoms or to denounce individual choice. We are here to ask the questions: why are we being treated so much, and so increasingly, like children? And why are we colluding in it?

And perhaps the answer is that we no longer know what we should be like; we no longer know what it means to 'be ourselves'. It's a truism to say that our sense of ourselves is, individually and collectively, fragile; but perhaps we do not see (partly because of careful concealment; partly because, like a lobster brought slowly to the boil, it has crept up on us incrementally) the dedicated and relentless degree of manipulation which has been brought to bear to turn us into true citizens of the infantilised society.

Democracy, or, Your Social Duty Explained

This, at least, is simple. Our social duty is to do as we are told, and go shopping. It is. Look around you. *It is.*

What Do You Lack?

If our passive duty is to do as we are told, then shopping is our active duty: the thing that primarily makes us good citizens, and so our most powerful social or civic urge must be wanting. Credit-card companies and other debt-mongers play on this, absolving our potential guilt and fear (but just you wait until you miss a payment: then the buggers will be on the phone, then the letters and the penalty payments will start, then you'll be BAD) with false-friendliness, the leer, the coaxing, the absolution in advance. Debt? We don't have debt, with its overtones of the sponging-house, the Fleet prison, bailiffs and tipstaffs abroad.* Bring back imprisonment for debt and watch the credit 'industry'

> ⚠ 'Bad debts at Barclaycard, Britain's largest credit card company, could exceed £1.5 billion this year ... finance director Naguib Kheraj [said] 'It's not a question of more customers getting into difficulties or defaulting, but that balances of customers who do get into difficulties are higher ... *In a sense, that's encouraging* [my emphasis].'' (*The Guardian*, 26 May 2006)

(not, of course, an industry at all; more a parasite on others' industry) disintegrate. Where would we be without it? Happier, perhaps? As of March 2006, UK and US consumer debt was over four trillion dollars; that's an awful lot of bills, an awful lot of interest, an awful lot of computer-generated letters, an awful lot of people poised to spring – unfortunate people mewed up in call centres from Mumbai to the Wirral, reading off scripts to

---

* Except for Sundays, when a man could walk about the streets without fear of arrest; 'Sunday gentlemen' they were called, and you wouldn't want your daughter to marry one.

scare the poor idiots who believed in the grinning credit-card advertisements, who identified with the bemused victim in the debt-consolidation advertisment, pictured on the telephone, arranging the loan which will soon wipe him out: 'We just want it all in one place so we know where we stand.'

'Why wait? Treat yourself today!' Why wait, indeed. Not waiting – not being able to wait – is characteristic of the infant in all things. The infant can't wait for food; the infant can't wait to empty its bowels or bladder. And the infantilised society cannot wait (or is persuaded it can't, or needn't, or shouldn't) for the analogues, the metonyms or metaphors of consumption and evacuation: gadgets, houses, faces, six-packs, clothes, music, food, more food, yet more food, anger, sex, violence, excitement, shouting, punching, attention, drink, oblivion, money, novelty, diversion, distraction, success, fulfilment. Now! *Now!* Can't wait? *Why* wait? *Won't* wait! Howard from the Halifax – a real-life bank clerk dressed up as a spaceman, with a matey smile and Bunter spectacles – says we needn't wait . . . so we're not *going* to wait.

And so we move towards a world in which not-waiting becomes, in itself, a good, and consumption becomes a marker of *being* good. But what an infantile being-good it is. Good baby ate it all up! Good baby did a poo! Good baby pleased Howard from the Halifax (and good baby, of course, doesn't see the men, the white men, the middle-aged middle-class white men, behind the scenes, pulling the strings, taking the long view . . . unless one of them screws up and announces that only a fool borrows on credit cards).*

But if not waiting is a good thing in itself, what are we not waiting *for*? Before we can refuse to wait, we have to *desire* something, *need* something, *want* something. Infants' desires are stimulated by waving whatever-it-is in front of their eyes: look what baby can have if baby wants it enough. And, sure enough,

---

* 'I do not borrow on credit cards. It is too expensive. I have four young children. I give them advice not to pile up debts on their credit cards.' Matthew Barrett, CEO of Barclays, to the House of Commons Treasury Committee, 16 October 2003.

baby goes mad with wanting, mad with wanting *now*, mad with not being able to wait.

And Big Babies are no different. 'Advertising,' George Orwell wrote, 'is the rattling of a stick inside a swill-bucket,' but, like so many memorable figures, it doesn't deconstruct well. The implication is that, by responding to advertising, we are pigs: subordinate creatures, gullible and unclean; so unclean that we eat swill. But for a pig, swill is nourishment and without it he dies; the rattle of the stick merely says 'Here is something you genuinely need; it is good for you; you have probably been waiting for it; it is here now: come and get it.'

⚠ 'It isn't a fragrance for fans of the band exclusively. It's about being a free thinker who blazes their own path and lives life according to their own rules realizing that there is no rehearsal for life. I find it a real turn-on – it's very feminine without being frilly. When I smell more women wearing KISS Her, my head will be turning to a point I need a brace. It's very sexy, flirtatious and very hot. It takes a certain kind of person – one with a little wildness waiting to come out.' The fragrance created by IFF perfumers includes 'top notes of apple-tini, wet fig leaves, racy bull accord and red peppercorns; middle notes of red poppy, black orchid, sueded frangipani petals and calla lily, and base notes of amber crystals, musky bare skin accord, patent leather and mahogany.' (Perfume PR, quoting a guitarist in the band Kiss)

'Fragrances are among the most common causes of allergic contact dermatitis, and they are certainly the most common cosmetic ingredient causing allergic contact dermatitis. They can also cause photodermatitis, contact urticaria, irritation, hyperpigmentation and depigmentation of skin.' (Auckland Allergy Clinic, October 2001)

Advertising – the advertising directed towards Big Babies* – is not about announcing what Stephen King christened 'needful things', but about making us want something. 'I want it now,' we cry, and ring up the call centre and listen, thrilled, to the scripts of pallid manipulators in drizzling northern towns which promise us more, now, and later will never come. The people we speak to have no authority; they are simulacra of human beings, mechanized rather than infantilised in a horrible inversion of the (un)natural laws of machine interaction, in which people become the avatars of computers. But all the same, they can give – *give?* – us what we want.

What do we want?

What do we *lack*? The words, at root, imply the same thing (though we choose to forget it): a deficiency, something missing, an incompleteness. It is still possible, still the lot of a large portion of humanity to die of want: want of food, want of shelter, want of health, want of medicine. Now we are merely encouraged to *feel* that we will die of a consumerised shadow of want: want of the latest upgrade, the smallest iPod, the smartest house, the fastest car. When we believe we want organic home-cured ham with the Prince of Wales's name on it, want a platinum-nibbed Mont Blanc pen, want a Jaeger Le Coultre Reverso watch which tells the time somewhere else in the world, want Botox, want to lose twenty pounds, want orgasms on demand, want it *all*, and want it *delivered* . . . what we are really saying is that we have a sort of free-floating sense of lacking something, an everything-shaped hole in us which can never be filled by anything. It is the characteristic of the mental landscape in which the Big Babies live, a landscape of immeasurable plenty but never enough, of feast and famine springing from the same source; it is, in short, a universe – a

---

* Who would never – for example – fall for the old advertisements for Three Nuns tobacco, which (successfully) encouraged young men to buy it because that was what the Vicar smoked. Then, the Vicar was one paradigm (however faulty or absurd) of being grown up; now, the Vicar wants to do what the young do.

Mummyverse – in which, like infants who believe that Mummy has gone away for ever, we are rendered so anxious by being *advertised at* that we never stop long enough to see that there *is* no want; that, in reality, we lack nothing; nor do we realise that when advertisers rattle the stick in the swill-bucket, they are trying to sell us bucket and stick, and there is no nourishing swill inside.

Zigazig-*ah*

'What do ye lack?' the old street-peddlers of London used to cry. 'What do ye lack?'

Marginal men have always moved in liminal spaces. They come in from the outside and take the streets as their territory, their shopfronts, their markets. And as their stage.

In his great biography of London, Peter Ackroyd writes of the beggars and hawkers and street musicians and of

> [the] many professions and trades where the actual principle was that of acting . . . Suffering and mimicry, penury and drama, are aligned with each other to a degree where they become indistinguishable.

And the cry of one of these lemmata, these human scribbles commenting upon the great text of London from the margins, could only be identified as: *Happy happy happy now*.

The question-mark is implicit. 'Happy happy happy now?'

Never. Not now. Because round comes the interrogation again. What do you lack? *What do you lack?* And a whole industry, a whole economy, has been built on maintaining us in a constant state of lacking. *What do we lack?* It was never a reasoned appeal, but a call to contemplation. Yes . . . what *do* we lack? Something. We know it's something or we wouldn't respond. Who now can say 'I lack nothing' without feeling that it's that admission which

48

is somehow shameful; that to be beyond desire is simultaneously smug and anti-social? The statement seems to us now provisional, contingent, conditional; if we hear (or say) 'I lack nothing' we expect a continuation: 'but', and then the truth. 'I am still not happy.' 'I feel incomplete.' Like the infant, the child, the adolescent, we seem to ourselves to be people-in-waiting, liminal creatures, things of the in-between. We may not be the Undead; but we are, all the same, the not-quite-alive. After a little over half a century on the planet, I still feel uneasy about declaring myself to be a man; to myself, in privacy, I am masquerading; I know I am not a boy, nor yet an adolescent, yet in my deepest self I know I am somehow lacking, that I am not, entirely, a man. And yet, at the same time, I also know that it is a public good that I am not quite a man; it is the postmodern way to be ironical, constantly under (re)construction, to be . . . provisional, contingent, conditional. My grandfather knew he was a man; my father knows he is a man. For me, born in 1953 in the middle of the Baby Boom, I know, perhaps, that I could be a man if only I could identify, and make good, the lack.

When we say we 'want' something, we mean we *lack* something. Sometimes (as in the case of a starving man) the lack and the want are the same: food. Sometimes (as in the case of a fat man crouched before the fridge in the middle watch) the want may be food but the lack . . . the lack is of something else altogether. But want and lack are always linked, inextricably. To promote our want is to make us always lacking. Lacking something we can't identify. A decade ago, the Spice Girls made a fortune demanding to know if they should tell us what they really, really wanted. Most of us weren't that interested – the question seemed pushy, rude and somehow terribly *un-English* – but they were quite insistent, and the answer to what they really, really wanted, as far as one could make it out, seemed to be this:

Zigazig-ah.

'Zigazig-ah.' The amorphous nothing; the unattached 'want'. We might almost say that here, at last, is Jacques Derrida's 'transcendental signified' which transcends all signifiers; a meaning which transcends all signs. Nor is it coincidence that the song was called 'Wannabe'; the want – the identified lack – is not about wanting to have, but about having a want. And the want is the *wanting to be*. The *becoming*. And it is 'becoming' which lies behind the rites of passage identified by the anthropologist van Gennep; condemned to perpetual liminality, though, we never complete the rites; never become; lack, always.

The rites of incorporation are never completed; at least, not in a way that we can understand. No bell is rung to say that we are grown-ups now, with the rights, the privileges and, God help us, the *duties* of grown-ups. We have become a society of impostors, acting the part; or, rather, overacting the part, so that we can see each others' lips moving like duff ventriloquists. The scenery of our mock-adulthood is badly done; the walls wobble when we slam the door; we worry endlessly about our costumes and suck up Sunday supplements by the forest-load to see whether we are getting it right.

And, of course, we are *not* getting it right. Look at your Sunday papers. What are they for? They are for lodging new neuroses, new doubts, in you, and twisting and tweaking the old ones so that you reach the dreadful despair of Sunday teatime somehow oddly diminished, less than you were, sure that other people have more money, better lives, more and better sex, faster cars, smarter houses, more fulfilling jobs; they are better-read, more fun, funnier, fluent conversationalists, adept seducers, money-wise but open-handed; they struck it lucky, timed it right, knew the people worth knowing, played their hands well. And now they consume the *entire world*: they have holiday homes on this coast or that island, they live in the smartest part of the smartest town, they mingle with the movers and shakers (moving what? Shaking what? What is this stuff that needs moving and shaking, and why can't it just be for God's sake left alone?) and

50

the worst thing of all is that we are *jealous* of them. We envy them. And by feeling envy, we are infantilised all over again.

We know they are loathsome. We know that we would rather be dead than travel from Paris to, my dear, Menton in the same railway compartment as them. We know that there is something wrong with anyone who spends that much time and that much money on their house, their car, their looks, their clothes, their self-promotion. We know their remarks are inane; our eyes bubble with disbelieving contempt at their astounding vapidity and their even more astounding self-regard.

But we *envy them*.

We partly envy them because we have been *told* to envy them. No human mind can resist engaging with the onslaught of the Murdoch machine or the Fox buggers for long, but even while we are being suckered, we know it is happening, and loathe ourselves for our weakness, our inability to defend ourselves, the way in which we are turned into mere punters . . . because the characteristic of the punter is that he colludes in his own self-delusion.

Check out the literal punters on Punternet,* an Internet site where men with gauche, galumphing nicknames (hornyguy57, MaxPussy, BIGDICKUS, uglyandfat, lickitoff, knobsquirter, MikeTheTongue, labialover, funboy23 . . .) write reviews ('Field Reports') on prostitutes. No reason why they shouldn't, of course; in a civilised world (you might argue) the Sunday papers should have whore critics just as they have restaurant reviewers.† Nor should we sneer at them too much for their horrid attempts to normalise their transgressions, referring to their pastime as 'the Hobby' and constructing little abbreviations for their practices: A for sodomy, OWO for fellatio without a condom, CIM

---

* <http://www.punternet.com> Now wash your hands.

† And there are historical precedents, too; see, for example, Hallie Rubenhold, *The Covent Garden Ladies: Pimp General Jack & the Extraordinary Story of Harris's List* (Stroud: Tempus, 2005).

for ejaculation in the prostitute's mouth, 'mish' for missionary position . . . fair enough, even if you want to take a shower after reading the chummy, hopeful, geeky nomenclature, designed to create a normative illusion around what is an eerily marginal pastime.

But then comes delusion. 'GFE' is the phrase, and it stands for 'Girlfriend Experience', and a prostitute who offers the 'real GFE' is accorded hollow plaudits. 'She is a gem, guys. Treat her with the respect she deserves,' respect which you may think might start by not giving her money to sodomise her and ejaculate down her throat, but then 'the respect she deserves' can be parsed in several ways. The phrase 'Girlfriend Experience' is far from any reality. The real Girlfriend Experience would involve minor arguments about food and car keys and what film to see and whether *The Simpsons* has lost its edge, and if there are interestingly perverse bedroom scenes, they are more likely to be about changing bedlinen, and how, precisely, he has managed to get himself entirely engulfed in the duvet cover and wedged behind the duvet (which he has pulled in after himself), and whether there is anything she can do to help or whether it's best to leave him to worm his way out, and whether she's going to wet herself if she laughs any more, and whether he is having a heart attack in there or has just seen the funny side . . .

But Girlfriend Experience, on Punternet, means the illusion of mutuality. It means a prostitute who gives the impression that she likes it as much as her client. It means, in short, tongue-in-mouth kissing and something like foreplay: a glass of wine, a fumble on the sofa, a tangle of clothes and orgasms for two. Or, rather – bearing in mind Thomas de Zengotita's observation that in, for example, Yellowstone Park, 'you won't see wolves, you'll see "wolves"' – we should call them 'orgasms'. No boasting, they write, but either 'she came three time's, v noisely, or shes a very good actress'. 'Natural things,' Zengotita goes on, 'have become their own icons.' The wolf, under our gratified consuming gaze, enacts 'wolf'; the prostitute, 'orgasms'.

And the 'field reporters' know the truth: that she had *no orgasms at all*. They know that when she put her tongue in their mouth – which is not something you'd do for money, is it? – she was doing it for the money. They know she *is* a very good actress. And they know that it is a performance, a mimesis, in which the punter's role is to perform the part of someone who doesn't know it is a performance. Their part in the trade is to conflate orgasms and 'orgasms', and to be satisfied with the bargain. The alternative – to acknowledge that they are cheating and being cheated, that they are paying for a (dis)simulation of reality, a Reality Lite – would be too demeaning.

MaxPussy, uglyandfat, lickitoff and knobsquirter are our avatars here, the quintessence of our postmodernist, infantilised condition, colluding in their own existential cuckolding. It's what we all do all the time. Nothing in this world of Reality Lite is quite genuine. We know we are being sold a set of illusions, and we know our role in the illusion is to pretend to be taken in. Because if we don't pretend to be taken in (even though we aren't taken in, and can see the cogs whirring, the smoke and mirrors, the lie-detector juddering off the chart, the tacks showing and the sawdust trickling out of the back) the whole illusion could implode, and leave us nowhere.

Or, worse still, leave us *nobody*.

Because our identities hang by a thread. How can we tell we are real when the reality of being grown-up, of being autonomous, of being . . . incorporated, are all contingent and provisional?

On Being Onscreen

By being on television, that's how. By being *famous*. By being recognised: a *celebrity*.

Some years ago, I accompanied the great cartoonist Michael Heath (whose work will tell historians of the future far more about how we lived in the late twentieth and early twenty-first centuries than any amount of earnest social anthropology) to New York. He was going to do a book, *Welcome to America*, but had never been further than the Isle of Wight before, and took against the Boeing 747 immediately. 'Nightmare,' he said. 'It's too big and who are all these terrible people with their terrible children, and what are they *wearing*, it's a *nightmare.*' But it got us to JFK and we made it to the Chelsea Hotel on West 23rd Street. By some foul-up in the booking system (later revealed to be due to the reception clerk, who said 'You were obviously two English faggots') we had to share a room, and I was woken before dawn the following morning by Heath, who was sitting in his under-wear gazing at the television and yelling with outrage. 'Christ,' he was shouting, 'Look at this nightmare! This guy! Look, the guy who's interviewing this man, he says he's famous! He's a success! The guy's a success and that's all the other guy is saying! But he's not saying what he's a success *at*! How can you just be a success? Does that mean *we're* successes?' He opened the window and bellowed out into the central well: 'Hey! We're *successful*! We're in here and we're *successes*! It's the *American Way*!'

Lurking in the absurdity, as is so often the case, was a funda-mental truth: that being onscreen is in itself enough, in the infantilised society, to guarantee a kind of reality.

Once, being onscreen generated a sort of super-reality. If we were real, they were more so, and the nature of the more-so-ness was not that far removed from (as far as we can reconstruct it) the idea of the ancient Greek gods. Not, of course, in the question of agency – nobody (apart from a few lonely people with a thin grip on reality, or the more flagrantly delusional) believed that being onscreen conferred the power to intervene in human destiny – but in the sense that they were like us, but bigger and realer and somehow more consequential. But for them to be those things required that we believed ourselves to be already big, real and consequential – three things that the infant (or the infantilised) most certainly is not.

> ⚠ There is television in taxis now, with – of course – a safety briefing (because all transport now aspires to the debased condition of the passenger aircraft) and then there is BBC Comedy because our minds need to be distracted from being in a taxi, in the world, in the street. And we *can't turn it off*. There is *no way to turn it off*.

But in a world where we never quite get to grips with the business of growing up – which is about autonomy and agency – then being onscreen is no longer about being ultra-real, but about just being *real enough*. We talk of 'reality TV' although the phrase is a nonsense, both in how it manifests itself (are those people on *Geraldo* or *Oprah* or *Big Brother* 'real'? Do we know any 'real' people who carry on like that, except for petulant children and those suffering from the psychosis of adolescence?) and in the phrase itself. Television is *not real*. Anything that happens on 'reality TV' is at worst a parody, at best a simulacrum, of reality itself. The observer alters the thing observed, and, on television, everyone acquires the status of Schrödinger's Cat: the moment the red light flicks on, the question is answered, the wave-form collapsed. They become *who they are* as soon as, and only when, we can see them.

And it is precisely because the wave-form is collapsed by the television lens that being onscreen confers reality. Unlike the onscreen gods, we ourselves – not the Undead, but the Unreal – are still oscillating between states of being, and given a burst of energy by the Sunday newspapers and all the rest of the media Heisenbergs, trading on uncertainty. We may be rich but are we happy? We may be happy but are we beautiful? We may be beautiful but are we posh? We may be posh but *what do we lack*?

Locked in our endless becoming, our own wave-forms forever uncollapsed, we gaze, with half-formed eyes, on those who have *become*. Well, of course they have; how otherwise could they be *onscreen*?

And yet there is still something uneasy about them. It is a curious phenomenon, but the President of the USA and the Prime Minister of Great Britain seem less substantial than Homer Simpson. Television is the natural element of all three; but only Homer was *made* for it. The other two are not-quite-televisual, just as, when they are not onscreen, they are not-quite-real. The only way we can deal with it (short of mass uprising and civil war) is to join MaxPussy, uglyandfat, lickitoff and knobsquirter. *She came three time's, v noisely*, we tell each other; *he's the President; he's the Prime Minister; treat them with the respect they deserve.*

But we know they aren't real. And we think we might not be, either.

I Believe in One Me

Maybe we're right. Maybe we aren't real. But the great post-modern (knowing, ironic) fear is that there isn't a 'real us' for us to be.

We used to cope by installing a sort of imaginary retort in ourselves, a distillery of essentialism which we called our 'soul', and this soul contained or exemplified or in some other way, always ill-defined, defined the One True Me.

Being grown-up was taking responsibility for nurturing our One True Me. Whether or not we dealt with the person of God directly (very different he was from the unctuous, ingratiating, 'personal god' of modern supermarket relativism, the roll-your-own Gentle Jesus, which makes one believe that, while it may have its troubles, Islam has at least not infantilised its actual *God*), adulthood came at the point at which we took that responsibility. If it was the duty of a man to save his own soul, then looking after that soul defined you as a man. Up to that point, others looked after it for you; after that point, you were on your own.

If you defined your soul as around half to three-quarters of an ounce of something-or-other resembling interstellar ether,[*] that was what you looked after and attempted to save.

If you defined your 'true self' as not being a soul at all, but the aggregate of your experience, an error-prone catalogue of unreliable sense-data, a solipsistic hallucination, or a by-product of the workings of the speech centres in the brain, you attempted to develop and look after *that*.

> ⚠ Big Babies do not know who they are. They have no idea, left to themselves, where they stand. So even on the fifteen-minute train ride from London to Heathrow, there is a First Class carriage, for those whose sense of self is so unspeakably fragile that they cannot go quarter of an hour without reassurance.

But, in any case, there was a *you*, your own One True Me, and you believed in it, and nurtured it. And doing so was what made you an adult.

What, now, has taken the place of this essential 'you'? We feel, perhaps, that we have come a long way; that each of us can define ourselves as we wish; that the old tyranny of 'adulthood' has been done away with, and each of us can fulfil the only true sacred trust of modernity, the full realization of our own selves.

The trouble is, we don't much believe it any more. We may talk about ourselves, and finding ourselves, but what we talk about, and what we hope to find, is the correct permutation of aspirations, desires and diversions which will do the job for us. A

---

* That was the proposed weight of the soul suggested in a series of experiments carried out by Dr Duncan MacDougall, of Haverhill, MA, and published in *American Medicine* (April 1907). A few years later, Dr MacDougall tried to photograph the soul, using X-rays, declaring that it gave off a 'light resembling interstellar ether' (*New York Times*, 24 July 1911).

dash of Buddhism, the right kind of iPod stuffed with the right kind of music; the appropriate house, an interesting erotic *truc*, the best possible sport, an unspoilt holiday destination, the right sort of children in the right sort of school, the clothes appropriate for the image we have been exposed to in order to make us believe that the sort of person wearing those clothes is the sort of person we would like to be, the fragrance and grooming products ditto . . . the One True Self we once believed in (or thought we believed in) has been reduced to a set of ingredients; and the saving of our souls has been converted into a slaking of desires. This is not the condition of an adult; this is the state of a child.

And don't They just know it?

I Am What I Am

Does it matter? Does it matter apart from the annoyance we feel, the sense that something has got a bit *thin* in our lives, that we are being buggered about with so that someone else can benefit, either by getting rich or getting power? Is there any significance other than the raised blood pressure, the desire to kill when yet another unutterable fool tries to tell us what to do and, by doing so, implies that he knows what is good for us because he knows who we are?

One of the primary tools of infantilisation is denial of autonomy; or, to put it another way, identity control. We feel most autonomous when we can control what is known about us. If we have no such control, we cannot give ourselves freely. The chief desire of the lover is, perhaps, to be known by the beloved, but if being known is a condition of our citizenship, then it is debased and worthless. Perhaps this is why we feel so disturbed when the government wants us to carry identity cards containing encoded biometrics which prove who we are. We know that a few dozen bits of data can prove no such thing; that we are immeasurably more than the sum of our credit rating, address, DNA, tax history and criminal record. We know instinctively that, bleat how they may about security (if governments) or Improved Customer Service (if corporations), people who want to collect and monitor this sort of data are doing it, not for us, but for them. It is one thing to reveal, to one's beloved, a secret craving for Cheez Whizz or Bailey's Irish Cream; another to have interchangeable super-market executives knowing it. The old saw 'the innocent have nothing to hide' fails to persuade us because it is a category mis-take. Having something to hide is not contingent on guilt but on autonomy. Choosing who knows what about us, and when, is a sign, not that we are guilty, but that we are grown-up; and when we have to show ID to get on an aeroplane for a domestic flight, when we have to account for ourselves at every turn, when we are hectored about health and safety, and photographed by auto-matic cameras, and forced to talk to strangers – people thousands of miles away who neither know nor care who we are – about our money (which is in itself a powerful symbol of adulthood), we feel cheated, manipulated, undervalued, traduced and gen-erally buggered about.

In 1934, the irritatingly bluff, pipe-smoking cartoon 'Yorkshireman' J. B. Priestley took a journey (in his big motor car) round England and wasn't altogether pleased with what he found:

> Notice how the very modern things, like the films and wireless and sixpenny stores, are absolutely democratic, making no distinction whatever between their patrons: if you are in a position to accept what they give – and very few people are not in that position – then you get neither more nor less than what anybody else gets. Just as in the popular restaurants there are no special help-ings for favoured patrons but mathematical portions for everybody.

59

There is almost every luxury in this world except the luxury of power or the luxury of privacy. (With the result that these are the only luxuries that modern auto-crats insist upon claiming for themselves. They are far more austere than most of the old tyrants ever were, but they are all greedy for power and sticklers for privacy.)

. . . Too much of it is simply a trumpery imitation of something not very good even in the original. There is about it a rather depressing monotony. Too much of this life is being stamped on from outside, probably by astute financial gentlemen, backed by the Press and their publicity services. You feel that too many of the people in this new England are doing not what they like but what they have been told they would like. (Here is the American influence at work.)

. . . I cannot help feeling that this new England is lacking in character, in zest, gusto, flavour, bite, drive, originality, and that this is a serious weakness. Monotonous but easy work and a liberal supply of cheap luxuries might between them create a set of people entirely without ambition or any real desire to think and act for themselves, the perfect subjects for an iron autocracy. There is a danger of this occurring in the latest England.

It has occurred, both in Britain and the United States: autoc-racy of a kind unimaginable even twenty-five years ago has snuck in, honey-tongued, smiling and nicely groomed, and we have just rolled over and sucked it up. Undemocratic and possi-bly illegal war is waged in our name but without our agreement. Our governments are run by men with tyrannical instincts, both of them clearly wrong in the head, both claiming democratic mandates which they do not possess. In Britain, the government warns parents that they will be 'forced' to accept government advice, while instituting a vague 'action plan' based on the maundering and witless assertion 'Give respect, get respect', as if 'respect' is a medium of exchange (you give it, you therefore get it) rather than a fine and discriminatory judgement, and hapless, witless 'respect tsars' are appointed (by this book-fiddling, lying, evasive government) to make us toe the line; we are told that we 'owe all faiths respect' in defiance of all reason (or at least that moment where reason tangentially glances against faith). In this, as in so many other areas, we are treated like naughty school-children. And instead of siphoning petrol out of the car, collecting milk bottles and tearing up old rags, we simply lie there and take it. We don't seem particularly to mind. If I'm not much mistaken, we're enjoying it. Unless we are very good actors. Treat us with the respect we deserve.

Avatars R Us

If you can tell what a society values by the prices it puts on things . . . why, we've had it, because what we seem to value most is being out of society, at home: shutting the front door, drawing the curtains, turning on the television and hiding out. In terms of opportunity and of action, we have become idiots in the classical Greek sense of *idiotes*, people who take no part in public life. We spend all our money on our homes or our private amuse-ments. Endless magazines cater to the voluptuous, cloying dream of 'home', the place where we can be the magic self which those endless magazines show to us. Apparently normal people sit for hours dribbling gently in front of pictures of houses owned by people who are clearly barking mad; interior design magazines run features on the houses of interior designers, which readers then imitate so that their houses look just as if they belong to interior designers. The One True Me an interior designer? But why not? Interior design is about creating an avatar: if you are nobody yet, if you are unformed, if you have not yet *become*, then your home (left to your own proper devices) will be no more than a staging-post, boxes unpacked, stuff strewn at random, your furniture saying nothing about you. This, apparently, is the worst thing that furniture can do, and if you think that the only thing your chair can say about you is 'This is what he sits on', you are missing something crucial in life.

And the crucial thing in life is this: nothing is what it appears to be. Our life has been reduced to an exercise in branding, and there is no escape. The only way out is blocked by what we might term the Muji Effect.

Muji started off as (they would have us believe) an anti-branding exercise. Their stuff – clothes, furniture, stationery, bicycles, luggage – was supposed simply to be good, cheap, plainly packaged. But what happened? Shopping at Muji became a way of making the statement that you were not taken in by branding, and so it was that Muji acquired its brand, and a very powerful brand it was. John Donne would have liked it. 'If I an ordinary nothing were,' he wrote, 'As shadow, a light and body must be here'. *Muji: Not Just an Ordinary Nothing.*

You can't get away from it. I use a shaving cream from my barber in London, Trumper's. It used to come in a pot which just said 'Trumper's Shaving Cream' on it. It didn't need to show off or brand itself; it was what it was; Trumper's was a famous barber which had been around for ever. Then marketing took over. The pot was redone in mock-Victorian lettering, with mock-Victorian 'heritage' text, nonsense about how it was 'Prepared at his celebrated Establishment'. It had been branded; but what was particularly odd was that it had been branded in order to give the impression that it was *what it actually was in reality*. The thing had become its own avatar and, by insisting, semiotically, on its own authenticity, it had mythologised itself at the cost of the authenticity upon which it was insisting.

Sound familiar? It *is* familiar. I can look around my apartment and see innumerable examples of precisely the same process. Here, in the refrigerator, is another tiny example: a pat of Italian butter. I have been buying this butter for some years. It has an embossed cow on it. Recently, on the packet, it has taken to announcing that this is *butter with Cow embossing*. The signifier and the signified have changed places.

This is precisely the mechanism of adolescence, the final blast of transitional infantilism before the adulthood that we can no longer quite attain, when our identities are so provisional, so strained, that we cannot clearly articulate them and must send avatars out into the world to speak for us. Adolescents are beaten up for wearing the wrong sort of trainers, or beaten up for wearing the right sort of trainers because another adolescent needs, but hasn't yet got, them. We, the Big Babies, have taken it a step further. We invest everything in our homes and in our homes we stay, surrounded by avatars – attorneys-of-taste who will speak on our behalf, but who speak only to us.

But what are they saying behind our backs?

CHAPTER 3

What Do You Think
You Look Like?

They are, for example, saying: 'What does he think he looks like?'

Of course they are. And the strange thing is, in the visual, post-literate world, assailed by images from every side, exemplars choking the always-on pipelines of the Internet, television, advertising, magazines and newspapers – so many images, so that we ourselves become images, and think of our image (and hire image consultants if we can afford it) – the strange thing is that, among all this visual noise, this visual panic, we don't have any idea what we look like.

How else would you explain it?

Again: don't take my word for it. Go out into the street and look at the people around you. Look at yourself, if you like. If you are truly postmodern, a child of our times, the first problem is to decide whether the visual thing that walks about and interacts with the world is, actually, you, or just a sort of representation of, or an advertisement for, you. I can only answer for myself, but the answer is alarming. I see before me one who is not me, but who could be, if changes (every bit as startling and radical as the changes we undertake in puberty and adolescence) were enacted. I see a man shorter than 'I' am, with a larger belly than 'I' have. I see a man worryingly not bald in the slightest. 'I' am bald, as a marker of manhood. My father was bald by the time he was twenty-eight and, as a boy, I assumed that you knew when you were really, actually a man because you went bald. It never happened. So I am not bald, but 'I' am bald.

Already, I am provisional, in the process of becoming 'me'. This is not, I fear, egregious. It is the condition of the postmodern man.

The postmodern man is never quite himself; never quite comes to terms with what he is. He tries to elicit desire by artificial means, unaware of his ability to do so naturally which is kept from him by the torrent of admonition from television, magazines, advice on the Internet. The postmodern man believes that he can only be acceptable if surrounded by things – honours, possessions, riches, testimonials – which vouch for him. A hereditary peerage, a chiselled jaw, £20 million in liquid assets, a Ferrari, a Nobel Prize, an Oscar, a Regius Chair, a place on the national team, an extra five inches of stature, an expensive wardrobe, whipcord muscles, piercing blue eyes, a senior partnership: then postmodern man could be himself, acceptable and authentic.

> ⚠ See the sophisticated person drinking her small *ristretto* at a pavement café, in the morning sun. Now see the AmeriBrit, clutching a cardboard pail of fluffy frothed milk dusted with sweetened chocolate, dosed with NutraSweet, sucked through the Suk-U-Like™ lidspout like a toddler's training beaker, and believing himself a sophisticate. (The soul-sucking Starbucks now has instructions on how to order your coffee. Coming soon: Why Despite Everything You Should Try to Enjoy It or You Will Get a Smack, We Apologize for the Inconvenience, Have a Nice Day.)

This is not a sensible way to carry on. Nor is it adult behaviour. It is the self-absorbed dislocation of the childish self, the self of shadows, the identity of a flickering turnip-ghost, the yearning self-deception of one made hopeless by the certainty that there is nobody there, and the few fragments that are there will somehow not do unless amended.

It is, in short, an infantile way of behaving. Or, rather, we have been infantilised.

Everywhere we look, we see games of let's-pretend. I, for one, am playing let's-pretend, spying life through my CibaVision Night & Day contact lenses, which I wear largely to give the impression that I have perfect vision, instead of the short-sighted truth. (I have worn glasses since I was five. Wire earpieces, mocha-and-flesh-coloured plastic frames. When I put them on I could see clearly; and what I could see clearly was that the world had changed for ever and from now on I was damaged.)

We might distinguish here between deception and let's-pretend. My contact lenses certainly give others the impression that I do not need glasses. That is an innocent deception. But they also give me the same impression; and that is let's-pretend. In tending to our appearance, how much is deception, and how much let's-pretend?

One more personal example. I wear a Tilley T4 outdoor hat, not because of its undoubted fine qualities, but because its clever marketing persuades me that it possesses an iconic quality which signifies an outdoors man. Not being an outdoors man, this is important to me; otherwise why would I be wearing this hat indoors, with nobody to see? I am playing let's-pretend, and I have just spent an hour on the Web shoring up the fantasy of my own outdoor-manliness, where I have made a list of other Tilley Endurables – 'Endurables'! – I need to buy: rugged trousers and easy-wash adventure shirts and a photojournalist's jacket, all of which are rather nasty-looking and remind me of the sort of person I dislike . . . except that if I were to wear them, I wouldn't be like that sort of person; in imitating them, I would overleap them and become, magically, the exemplar whom *they* were trying to imitate (chiselled, tanned, rugged, authentic), and so somehow emasculate and defeat them. Like a small boy playing cowboys and Native Americans.

On the Web, there are hat reviews. There are reviews of everything. You name it, it's been reviewed, by astonishingly detailed obsessives. Sometimes I read reviews of things I already have and like; the computer software on which I depend, for example. I chose these tools on sound grounds. But still I need to read other people saying so; eighteen-year-olds, on the whole, because they are the sort of people who post software 'reviews' on the Web. Why do I need my adult choices to be ratified by these people?

Because (I think) I am a postmodern man.

The postmodern man has no real confidence in his own idea of what he should be, and so no idea of what he is and how he is measuring up. This is a defining condition of being infantile. Poor postmodern man becomes entirely dependent on external ratification. The sense of being autonomous, self-defining, possessed of the adult faculty of choice is, deep down, an illusion. Postmodern man knows, in his heart, that authenticity is the one thing he will never feel.

God reportedly defined himself in the declaration 'I am what I am'. A more alarming gloss on the original says that it is better rendered as 'I am that which I shall become'. Which is it to be? If God is what He is – that is to say, pure authenticity – then perhaps it is not unreasonable that we poor fallen creatures can only aspire, hopelessly, to that condition. If, on the other hand, God is that which He will become, then (god help us) He is in the same boat we are: adrift in an endless becoming, his own rites forever unfulfilled: a liminal god for a liminal creation.

67

What Do You Lack (Again)?

And once again our deficiencies come round. What do we lack? What do we want? What is it that can quench our neediness and make us feel good about ourselves? – or, if we're honest, feel at least tolerable about not being ourselves. Feeling good about ourselves – our clever, examined, constantly recalibrated post-modern selves – is a delusion. The self-esteem industry doesn't work; and being 'given' our 'self-esteem' is one of the lowest tricks of the infantilisers. 'Good baby,' they say as we hand them the money and wriggle on our rugs; 'Who's my very special goodest bestest baby?' as we trickle down the plughole, giggling.

At first glance, of course, it seems an absurdity. Surely now, more than at any time in history, are we not free to be who we really are? Modernity has made self-invention not only accessible, but the highest good of all. But we are so surrounded by images of others who present a sort of unattainable authenticity that, from the word go, we know we can never match up. There they are, on television, on hundreds of separate satellite channels, available on demand, bigger than us, *more so* than us, *better known* than us (when a life lived in obscurity is no life at all) and, above all, *onscreen*.

We see them. We see them all the time. In a single 24-hour period, the average American household spends, in aggregate, almost a full working day watching television.[*] In that time – never mind the murders and the sales pitches, the violence we have to rein in, and the passionate sex we aren't going to get, the places we aren't going to see and the celebrity we are never going to enjoy; never mind all that – they are being exposed to people who are more so. More handsome or beautiful; more suntanned; better dressed; fitter; more articulate; more free;[†] above all, more themselves. In the face of their overwhelming

---

[*] Davenport and Beck, *The Attention Economy*, 101

[†] It is strange that – with the exception of doctors and policemen, the only two social groups considered continuously worthy of dramatisation – nobody on television ever has to go to work.

'authenticity', we fade into sepia, bleach out, become unworthy of consideration, even to ourselves. No generation has ever been so constantly or so easily entertained – entertained almost by right, the lack of a television being one of the formal markers of poverty – than the one ruled by the Boomers. No generation has ever had so many exemplars thrust in front of its weary, red-rimmed eyes; nor have any previous generation's exemplars been so – literally – inimitable

There was a time when our exemplars were local, and what they exemplified could be reasonably emulated. Our exemplars now – exemplars in that they command our most valuable, and most competed-for, resource: our attention – bear the same relation to their forebears as the call centre in Mumbai to the local repair shop: they are outside our immediate cultural sphere, they cannot be appealed to (in the communications age, this communication is one-way only), they do not know us, and we cannot become them. Our exemplars have become industrialised; and their most striking characteristic is not the example they set, but that they are exemplars.

I grew up on the cusp of this change. My primary exemplar was my grandfather, but there were others. Frank the grocer I admired for his dexterity and the way in which he made his work (behind the counter, fetching tins, scooping rice, slicing bacon, shrouding the cheese in waxed paper) into a theatrical performance. Dr Chand next door (his real name, it was said, had many, many more syllables) I admired because he had tufts of hair growing out of his ears and introduced me to the then unheard-of glories of the sitar. I admired Len the caretaker at school because he smoked Erinmore Flake in a short black bulldog pipe and knew everything, and I admired the omnipotent headmaster, Kenneth Imeson, because of his preternatural dignity and because, having a liking for mavericks, he admired me, and because we shared a taste for Sibelius. I admired my Latin master and my organ teacher, and I was, I now recognise, in love with the conductor Nicholas McGegan, who was a couple of years older than me; I imitated his haircut, his glasses, his Tyrolean pipe and his aromatic Dutch tobacco, his corduroy shoes,* his books, his handwriting, his manner of speaking and his approach to music; had I known how to go about it, I would have tried to seduce his mother. Had I thought a bit more clearly, and recognised my devotion for what it was, I might have tried to seduce him. Above all, I wanted to *be* him.

⚠️ We consider it odd when we see, in old paintings, the way children are dressed like miniature adults. It doesn't sit well with our idea of childhood as a special period to be demarcated from the rest of life in a sort of protected innocence. Now walk around the city. How many adults are dressed like grown-ups? Conversely, how many are dressed like children? (Ill-kempt children, hair awry, unwashed, crumpled, shirts untucked, trousers falling down, slouching, sucking things, gobbling things, licking things, munching things, shambling along blocking the pavements, heads wagging to the ear-plugged beat.) This is more than just an aesthetic affront: it represents a recalibration of public space. Once, people got dressed up – or at least dressed with care, with an accepted minimum of necessary grooming – before going into public, because the public space was shared with our fellow-citizens and they were to be accorded a baseline respect. Now the public space has become an extension of the private; in some cases, an extension of the lavatory. The clear message is one of, at best, lack of recognition, and, at worst, complete contempt for the people we live alongside. But civility, in its broadest sense, is a marker of adulthood. Only the infantile cannot see that they are part of a wider community.

---

* They enjoyed a brief day in the sun around 1970. Blink and you'd have missed it.

And I could (all other things being equal) have *been* him. I could have been any of them, and to a certain extent I now am. Elements of all these people I admired are now incorporated in the man I presently became. The crucial point was their accessibility. They were *real*. They were there, going about their lives, which were directed to their own ends, not to provoking my emulation. And in that, they differ from the exemplars who hold our gaze on the television screen, or hector us from newspapers and magazines. The communication was what information technologists call 'duplex'; it worked in both directions. The people on television are not. We cannot talk to them; and they only *appear* to be talking to us. In reality (and we all know this, but how hard it is to remember) they are, at best, utterly oblivious to our existence, and, at worst, filled with a fine blithe contempt, because we are civilians and they are not.

They have, in other words, crossed a barrier. The celebrity's primary job is to be a celebrity; everything else is small beer and counts for nothing; and the barrier which they have crossed is the eyeline of the camera. As for the actors – has there ever been an age more obsessed by actors? – the truth is that, whatever or whoever they are pretending to be, what they really, and always, are, to us, is . . . onscreen. Even when they aren't in front of the camera, they still have access, and are bathed in its numinous magic dust. They are in front of it; we remain behind, watching. Being an exemplar now is something you do, not something you are; and even if we could find someone insane enough to want to be Graham Norton or Rush Limbaugh, that person could not pull it off just by trying. The nature of the game has fundamentally changed. And the result is that they have a secret knowledge which we cannot acquire. It makes them – the celebrities – what they are, and, in the face of it, we are condemned to sense our own lack of authenticity.

This, one might argue, is nothing to do with being infantilised, but the result of a very adult sense of dislocation. But the realisation of our own authenticity, the understanding that we are real, is something that escapes the infant, the toddler, the child, the adolescent. The first sixteen years of life are, and should be, a wrestling with the sense of our own individual reality, but there is no sense of authenticity about it; the idea doesn't come into question until adulthood, and it may be that a crucial component of being a grown-up is being able to say, and to genuinely feel, 'I am my own authentic self.' To lack that sense is to be less than grown-up.

If we cannot achieve authenticity ourselves (being infantile, and infantilised), there are plenty of interests out there only too keen to sell us the illusion of, and the accessories to, a *pretence* of authenticity. Native American wisdom is said to include the assertion that you won't understand another human being until you've walked a mile in his moccasins.* Modern American wisdom (and what could be higher wisdom, tricksier and more exhaustive in its ability to understand the human soul, than marketing and advertising?) says that if you buy moccasins like he wears (or bearing his name or a picture of him or a picture representing him), you will become like him.

World Enough (Time Extra)

Examples are all around us. Just go out (or open the paper) and you'll see for yourself. But one of the best examples, for men at least, is the wristwatch. That prototype of Romantic authenticity, the egomaniacal and paranoid Rousseau, sells his watch, telling himself delightedly that he will no longer need to know the time. No modern man would sell his watch unless it was to buy a more expensive one, or, perhaps, one with a different narrative. A

---

* And it has been pointed out that, should everything then go awry, at least you're a mile away and you've got his shoes.

particularly fatuous advertisement for the unexceptional, middle-of-the-litter Seiko range of wristwatches shows the sort of man that gay men think heterosexual men will find handsome[*] declaring that 'It's not your car. It's not your friends. It's not your job. It's your watch that says most about who you are.' The even less distinguished Pulsar watches are even more fatuous. Their man is described, in the sort of winsome lists that people provide on Internet dating sites or applications to be on reality TV, as 'Addicted to reality TV. Hates coriander. Believes in ghosts. Has two pet chihuahuahs.[†] Likes 80s music, 70s décor. Champion sandcastle builder. Reading Dostoevsky. Loves stripes. Former vegan. Wears a Pulsar.'[‡]

At the other end of the scale, Patek Philippe advertise a different sort of authenticity for those with deeper pockets but equal insecurities. 'Begin your own tradition,' the copy runs, above a picture of a casual, 'accessible' man in his thirties with tousled hair, frowning over his son's homework (you don't have to be clever to really, really need an expensive watch). The copyline runs:

> You never actually own a Patek Philippe. You merely
> look after it for the next generation.

The pitch is, of course, masterly, and unpacks with enviable agility, coaxing, deluding, suckering and wheedling with all the skills of Mummy trying to persuade her child ('Who's my goodest bestest baby?') to eat its broccoli:

---

[*] Heterosexual men, curiously, cannot tell whether another man is attractive. We always get it wrong. So do the gay men who try to guess; so the men in these advertisements are always those ones whom *nobody* finds attractive.

[†] See? Gay. But what gay man would fall for the tacky old chihuahua *shtick*?

[‡] Pulsar is Seiko's subsidiary. As the pseudonymous blogger eehbahgum observes, what wearing a Pulsar *actually* says about you is, 'I can't afford a Seiko.'

1. 'Begin your own tradition'. The sucker potential customer can come from either side of the establishment fence:

    (a)   The grandee, aristo or long-lineage Eurotrash, will linger on the word 'tradition', the absolver of all ills, modified by the soothing 'your own': his own tradition, as opposed to all the traditions he has inherited. Buy This Watch and Do Your Bit. Whereas

    (b)   The *arriviste* will focus on 'Begin'. Self-made money is not (the ad assures him) transient and, with the aid of a wristwatch, *sic transit gloria mundi* can be held at bay. The gap between *arriviste* and *aristo* can thus be narrowed.

2. 'You never actually own a Patek Philippe.' Further absolution. If you never actually own it, you never actually *buy* it. The money therefore doesn't really matter.

3. 'You merely look after it for the next generation.' That 'merely' is masterly; it's a bagatelle, a mere nothing, how can I not afford it? Particularly as it's not for me, but for little Harry. Note also:

    (a)   If it's for little Harry, then wearing it in the meantime – merely to look after it – means that, whether prince or property shark, I am not the sort of inauthentic man who is so anxious about what other men will think of me that I need to wear a very expensive watch – a more expensive watch than any of their watches – so as to announce the fact that, hey, I am wearing a more expensive watch than any of them. No sir! I am not that inauthentic man at all!

    (b)   The watch – this watch – cancels out its own mortality. The beating of its little mechanical heart appears to count the seconds to the grave, but, in

74

reality, it is a powerful spell to keep away evil. It will go on to the next generation; with it, I can project my avatar into an indefinite future of generations, to the tick of doom.

And all this in a little circle of gold . . . originally regarded as effeminate, because a real man – an authentic man – kept his watch in his pocket.

> ⚠ **Canary: like to chat? Racoon: resourceful and industrious? Dolphin: fun-loving and sociable? Panther: always on the go? These are call plans for Orange mobile phones. *Call plans*. What about Anaconda: getting quietly but increasingly angry and any minute now about to crush the life out of you and swallow your head? Now *there'd* be a winner.**

The wristwatch is such a perfect example of the way in which we buy (or are sold; and in either case, fall for) substitutes for our autonomy, our authenticity and our *selves*, that it is worth looking at one more manifestation of this curious confidence trick, the so-called 'pilot' or 'navigator' watch. The term is applied to any wristwatch with white Roman numerals, preferably luminous, on a plain black face; it derives from the navigators' watches of the 1930s and 1940s. So far, so very simple. But when we fall for it, when we take it up and strap it to our wrists, we are like children; they too dress up, they, too, fall for the idea that it's the costume and the accoutrements which define the role they want to ply. Put on the cowboy hat and they become the cowboy. Put on the pilot watch and . . .

And pilots, of course, do not wear pilot watches. Even the humblest of rental Cessnas has a decent clock in the instrument panel, and the glamour-free zone of the airliner flight deck has digital timers wherever you turn. Nobody in their right mind would use a wristwatch to time, for example, a non-precision (that is, dodgy) approach to a short runway in heavy cloud, driving rain and bouncing turbulence. The only reason a pilot needs a watch at all is to get to the briefing room on time. Pilots do not wear pilot watches.

Indeed, a pilot who *did* wear a pilot watch would be regarded with suspicion, as being a little amateurish, a bit of a wide boy, more money than sense and the sort of ego which would make you want to get plenty of airspace between him and you. There are even jokes about it. 'What do you get if you cross a pilot with an ape?' 'I don't know. What do you get if you cross a pilot with an ape?' 'An ape with a big watch.'

If the silliness stopped there, it would be fine. But it doesn't. One of the odd and alarming things about writing a book like this is that you start off full of righteous outrage, determined to show the damned people what fools they've been making of themselves and how they've been taken for a ride by the forces of, in this case, infantilisation. But as you work through it, you find, very strangely, that you yourself are the epitome of foolishness and exemplify much of the gullibility you (I, in this case) are attempting to whop everyone else over the head for.

Actually, of course, it's not odd, alarming or strange at all. It's what one would expect; otherwise why would the idea have occurred to one in the first place?

Which doesn't alter the fact that (1) I am a pilot; and (2) I wear a 'pilot watch'.

By 'I am a pilot', I mean that I am qualified to fly various sorts of aeroplane in various sorts of weather, and have done so for many years. By 'I wear a pilot watch' I mean I wear the sort of watch which no pilot needs to wear – an IWC Mk XII, if you want to know – and which is generally worn by people who aren't pilots but who want to give the impression that they are. They want this not because they want people to think, 'Oh look, that fellow's a pilot, I feel oddly diminished beside him' – or, if women, 'Oh look, that fellow's a pilot, I think I will offer to have sex with him' – but because they want to be thought to possess the *qualities* of a pilot.

But the children's game of make-believe doesn't stop there. What *are* the qualities of the pilot? Primarily – and this is true of all pilots I know, and was inculcated in me from the moment I first sat at the controls – a rather hypertrophied sense of caution. Pilots are obsessed with risk, and correctly so; if things get out of hand in an aeroplane, your options are severely limited. Pilots are obsessed with the weather, obsessed with maps, obsessed with fuel consumption, obsessed with elapsed time and time-to-run and point-of-no-return and visibility and cloudbase and runway length and stopping distances and glideslope and drag and asymmetric thrust and checklists and maggots in the pitot tube[*] and weight-and-balance and just about anything else that one could reasonably be obsessed with. Pilots fret about oil filler caps and cowling latches and seals; pilots fret about interlocks and warning lights and tyre creep and brake wear and oleo extension. Pilots . . . *fret*.

And is that why people who aren't pilots wear pilot watches? So that other people will spot the watch and think: 'That chap frets'?

Of course it isn't. The person who *isn't* a pilot wears a pilot watch so that other people will associate him with the qualities which someone who doesn't know anything about pilots assumes that pilots have: daring, courage, cool command authority, unflappability, devil-may-care smiling in the face of fate, nerves of steel, wrists of iron, ability to see in the dark, extra-sensory perception, an enormous penis and a complete absence of fear. There are probably also manly overtones of castor oil, cordite, black labradors, Howard Hughes, David Niven, the stars over the desert, that woman with the wet dress in *A Town Like Alice*,

---

[*] I have *had* maggots in the pitot tube and it is no joke so wipe the smirk off your face.

heroic endurance, prosthetic limbs, Irvin flying jackets, funny helium *Dambusters* voices, dust storms, solitude, sleepless nights, *A Matter of Life and Death*, James Cagney flying through the fog-bound pass, Spencer Tracy slapping his chewing gum on the cockpit canopy, *The Right Stuff*, women with long legs, dead-stick landings on blacked-out airfields . . . in short, testosterone and its magical distillate, *manliness*, defined (albeit reluctantly) by author Harvey Mansfield as 'confidence in risk', which is something (like manliness itself) which we are really, really supposed to be against these days, because someone might get hurt and how would it be if everyone did it?

So the pilot watch on the non-pilot wrist first of all says 'pilot', which in its turn says 'make-believe pilot', which in its turn says 'lost epitome of manliness which never really existed'. The pilot watch is an icon of *saudade*, that Portuguese musical genre which sings of the yearning for something which never was. More than that, it is yet another avatar: something we send out into the world to speak (and act) on our behalf, because we cannot even aspire to the 'authenticity' which the avatar unpersuasively dissembles. There is nothing authentic in the entire charade; and yet we still do it; and at the far extreme of this idiocy I take my place. Let me remind you: (1) I am a pilot; and (2) I wear a 'pilot watch'.

Actually, I slightly lied just now. I do indeed wear an IWC Mk XII, but I also have, and wear, a Fortis 'pilot watch' which instead of having the numbers 1 to 12 round the edge, has the numbers 5 to 60. Minutes! Minutes are so much more *piloty*, would you not agree? Who but a pilot would have *minutes* on their wristwatch?

Men: you know precisely what I am speaking of, even if your own version takes a different form. Women: now you know the truth. Me: I am more bewildered than when I started. Do I wear the pilot watch because I do not have a sufficient sense of authenticity to believe the evidence of my own experience? Am I so infantilised that I have to play at being something I already am? Do I not believe I look sufficiently like a pilot to *be* a pilot?

Or is it that we, like children, can only now play at being our-selves, and cannot trust ourselves to look like what we are without the accessories ('Look Daddy! I'm a cowboy!')?

We Praise Thee, O Great Reborzo bin-j'Ja'abli

Some years ago, my then wife, a theatrical set designer, had a large block of expanded polystyrene, some 4′6″ by 3′ by 6″, delivered to our house to be turned, presently, into a giant medal-lion of Le Roi Soleil for an opera. I found it standing in our sitting room when I came in from lunch with an old friend, Fr. Joe Christie, a Jesuit priest of some distinction.

Joe and I had lunched well. We were modestly illuminated. And where others would simply have seen a giant block of poly-styrene, we saw an theocratic opportunity. The first thing we did was to invent a god. We already had a perfectly good one – the god of Abraham, of Isaac and Jacob and their seed forever, available at good churches, mosques and synagogues every-where – but we felt a new one was needed, and the Great God Reborzo bin j'Ja'abli fitted the bill.

In the Great God Reborzo bin j'Ja'abli's honour, we decorated the block of polystyrene with an embroidered tablecloth, a number of brass candlesticks, a miniature chest of drawers ('The Ark of Fna'a,' said Joe), a number of small offerings – oil, wine, a plaster doll's-house roast chicken – and a Chinese brazier burn-ing incense. We then put on dressing gowns (his was my grandfather's, heavy silk brocade; mine, as befitted a mere deacon, was green wool with red piping), co-opted Alice, my Siamese cat, as a sacrifice, and began intoning the Megalodos of Reborzo (*tonus tertius*), at which point my then wife came in and froze in alarm and bewilderment.

'What,' she said after a while, 'the *hell* are you doing?'

There was another pause, then Joe – Father Joseph Christie,

SJ, orator, preacher, administrator of the sacraments, clerk in Holy Orders and a priest forever according to the order of Melchisedech – said, with commendable dignity:

'We are pretending to be priests.'

It was a splendid *jeu d'esprit* but, for all its innocence, it summed up the state in which so many of us find ourselves: that of having to somehow pretend to be what we really are, because what we really are is no longer convincing, even when we know what it is.

Living in the Dressing-Up Box

A childhood without a dressing-up box (or, at any rate, without dressing-up of some sort) would be a sorry affair. When we are little, we have to try on different identities; they are part of the long rite of separation and incorporation – of parting from the ostensibly warm embrace of mother and home and joining in the more diffuse but less forgiving world of adulthood.

Dressing up is an appropriate activity for children. In costume, we are neither ourselves nor other, but a transitional sort of creature, trying life on for size, which is exactly what children should be doing, and exactly what children are for. But what happens when we are encouraged to go on dressing up for the rest of our lives?

'When I was a child, I spoke as a child, I understood as a child, I thought as a child,' wrote St Paul;* but childhood, for him, was a transitional, preparatory state. He goes on to write: 'but when I became a man, I put away childish things' – and it

---

* Or, more likely, wrote someone else in his name. The tactic of the faked epistle flourishes now as never before: admonitory letters come through the door every day, not from some pseudepigrapher pretending to be an apostle, but from computers pretending to be people. We live behind a glass, darkly; and that glass is the computer screen.

is not an admonition, but a statement of fact at which his readers would have nodded in recognition. Now, advertisers, whether commercial or political, urge us to resist. 'Don't put away childish things!' they urge; 'Why *should* you? *Release your inner child!*'

And what the inner child does, more than anything else, is play at make-believe. The inner child lives in the dressing-up box.

When I was little, I was a cowboy, an Indian, a bridge-builder, a steelworker. I operated the gates on the Sandbanks Ferry, drove oil-fired trains through the night (from the innovative prone position in my bed, viewing the onrushing tracks through an imaginary periscope; the control levers and valves conveniently to hand) and was propelled into space. I was an Egyptian priest, a Roman centurion, King Richard II and the Sibyl at Cumae. I was Robin Hood, Piglet, and a Three King (of Oryan Tar, wherever that was). Sometimes I was a stern judge, sentencing people to death and throwing them (with, of course, a kindly word at the end) into the Deadly Death Pit of Death; sometimes I was a fearless explorer, blackened and shrivelled by the sun, hacking my way through the Amazon (though the dispassionate observer would only have seen a watery grey English sky and a child with a bamboo stick poking at the dense elder tangled between the garage wall and Mr Beardall's fence next door).

Sometimes I operated upon my sister, still, in those days, harmless and compliant; my first published work was a pathology report written after one of those operations, in which, aged seven, I expressed alarm about the nature and number of faggasites in her blod striem. (My father sent it off to a medical magazine, which published it as a novelty.) Subsequently I became a maker of polio vaccine (vinegar, sugar, a sprig of earth for germs), then a nuclear explosionist (copper sulphate, hydrochloric acid and a trip to hospital) and a demolitioneer (hoarded fireworks, weedkiller, a bang and black smoke in the spinney), before turning my hand to fortune-telling at a youth club fete (all copied out of Agnes M. Miall's *Complete Fortune-Telling*),[*] becoming a world-famous magician ('Was it meant to do that, laddie?'), an international spy ('Have you been fiddling with my cine-camera, laddie?') and Paul Revere ('What the hell have you been doing with your bike, laddie?').

> ⚠ **Lloyds Bank, Sidney Street, Cambridge; 4.15 p.m. A traditional banking hall: an elegant, slightly over-done, Rococo-Byzantino-Gothic marzipan sandcastle Battenburg-cake building, where banking (a reasonably serious business) is carried on. He is wearing baggy orange shorts with a logo on; he is wearing black socks and huge trainers with a logo on and with lights which flash on and off as he jiggles up and down to the secret pulse of his iPod. He is wearing a T-shirt with a cartoon on it. One hand is in his shorts pocket, waggling his testicles; the other is holding an enormous ice-cream cone which he licks at greedily. On his head is a baseball cap, sideways. He is waiting for a woman to finish her banking. He is at least fifty years old.**

And the majority of these transitional personae involved some sort of costume. 'Distrust any enterprise that requires new clothes'? No. Thoreau was entirely wrong. Much of the enterprise resides in the new clothes. Any actor will tell you that it doesn't come entirely right until you get into the costume; any

---

[*] And very distressing it was. My first customer sat down. I looked at her hand and cross-referenced it with the crib sheets scattered about my tent. 'You have been ill twice with respiratory sickness. You should have had three children but I only see two. You are making a journey next year . . .' She stared at me. 'Is this some sort of joke, sonny?' It turned out that she had had tuberculosis; her middle child had died; she and her husband were emigrating. I never trusted Agnes M. Miall again.

businessman, or any petty criminal in the dock, will tell you that the costume – in this case, the slightly sharp suit – is the *sine qua non* of the enterprise. Dressing gowns, sheets, turbans, hats, pipes, walking sticks, briefcases, boots, scarves, dark glasses . . . all the contents of the dressing-up box (and some of the contents of my parents' wardrobes, stolen under cover of daylight) were pressed into service as fetishes in the religion of endless self-invention.

Which is, of course, how it should be.

But not when it continues endlessly into what should be adult life. We – the Big Babies – wear costume when once our predecessors would have worn clothes; we dress up when they would have simply dressed. Our lives have become performances and our clothes have become parodic vestments shrouding the uncertain pastiche beneath.

Zengotita's Law of Wolves – that in Yellowstone Park you see no wolves but only 'wolves' – applies as much to clothing as it does to so many aspects of our infantilised lives. After the decline of hat-wearing during the presidency of John F. Kennedy[*] it is impossible to wear a hat in England or the USA; now, you can only wear a 'hat' and despite the existence of a few decent hat shops, they are no longer hatters but 'hatters'. The Australian bush is perhaps the last place on earth where one may wear a hat free of all subtext. There, the details of the hat – its shape, its colour, the degree of wear, the nature of the bash – reveal things about the wearer. But the wearing of the hat itself says nothing more about you than that, on your head, you are wearing a hat. It is an unreconstructed paradise; it is Eden.

Everywhere else is east of Eden, in the Land of Nod. Whatever your chosen hat – Borsalino fedora, musquash Ushanka, Bates velours, Lock trilby, Panama, boater, Persian astrakhan, Az-Tex 50X Windcutter, whatever – it is, first and foremost, a 'hat'. It announces that you are wearing a hat, and

---

[*] Splendidly chronicled in Neil Steinberg, *Hatless Jack: The President, the Fedora and the Death of the Hat* (London: Granta, 2005).

invites the question 'Why is that person wearing a hat?' and the supplementary question 'Who is he pretending to be?' You may feel that a hat adds a certain style; that it completes one's dress; that it establishes a sense of continuity with the hat-wearing past and, by doing so, offers a palliative to the competing sense of being adrift in a perpetual present, perhaps the defining characteristic of postmodern man. This is all very well; but what a hat really does is announce to the world that one is incomplete; that one is playing a part, even if only to oneself; that one is *pretending*.

Sometimes we read the pretence as risible: the Englishman with his spindly white legs and easy-care shirt who, in his Dordogne holiday home, adopts a Basque beret, is, if anything, slightly more ludicrous than his academic counterpart who wears one while cycling through the Cambridge drizzle.* The latter we forgive on the grounds of rational practicality, almost admiring his pragmatism and lack of dress sense; he may be in costume, but it is the correct costume for the unworldly man of intellect. The former we cannot forgive, because his costume is not only wrong, but reveals his delusion: he is attempting to pass himself off as a Frenchman, partly to the actual French people, but mostly to himself. He has been at the dressing-up box; but what upsets us most is what upset Billy Connolly about the Australian politician's comb-over: that he thinks we will fall for it. That he thinks we are so easily fooled.

More peculiarly, we might ask ourselves what we would think of a Frenchman in a beret. The answer is odd but revealing. Unless he were very old and fully submerged in *la France profonde* we would think: 'Here is a Frenchman pretending to be French.' A man pretending to be himself: it this the nearest we Big Babies

---

* The beret is among the signifiers of pretension and self-delusion in Kingsley Amis's *Lucky Jim* (1954); indeed, it figures in the defining moment at the end of the book, where Welch and his terrible son Bertrand swap hats. Wearing the wrong hat is bad enough; now they are wearing the *wrong* wrong hats, and their fate is sealed.

can get to authenticity? (And what could be less authentic, now, than 'national costume', whether it is cowboys in chaps, Frenchmen in berets and *bleu de travail*, Welsh women in witches' hats, Scots in kilts, Mexicans in sombreros, Austrians in lederho-sen,* Dutch people in clogs or Fijians with their bottoms out at rugby matches? 'National dress' has become 'what nobody really wears', a costume for souvenir dolls, which aren't proper sou-venirs at all because instead of jogging the memory, they trigger a conditioned response to a piece of false branding. A real sou-venir of the American West would be a doggy bag with the rest of your all-you-can-eat Surf-'n'-Turf dinner in it; of France, a speeding ticket; of Amsterdam, a recording of English people, drunk and shouting, in the Wallatjes red-light district. And, everywhere, national costume would be what was fifty years ago (when Ray Bradbury wrote *Dandelion Wine*), the magical uniform of American boyhood: sneakers, blue jeans, T-shirt and, of course, the baseball cap.

The baseball cap is fascinating. It should, more properly (since no pro baseball player would wear one to play baseball in), be called the 'gimme cap', so called because they used to be handed out at county fairs, advertising feed merchants and tractor man-ufacturers. 'Hey uh gimme one of them caps willya?' farmers would say, and everyone was happy: the farmer was protected from the perils of scorching sun, thin dispiriting rain and flying shit, and the donor got his logo on the front of the guy's head.

Now, the gimme cap is universal, and probably (outside Australia) the last surviving unironic headgear. It is one of America's great gifts to the world: cheap (or free), practical and democratic (things don't come much more democratic than one-size-fits-all, except for those whom it doesn't fit). And yet it arouses outrage. Is it because it is associated (incorrectly) with sports: with play and inappropriate levity? Is it because it is so insistently democratic, obliterating distinctions between rich and

---

* Now hijacked in some circles (gay ones mainly) as a gay icon.

85

poor, urban and rural, white and black, infantile and adult? Certainly there is no corporation, however insistently casual its compulsory dress-down Friday may be, that would tolerate the gimme cap; and any business that tried to impose logo-branded gimme caps on any but its bottom-of-the-heap helots would find a rebellion on its hands.

But perhaps the main reason for the gimme cap's power to enrage is the message it now delivers: not its original narrative of honest rural toil, but its adopted discourse. 'I am young, free and transitional,' it says, 'and I am not playing your game. I am young! I am young! *I am young!*'

New Identity, One Size Fits All

'Here's the famous World War One fighter ace,' says the beagle Snoopy in Charles Schultz's *Peanuts* strip as he sits atop his dog-house, his silk scarf streaming behind him in the imaginary slipstream: so potent is the force of imagination that, as he recites his internal monologue, even meteorology bends to his will.

This is what children do: hold imagination so dear that it not only acts upon itself, but shapes the external world. Being grown-up is, in part at least, realising that this belief, this valorising of imagination, is an illusion. And yet we seem unable to abandon it. The hat – the 'hat' – is just a symptom.

And there are many more, similar symptoms. Walk about your town. Look, with unaccustomed eyes, at the shops. What are they? Mostly, they are *clothes* shops. Walking through central London, it comes as a shock to look, as if for the first time, and see just how many shops are selling just how many clothes. There are whole streets, whole *districts* of clothes shops, and although it would be fatuous to claim as original the idea that they aren't really selling clothes, but costumes – the whole street or district just one huge dressing-up box, for one huge game of let's-pretend – it does however seem a fantastical lunacy, a support industry for a society based on make-believe and self-deception.

Think, too, of the magazines full of clothes, devoted to clothes, advertising clothes, talking about clothes with the detailed precision of obsessional psychosis. Think of the ships laden with clothes, the models famous for putting clothes on and having their picture taken, the designers of clothes feted in (and sometimes shot outside) their tremendous palaces. Think of the commentary about clothes, no interview complete without an analysis of them. Think, most curiously of all, how very little television advertising is devoted to clothes.* There is something about clothes that simply does not translate to the small screen. It can't be that clothes won't work in two dimensions; fashion photography, with its witless false 'narratives' and its celebration of the disordered and the marginal (anorexic girls photographed with homeless people, indigent Africans, bewildered islanders, the whole generality of victims, schlumps and yutzes), nevertheless manages to shift clothes like nobody's business. Like nobody's business except the clothes-pushers, who are doing very nicely.

But perhaps clothes aren't sold on television because the message conflicts with the medium. Clothes are sold to us – and, obediently, we buy them – so that we can play make-believe, be onscreen for as long as (like Cinderella) we are wearing them. Show the clothes actually onscreen, then the magic, the promise, is obliterated – not least because another part of the magic is that our clothes uniquely present ourselves to the world and, unless we are imitating someone else's dress, like the Indiana Jones groupies, seeing our clothes on television would explode the illusion, cancel out the make-believe.

Where everything is make-believe, pure make-believe cannot be effectively pushed upon us. Or perhaps the powers of the

---

* Except, of course, for jeans – perhaps, significantly, the only item of clothing we actually *wear* rather than dress up in. *We* don't come up with a let's-pretend when we put our jeans on; so the advertisers can come up with one for us.

great infantilisers, the advertising industry, just haven't quite worked out how to do that; just as they know they would fail if they tried to sell holidays in the Maldives to people on holiday in Mauritius.

> ⚠ **Food (1):** A packet of fish fingers. On the packet is a picture of the fish fingers on a plate. 'Serving suggestion', it says. Why? Are we stupid enough to serve them in the lavatory otherwise? Or are they worried that we will sue them ('When I opened the packet *there was no plate* or indeed sprig of parsley either')?
>
> **(2):** Jamie Oliver, the cockney chef, in an advertisement: 'Slam in the lamb.' That is our level. No effort. No care. An undertone of violence. *And it rhymes.* We can remember things if they rhyme.
>
> **(3):** Waitrose. You don't buy salt, chillies, balsamic vinegar. You buy *a pinch of*, you buy *easy on the*, you buy *a drizzle of*. Complicity is everything. *They know how we feel, innit?*

But even without television advertising, we are submerged, drowning, in a world of appearance. Instructions and exhortations to change our appearance fretfully admonish us at every turn, so that even getting dressed in the morning is both provisional and an act of make-believe. Once upon a time (and not that long a time ago) men, at least, had some degree of certainty. We wore working clothes during the working week, and informal clothes at weekends. My father wore a suit from Monday to Friday. Family legend has it that he once arrived late at a fancy-dress party, having been delayed by a difficult delivery and so not having had time to change.

'Why aren't you in fancy dress?' his hostess asked when he arrived in, of course, his suit.

'But I am,' he said with some dignity. 'I have come as a GP,' and his costume was declared a triumphant success.

At the weekend – including his Saturday morning surgery – he abjured his suit in favour of flannel trousers, a Viyella shirt and a tweed jacket, and what this said about him was that it was the weekend. He himself, within his clothing, remained unchanged.

Despite our having fallen victim to a less dramatic version of what afflicts women, men still have this tendency deeply rooted in our psyches. A man who finds he is dressed identically to all the other men at a party experiences a sense of profound comfort, something women find impossible to understand. For a moment, we cease to be provisional, creatures with a whole programme of self-realisation and becoming to accomplish, and instead can just relax and be what we are. The old-style school uniform, with no room for manoeuvre, had a similar effect; far from being infantilising, it was liberating. Everyone looked identical, so nobody worried. Far from being placed in the position of children, to whom everything is contingent, we were elevated by the uniform to the status of adults-in-waiting, whose ability to act in the world was based upon the actual self, not some manufactured and marketable advertisement for another, pre-approved self not our own.

The leisurewear revolution of the late 1970s, preceded by the brief explosion of peacockery of the Sixties, pulled that rug from under us. Now, men's clothes have become advertisements for the false self. I once lived in an archetypically middling London district, opposite a man who was never out of costume at weekends. He had a special outfit for his hunter-gatherer expeditions to the local supermarket: a green Barbour waxed-cotton jacket, a Tattersall check shirt, green Hunter gumboots, a flat tweed cap. When he drove his second-hand Lotus, he put on special Lotus-driving clothes: houndstooth trousers (which he probably called 'slacks'), Ray-Ban sunglasses, a white Orlon turtleneck sweater, an Irvin flying jacket, a Greek fisherman's cap. He was given to

DIY; his poky house was a riot of chipboard and undoubtedly a terrible fire hazard; but when he was Doing It Himself, he put on special clothes for that, too: steel-toed, yellow Nubuck safety boots, a one-piece fire-retardant boiler suit, a safety helmet with hearing defenders and safety glasses attached, and – completely inexplicably – a bright orange high-visibility vest. God only knows what he put on when he intended to have sex with his wife, a thin, careful woman dressed in Dralon chintz, with a permanent cold and red-rimmed eyes. But the rest of the time, he was like a child, but with the added complexity – at the very heart of the Big Babies syndrome – that he was *pretending* to do what he *actually was doing*. Snoopy again: the interior monologue as a sort of ritual act, making good his deficiencies. His scarf blowing backwards in the windless air.

Who Shall We Pretend to Be Now?

This terrible man was a harmless minor version of an equally harmless and affable lunacy enacted, with hats and suits and stockings and etiquette guides, on one of the most peculiar and engaging websites you will find. The Fedora Lounge[*] is the home to a number of grown-ups (American mostly, for obvious reasons) devoted to retrojecting themselves into the 1940s, when men were men and hats were hats, when there was risk and suits and dames and danger and the shadow of war and a world which, through the distorting glass of *post facto* affection, seemed profoundly more authentic than today's.

The denizens of the Fedora Lounge do not merely like dressing snappily. They dress with an almost insane attention to detail, posting pictures of themselves in their latest Stetson 'Open Road' or brown pinstriped suit or Hollywood-waist trousers. Their

---

[*] www.thefedoralounge.com

heroes are Bogart, Howard Hughes (whole debates are devoted to, and thousands of dollars expended on, getting the exact pattern of Hughes's rather horrible jacket) and, inexplicably, Indiana Jones. The quest for the exact Indiana Jones ('Indie') leather jacket, the exact Indie fedora, is endless, only occasionally broken in upon by someone remembering that it was only a film and Indie didn't exist and his clothes were made up by costume designers. But the rest of the time, it's *real*.

Clothes are merely another form of text, and their grammatology is shifting, endlessly deferred, refracted by culture and personal reception and inevitably poised in relation to an opposite which is only occasionally articulated. There is no hermeneutics of the hat.

The opposite with which the Loungers exist in tension is the leisurewear culture which has overtaken much of the English-speaking world: sports clothes on immensely fat sluggards, T-shirts with cartoon characters worn by people old enough to be dead; athletic shoes worn, reeking, everywhere; ball caps; jeans; shorts (and shorts which look like slimy underwear, out of which one would be alarmed but not astonished to see a rugose testicle slithering) in public, vests in public, matted dank armpit hair and an (imaginary?) reek of onions from the sodden oxter.

Baby clothes. Clothes for people who are called upon to do nothing, not even to present themselves in such a way as to enact the civilities of public life. A friend in her middle years was taken aside by a much older, and very soignée, woman who said: 'After a certain age, my dear, a little lipstick is a kindness to others.' The leisurewear culture accords no such kindness, and if it wears lipstick it is as a defiant statement of presence rather than a gesture of a sort of public commensality. Minority groups, far from wanting to demonstrate their commitment to social cohesion, insist on their right to distinguish themselves with their 'religious' dress (which is a peculiar concept since the God in whom they must believe sent us all into the world naked), but while they may indeed be showing respect to their gods, they are also saying 'fuck off' to everyone else. Grown women wear bright pink; civil servants cast away their neckties; priests abjure the Roman collar ('Call me Terry') and everywhere there is unseemly access to flesh (midriff, arse-cleft, armpit), there are prosthetics, there are beanie hats, stubble, the slump, the sweats, the tattoos, the piercings.

None of this carries any inbuilt freight; though we may believe that civility lies in a certain modesty and elegance, civilisation itself will not crumble if men wear shorts in London. It is, however, babyish. Infants (untended-to) are slovenly and egomaniacal; they are dressed to conceal their privates and to protect their flesh, nor do they care (or even recognise) what other people may see or think. The ostensible democratisation of clothing is, in reality, a regression into infantility: people coming into public as though they have dressed in the dark deliver the clear messages that, firstly, they do not consider themselves members of the *polis*, and, secondly, that they do not regard their fellow citizens as worthy of respect. Beneath the infantile exterior, all sorts of body dysmorphism may be going on across the gamut from anorexia, via bulimia, to down-and-out gluttony. (Fat people demand our respect too, now; but how can one respect someone for being fat? Despite it, yes; but because of it? How, exactly, is that done?) Never before in history has there been so little sense of social dressing; never such sense of the disconnected body, adrift in its mental perambulator, soothed with Botox and blepharo-plasty, gym-bellies and labial rings. Men, too, are suffering from the same delusional infantility, spending hours at the gym to acquire a six-pack (how are abdominal muscles useful to a Web 2.0 marketeer or a commercial solicitor?) which only, really, appeals to adolescent girls, exfoliating, moisturising, grooming, preening.

It is like a disease; by which I mean there are a number of components to the infection. Pressure is applied, in the form of advertising and editorial (editorial being only done to get adver-tising) in men's magazines, set up by Baby Boomers to fund their

92

Neverland lifestyles by trading off the insecurities of others. And those others must collude. But whether the result is direct, as in the leisurewear culture, or indirect and reactive, like the Fedora Loungers, both are in their own way acting out, both are infantilised. While the Loungers are retreating, either into a fictionalised re-enactment of a false memory of the 1940s, or even into a re-enactment of not the 1940s, but the '1940s', itself fictionalised from the very outset.

Surrounded by images and exhortations, both sides retreat into childhood: one, by a slack compliance; the other, by declaring itself a righteous and inspired church of refuseniks.

And what is missing is authenticity. Is it anywhere to be found, or do we have to wait until we just grow up?

CHAPTER 4

What Do You Want
One of Those For?

Big Babies bark and howl and cry in the night, just like little ones. But their cries are more varied and louder, their sleep more disturbed.

Big Babies are foxes. The Greek poet Artilochus observed that the fox knows many things, while the hedgehog knows one big thing. And the one big thing that the hedgehog of infantilism knows is how to drive the fox crackers with hopeless desire.

We are the foxes. And if what we really desire is the authenticity which comes with being grown-up, then the hedgehogs – the marketing hedgehogs, the brand specialists and product-name consultants with their databases and metrics, and, of course the advertising hedgehogs with their focus groups and a degree of concentrated expertise in human manipulation which, if more wisely applied, could bring world peace, halt global warming and abolish disease – know how to keep us thinking we are going to get authenticity, but without ever actually delivering it.

Well of *course* they don't deliver it. First, they can't. Authenticity isn't to be had at the click of a website or the snap of a credit card. And, second, even if they could deliver it, they wouldn't, because then we wouldn't need them any more. Instead, we would become hedgehogs: big hedgehogs with teeth, hedgehogs filled with terrible contempt, hedgehogs who would rise up and tear their brand-image departments to the ground, and wad up their expensive advertisements and poke them down their yapping throats.

Consider femfresh.

Femfresh is an 'intimate feminine hygiene product'. The idea behind it is simple and masterly, and it is this: women smell bad. No need to go into *where* women smell bad; it is the principle, and the crass, vulgar, heartless, grasping, misery-spreading, con-man dishonesty of the exercise that counts.

If you had never realised that – if you had thought that your honeypie, or, if female, yourself, had been gifted with a rather lovely beguiling body, designed by nature, in its most private and appealing regions, to be self-cleansing and equipped with an attractive, musky perfume which would summon men to declare their adoration and so to propagate the species – you are quite right. But you are a fox. It is different for the femfresh hedge-hogs, who cleverly saw a potential neurosis and thus the chance to flog a 'solution' and get your money. Which is the one big thing the hedgehog knows. He knows he wants your money, and he knows how to get it.

I say 'he' because it is certain that only men could have come up with the thoroughly nasty idea of lying to women that they stink and selling them the solution for this imaginary disadvantage. It's a simple and devastating stunt. 'Bad girl,' the pitch goes; 'Do you want to be a good girl? Do you want Poppa to love you? Do you want Poppa not to throw up when he comes near you? Then give Poppa the money.'

Gosh, Is It Really Still the Seventies?

Femfresh first appeared in the early Seventies – the time when infantilisation really took hold, after the Sixties had set up base camp and laid in supplies – but the surprising thing is that it is still going. Says the femfresh website:*

> There are times when you really could do with a shower (you're at Glastonbury, danced for three solid days and the lack of shower facility is taking it's toll, or when you're going to your boyfriends after a whole day stuck at your desk in a hot, sweaty office . . .) so you do what you can to make yourself feel clean. You deo wipe your under arms, swish mouthwash for fresh breath and spray perfume to disguise the day . . . but girls, we all know what we really need to feel *totally* clean, and that's freshness, down there . . . femfresh gently deodorises and refreshes for extra freshness everyday, not just for 'problems'.

The pitch is trying to appear subtle, but in reality it is as foul and blatant as any eighteenth-century peddler. See how every word is carefully chosen, either to promote a feeling of false chumminess or to present an irrefutable proposition. 'There are times when you could really do with a shower'. Who could disagree? Who is going to say 'No there are not. I could *never* do with a shower'? No; already, we are drawn in to collusion.

'You're at Glastonbury, danced for three solid days and the lack of shower facility is taking it's toll'. The pitch is *au courant* (Glastonbury), fun (dancing), funky (no showers! how, like, devil-may-care!) and already the target fox is caught like a rabbit, feeling herself start to stink.

'Or when you're going to your boyfriends . . .' Now we know where the apostrophe in 'it's' came from; it fell off what was once 'boyfriend's' and got blown back. But . . . no loser, the fox: she has a boyfriend; has a job in an office, too; independent (not just the job, but the boyfriend who she's not living with) but

---

* <http://www.femfresh.co.uk>

96

not-quite-valued-as-she-should-be; the office is hot and stinks. Let's hope it all works out with the boyfriend, who is called Kent or Chip or Gary or Matt, and works in finance or real estate and his, like, prospects are, like, really, you know, amazing, and the nice house beckons, and the Merc and the Porsche 4x4, and the bi-i-i-g refrigerator, Chardonnay on tap and the home gym, even, keeping in trim after the kids are born, and the bed linen from the White Company and Kent or Chip or Gary or Matt will love her for ever and there'll be a Home Entertainment Centre with 48-inch wall-mounted plasma TV and a Starbucks nearby and it'll be just like everything she's ever seen on television except *real* . . . But let's not get ahead of ourselves, poppet; let's do something about that stink first.

So 'you do what you can'; you 'deo wipe' and 'swish' and 'spray' (such friendly, informal, sea-clean, breeze-fresh words, apart from 'deo wipe' which is a tiny error, sounding some-how . . . rectal), 'but girls . . . we all know what we really need'.

We're All Girls Together

There lies the master-stroke: we are all girls in this together. And then the clincher: 'we all know'. This, above all, is the defining trope of modern advertising, the equivalent of the hectoring newspaper columnist who, lacking the tools of argu-ment or persuasive rhetoric, declaims 'Let's face it . . .', followed by whatever insupportable fatuity is about to form the Thought for the Day. It takes a stern reader to shout out, 'No, damn it; let's not face it, because it's tripe,' and the problem is that, by the time you have realised it's tripe, you've already faced it, hand-in-hand with your idiot guide. You're committed. It's too late.

'We all know . . .' Keep an eye open for it. You will see it, or its equivalent, leap out of advertisements everywhere: the phony

matiness, the bogus communality, the utterly dishonest alignment of our own foxy interests with the interest of the hedgehog.
Whether it is the petty annoyances of the mail-order catalogue
('We all know how annoying it is when we can't find the ointment
for the dog's warts') or the larger-scale insinuation of the pull-out
Dell computer advertisement ('Relax! You're covered' – the
advertiser shares your anxiety) or ridiculous, lying politicians
telling us they share our pain, the establishing of false common
interests is the persuaders' great standby.

> ⚠ **Big Babies can judge nothing for themselves. Not
> even the weather. Weather used to be delivered by
> meteorologists with ingenuous spectacles and off-the-rack
> jackets who spoke of isobars and depressions. Now it is
> delivered by young women who are little more than life-
> support systems for breasts and lipstick, telling us not so
> much what it's going to be like, as how we're going to feel
> about it. They tell us it's going to be a beautiful day when
> what they mean is it's going to be too hot and your
> melanoma will kick in. Hot does not equal lovely. Cold is
> lovelier, because if you are too cold it's easy to get warm.
> (But they don't tell us that. 'Be sure to wrap up warm,'
> they say. Yes, but surely we must remember to wipe our
> bottoms first?)**

It is the Hat Trick under a different disguise. Show us someone
we aspire to be like (insecure in our perpetual state of becoming,
adrift in the present and untethered from the past, we Big Babies
no longer have the confidence to want to be like ourselves or our
forebears), then tell us that people like us really enjoy whatever
fools' stuffing the hucksters are trying to peddle. 'Look!', we cry.
'This person who has been on television uses this cologne which
I don't use yet but which I will use because I am just like this

person on television, who also uses this cologne. What about *that*, then? Don't tell me that's a coincidence! I am *just like him*! We even use the *same cologne*!' And the hedgehog plods away with the money, passing his cut to the celebrity on his way to the bank.

It infects us all the way up to our political, social, sexual and intellectual affiliations, this nasty trick of pre-empting our responses. We vote for this party, we follow that philosophical line, observe this religion, go out with that sort of person, eat this sort of food, take vacations in that sort of place, give our children these sort of names, dress in that sort of way because of a simple and crass logical error:

1. We want to be like this person or belong to this group.
2. This person or group votes/ thinks/ worships/ dates/ eats/ vacations/ dresses/ whatever in this particular way.
3. We vote/ think/ worship/ date/ eat/ vacation/ dress/ whatever in that particular way, too.
4. See? We are obviously like this person or this group. Look how much we share!

On its own, this is fairly straightforward, and is perhaps at the root of all the things we do in order to confirm and simultaneously advertise our allegiances, whether in the music we listen to or the football team we support.

Been There? Or Done That?

The sense of belonging which this promotes (we have only recently found out, because we've only recently been able to do it) is little or nothing to do with actual community or actual belonging. For the ancient Greeks, the tragedies of Aeschylus, Sophocles and Euripides were part of a tremendous communal festival – the City Dionysia, in honour of the god of ecstasy, Dionysos – at which attendance was so important that a special, and legally ring-fenced, dole, the Theoric Fund, was set up so that even if you were poor, you could go to the theatre. (It would be as if anyone who didn't have the money today could get in to Glastonbury, like our unfortunate femfresh victim, for free.)

Things have changed since Athens in the fifth century BC; indeed, since the 1950s. 'Been there, done that' is the weary cry of the disaffected adolescent (who has, in reality, been hardly anywhere and done very little) but technology has enabled us to uncouple the two components, so that *doing that* no longer requires *being there*. Participation in major sporting events has become fragmented in space and time. No longer do we need to be there or even be then; we can watch at home, on our own,* go to a 'sports bar'† and watch with a subset of the crowd, or, using our Tivo, displace the thing in time and watch it whenever we want. Music, too, which is not only tribal but increasingly and frantically Balkanised (people despise other people because their music is ten beats per minute faster) is no longer necessarily communal: the I'm-just-a-big-kid-at-heart forty-year-old softening his brain-bones with his iPod‡ feels as much a part of his chosen tribe as if he were there, in the mosh pit or other locus of degeneracy; while, in a truly infantile display of both solipsism and bad manners, he detaches himself from the fellow human beings among whom he moves and from all who are not of his tribe.

---

* Interesting to see how, for example, Blockbuster Video attempts to synthesise the old cinema-going experience with its sacraments of popcorn and Coke, both served in a bucket; perhaps they should also sell urinal cakes for that authentic movie-theatre smell, and, ideally, you should, for a premium, be able to hire a pervert who would creep in, sit next to you and put your hand on his thing.

† A pub with a big TV, actually.

‡ Not forgetting to keep an ear open for incipient hearing loss, so that he can sue Apple for letting him turn the thing up too loud, of course.

The Trick of It

But the truly clever invention of advertisers has been to pre-empt our desires and guide them towards the club they want us to belong to. The trick comes before the first item in the list; instead of waiting for us to decide what group or individual we want to be like, the huckster tells us, sometimes with an almost embarrassing directness, as in the femfresh advertisement, some-times with greater subtlety, sometimes with so much subtlety that we can't quite work out what is going on unless we close one eye and squint. This is, if you like, the trick-of-the-trick, where the actual device telling us what to do is hidden, and only the all-important trace remains.

Often, the trace is television itself, hinted at without comment in the knowledge that we will reverse-engineer the pitch and then fall for it, in the manner of a man digging his own grave. 'Celebrity endorsement' more and more heads in this direction. There was a time when the celebrity would actually endorse the product, extolling its virtues with, presumably, the added credi-bility which comes from being on television, perhaps as an actor, a profession whose main task is presenting plausible lies. Now this is seen as callow, and, instead, the celebrity is simply, and silently, associated with the product: standing by it, sitting on it, eating it.

Sometimes there can be a double-bind, as in the case of the debt-consolidation company Firstplus; and what a clever, unethi-cal name that is. The pitch is banal: 'Worrying about money can leave you feeling as though life is passing you by. Firstplus is here to tell you it doesn't have to be like that.' The truth is more like this:

'Worrying about money can be just putting up with telephone calls from people in India with no power to do anything at all about your situation. Maybe putting up with endless, soon-to-be-illegal, surcharges of £30 to do something which actually costs the company roughly £0.05. Perhaps even debt collectors with cheap sunglasses and colo-rectal problems will come round and burp insolently on your doorstep. But with Firstplus, you can consolidate all these worries into one big worry: screw up one more time and we'll repossess your house.'

To sugar the pill, and to give Firstplus some curious credibility-by-contagion, they hired a woman called Carol Vorderman who does adding-up on a TV game show called *Countdown* and so has gained a reputation for being some sort of mathematical wizard and a miracle of probity. On the company website, Miss Vorderman stands there. Just stands there. The implication is clear: Miss Vorderman does adding-up on a game show, and is a celebrity, and is happy. Firstplus therefore will cast the oofle-dust of celebrity upon people who have been suckered into misery by credit-card companies, which will result in happiness, end the sensation of life passing us by and (because it is also associated with clever adding-up) not get us into further trouble, so that we will be free to go out and get more stuff which we don't want but which we do, very strangely, *need*.

A petition launched to stop Miss Vorderman 'endorsing' Firstplus gathered nearly 50,000 signatures in the forty-eight hours after its launch,[*] which is even more worrying, suggesting as it does that there are people who are so stupid that they will be unable to help themselves from pledging their houses because they have seen a picture of someone who is on television. Are we really that infantile? Or is Firstplus so stupid that it is wasting its money on Miss Vorderman? Either possibility is disturbing; but we should by now be beginning to get an idea of which is more likely.

And finally, there is the Great Oozalum Bird of advertising, so intricate as almost to defy analysis, exemplified by the packet of peppers from Sainsbury's which announced: 'As seen on TV'. If Carol Vorderman and her moneylenders are pulling the Trick on people infantilised into early adolescence – terrible untethered desire coupled with a mad suggestibility – then the Sainsbury's red peppers approach The Holy Grail of post-structuralist semiotics, the thing which rises above all need for embodiment or signification.

---

[*] <http://www.moneysavingexpert.com/carol>

> ⚠ Every time a friend turns on his Sony Digital Walkman it tells him to 'enjoy your music enjoy your life'. What is the purpose of this? Is it an injunction, with the implied opposite that if he fails to enjoy his music his life will be ashes? Is it an exhortation to jolly him along, in case he absent-mindedly listened to the music without any particular effect, or, worse, listened to it, hated it, became disenchanted with his life and garotted himself with the headphone-cord? Is it an elliptical, implied causal link: 'If you enjoy your music, you will then enjoy your life *and it will be thanks to Sony Corporation*'? Whatever it is, why can neither Sony nor anyone else just sell us the damned thing – whatever it may be – without telling us how we should feel about it? Why, in short, can't they just take our money and fuck off?

There is only one step further to go: that Sainsbury's begin to sell cellophane packets emblazoned with the words 'As seen on TV' but containing *nothing at all*. The transcendent signifier, to match the transcended signified. Words, words, words . . . £2.45 a kilo.

Meanwhile, Back at Glastonbury

And so back to our girl, a girl among girls, a girl who agrees that 'we all know what we really need to feel', which is, of course, '*totally* clean', 'down there'. So she shells out her money and yet another fox enriches the same old bloody hedgehog. Does she feel what she's meant to feel? She knows what she's meant to feel, and that's the main thing. She's got her chance.

And never forget: the hedgehog would starve if we were all grown-up enough to shout 'Bollocks' at it, and pelt it with stones and rubbish; and so the one big thing the hedgehog *knows* is not the one big thing the hedgehog *wants* (which is, of course, our money). The one big thing the hedgehog *knows* is how to make Big Babies of us all.

Remembering that the infantilised person – the perpetual child, the frozen adolescent, one who has not yet acquired identity or control – has no judgement, no *discrimen* (having surrendered some of it and had the rest taken away), it's easy to see that pre-empting response is the best way of controlling desire. The old advertising motto – 'Sell the sizzle, not the steak' – has never been more assiduously applied, nor more effectively. A £2 million campaign for a business which exists to sell nothing but emotion – the National Lottery – proves the point explicitly.

The television commercial is a tiny but perfect narrative of delight, set in an urban dreamscape to the backing of Patience & Prudence singing 'A Smile and a Ribbon'.* The result is unfathomably charming, as a tiny animated family in its idiosyncratic apartment is visited by happiness, which the oddly androgynous father distributes around the town. But in an accompanying press release, typed out by someone whose soul must surely have

---

* http://www.studioaka.co.uk/html/projects.php?p=nationallottery> And a curious song if looked at closely, tinged with a terrible sadness: 'To be a girl they notice / Takes more than a fancy dress / So I'll be noticed because I'll dress / With a smile and a ribbon in my tresses . . .' But what if it doesn't work? What if she is lonely and sad, and cannot smile? Tragedy hides behind charm, smuggled in on its coat-tails.

been sucked out by the Dementors of Azkaban, the gloves are off:

> Camelot this week unveils its latest big lottery winner –
> an animated character called Milo, who is the 'star' of a
> new £2 million plus TV advertising campaign . . .
> designed to capture the feeling of playing and winning,
> in a way that inspires players to live the lottery
> dream . . . the ad tells the story of a contented lottery
> winner sharing his happiness with the people around
> him. The scene opens with our animated hero being
> woken by a bag landing unexpectedly on his bed.
> Surprised, he checks the bag and finds it full of smiles –
> a metaphor for a lottery jackpot win. Checking his own
> face, he finds he does not have a smile, so tries one on –
> and immediately feels fantastic . . . inspirational ques-
> tions that urge players to act on their dreams . . .
> Camelot Marketing Director, Martin Pugh, said: 'This
> campaign is designed to capture what it feels like to play
> and win the lottery in a way that inspires players to
> dream and participate.'

We have to be told, you see. We have to be spoon-fed with the carefully disguised truth ('the lottery dream' . . . 'act on their dreams' . . . 'inspires players to dream') that what is being advertised is . . . nothing. A remote possibility of . . . happiness. A few hours of hope followed by (anyone who has ever played a lottery will recognise this) anger that, once again, one has been cheated.

That in itself is quite babyish enough. But the real monstros-ity is right at the beginning. 'An animated character called Milo.'
Milo.

Why does it have a name? Why does it have a name which is *never referred to*? Why do they *tell* us about this name, which has been made up? Which isn't real?

Why, so that we will *bond*. So that our emotions can be preempted. So that we know what to think, and so that (remembering that this is a press release) the journalists who read it can tell their readers what to think in their turn, trying, in the meantime, not to recall why they went into journalism in the first place, and putting aside all those thoughts of politics and wars and fedoras* and Edward G. Robinson in *Five Star Final* and other great hat-and-reporter movies, *The Front Page* and *His Girl Friday*, because that was when journalism was about *news*, about *crime* and *corruption* and standing up for *truth*, whatever truth may have been, and also about *smoking*; but now it is about celebrity, and celebrity is about show business, and show business is in the end about advertising, so journalism, too, is about advertising. Advertising and celebrities. Showbiz without the glamour.

Do you feel well served by your newspaper?

---

* Maybe *that's* whom I am pretending to be, when I put my hat on! A *journalist*! With a sharp suit in 22 oz Donegal tweed, and a Speed Graphic, and a cigarette case, and an apartment with a roll-topped desk, and nobody treating me like a Big Baby.

So how come you haven't stormed its offices, demanding to be treated like an adult?

Because they think they've got your number. Yours and mine. They know that, really, we're all girls together and what we really want is to wipe, swish and spray and, above all, to be clean and fresh *down there*, where our . . . *stuff* is. The stuff we don't really want. The stuff that we think we want because there's something missing. The stuff that all the other all-girls-together not only want but have, because all the other all-girls-together have it:

The digital camera to take photographs of things which we would remember better if we looked at them instead of taking photographs, and when we've taken the photographs, instead of forgetting to send the film to the chemist's and never seeing the photographs, we load the photographs onto our computer, and it looks at them on our behalf.

The SatNav system for the car, because it is a gadget and involves satellites! and pilots use them! and yacht people! and even if we never go anywhere ('Look! I'm exactly outside the front door and that's where the *SatNav* says I am, how about that?') we know we could if we wanted to, just like our old penknife with the thing for taking the stone out of a horse's ass, never actually used but it could have been if we had come upon a horse with a stone in its, no, hoof, though not now, because instead of that knife we have a Leatherman Wave, the ultimate survival tool although we are unlikely ever to need to ultimately survive except if we're in an air crash, in which case we wouldn't have the Leatherman Wave because it would have been confiscated, as would the Leatherman Juice which is smaller, and the Leatherman Squirt which is smaller still but, hey, the intrepid guy has to be prepared to ultimately survive at all times although he may have to do it without his Leatherman Squirt, which he can't find because it's so conveniently *small*.

Forty-seven handbags, including this season's must-have and

next season's must-have, which we know are must-have handbags because women in magazines whose job it is to tell us which is this, and next, season's must-have handbags have – now here's a coincidence – told us about this, and next, season's must-have handbags.

Philly. We want Philly. It used to be called Philadelphia Cheese Spread but that was a bit grown-up, like Pan-American Airways had to become PanAm and Western Pacific Bank had to become WestPac, and the National Biscuit Corporation had to become NaBisCo . . . so Philadelphia Cheese Spread is 'Philly' now, and the advertisements tell us what to think. '*It's chicken with yummy Philly penne.*' Yes? How old are we? *Yummy*, for God's sake? But, good consumers that we are, we forgive the 'Yummy' and instead lapse into a terrible reverie that here are people having chicken pasta (with processed cheese, excuse me?) with friends, and it's all easy and 'While your pasta's boiling, pan-fry the chicken in –' Just *one fucking minute* here: my pasta isn't boiling. I haven't got any pasta. Nothing is boiling. I am in my study.

How dare you hucksters make assumptions about what I am doing or what I like or how I am going to feel if some barking incompetent gobbogue offers me chicken-and-processed-cheese pasta? Hmm? HOW DARE YOU?

Happy Happy Happy Now

But before I can resolve to sharpen one of my Leathermen and punch the directions to Philly headquarters into the SatNav, I forget my anger, isolate myself with my iPod, buy a few more songs,* plunge into the male grooming section, think of new

---

* The iPod only recognises, as a unit of music, the 'song'. According to iPod, the first movement of Bruckner's 8th Symphony is a 'song'. They're not scary, you see, songs. Are they? Because we are all frightfully easily intimidated, and ain't that the truth?

⚠️ The difference between being a child and being an adult was once the ability to provide your own food. Now, we just watch others (whether Nigella, the universal Mother, or Jamie Oliver, the universal cocky little prick who we'd like to punch in the eye) cooking for us, and, thus inspired, spend money on *very* expensive knives and 'professional' kitchens in which we don't actually cook; instead, we make a fuss (like children playing at cooking) or alternatively buy pre-assembled, pre-chopped, pre-everything-except-pre-eaten kits of food-style product which we put together, coat with the special glutinous sauce, and wait for the credit. Look, Mommy! Look what I did done!

shoes and more new shoes and organic green tea and a Nigella model mixing-bowl set and a lovingly hand-crafted reproduction Viking keel-adze and a vintage potto hutch from eBay and a tan bridle-hide notebook-holder and an £875 Aeron chair and a new laptop and lots of new software which will change my life and make me happy and a new briefcase which will make me happy and a new electric razor and faster broadband and bigger television screen and louder speakers and a bigger sofa and an Irish linen safari jacket for sitting on the bigger sofa in while dreaming about the safari I won't take because that's not what Big Babies do, Big Babies may go on safari-style holiday packages, but they don't actually go on safaris. And there's an ultrasonic one with 40 minutes' anti-skip and non-return valve in a handsome, elegant Iridinium™ slip-proof casing with six (6) inclusive designer radiators and high-altitude delicates cycle for easily downloadable Laser compatibility on a Tbase-1000 scaleable system with 'natural daylight' posture adjustment and auto-sleep energy-saver mode, easily portable for rapid, deep-ocean functionality with maximum signal-to-noise ratio.

And what does it do? It makes me feel . . . hang on while I look up the advertisem – What does it do? Well, it . . . it . . .

It makes me feel in control.

It makes me feel like I am the sort of person who has one, just like the sort of person whose picture was on the advertisement.

It makes me feel . . . grown-up.

I am grown-up. And happy. They said I'd be grown-up and happy if I got one, and now I've got one and I'm grown up, and I feel . . . happy.

What do I want one of those for?

Because I smell bad. Okay?

So bring on the cartoon dog to sell me motor insurance! Bring on the talking food! Bring on the creepy spooky baby-in-a-suit telling the toilet-roll executives how to do toilet rolls, bring on the porridge ad with Windy Miller ('Ooh look, it's Windy Miller. Not having your usual fry-up breakfast today? Is that since you got the results of your cholesterol test?'). Read out a biscuit packet to me! McVitie's chocolate digestives. Read it: 'We're passionate about what we do . . .' And I'll pretend to believe them, if they respect me in the morning. I will. I will honestly believe that they are passionate about what they do.

I am a Big Baby. I need to be told what to think. Don't we all, girls?

CHAPTER 5

What On Earth
Are You Playing At?

Mum, Mum, I'm Bored

Big Babies are the first entertained generation in history. We could almost say that the point of life for a Big Baby is to be entertained. Taken in aggregate, the biggest endeavour, and perhaps the biggest business, in the advanced English-speaking world is distraction. What, exactly, it is we feel we need to be distracted from is harder to nail down. It could, perhaps, be the end of work, as work used to be considered: the ploughing and forging and building and heaving and hammering and slaughtering and tanning and loading and all those other things which are increasingly done by machines, or by Asians and Indians, in Asia and India, who, to the Big Babies, are better than machines because they need less servicing and require no capital investment (and, of course are self-replicating). The standard theory defined work as an essential requirement of human fulfilment because it offered a sense of status, of belonging, of being useful, but it could equally well be that work offered a diversion; and now that (as we shall see later) work is either vanishing or ceasing to be recognisable as work, we need to find our distraction elsewhere.

111

⚠ When we were little, there used to be join-the-dot puzzles which we hated but which we were forced to do on trains to stop us whining and grizzling, or, even worse, Having Thoughts and maybe even Fidgeting. Now grown-ups do Sudoku. They put numbers in squares. Why? How did this happen? What the *hell* is Sudoku, and what the *hell* is it for? (And let us not even think about the spectacle of grown men hunched over little screens on the train, playing pretend computer golf with little stick men and golfing sound effects.)

It may even be that distraction is the primary discretionary need. Once we have filled our bellies and got warm, after all, what do we do next? I recall once camping out in the African bush. I had foolishly left the spare gas canisters for the lantern in Harare, and here I was, supper eaten, the sun going down with a bang, as it does in those latitudes, ludicrously early and a long night ahead with nothing whatever to do and the impossibility of reading. I realised then that my belief that I would do fine in prison was a mistake, and that the truth was that I would do fine in prison providing I had a book and enough light to read by. 'Here I am, alone in the bush,' I thought. 'This is the solitude which millions of city-dwellers crave.' I lay there for a while in my tent, then I thought, 'Millions of city-dwellers don't know their arse from their elbow,' and then I thought, 'Sodding tent,' and then I thought, 'Sodding bush,' and then there was a terrible shriek and I thought, 'What was that terrible shriek?' and then I thought, 'Sod it, whatever it was,' and then I thought, 'Here I am alone in the bush, with my thoughts,' and then I thought, 'It's a pretty poor thing if here I am, alone in the bush, with my thoughts, and my only thought is "Here I am, alone in the bush, with my thoughts",' and after that I slowly declined into a terrible stupefied madness, the sheer banality of the situation keeping me awake with a kind of psy-chotic boredom until I fell asleep just before dawn, to be awoken about ten minutes later by the sun coming up again with an audible crack, followed by a terrible shriek, because, whatever you say about the bush, the one thing it's good for is terrible shrieks.

If someone had come along with a distraction – any distrac-tion – at any point in the night, I would have sold them my soul. A book and a reading light, an iPod, a video, a computer game, an Internet connection, a Game Boy, anything to take my mind off my situation.

Even work.

If that same somebody had come along with some work I could usefully do, I would have been as glad to do it as anything else. And so the boundary, it seemed to me, blurred between work and distraction: both exist to keep our minds off the central existential problem facing intelligent life on this planet which is, once again, that once we've filled our bellies and got warm, there's *absolutely nothing else to do*.

And you realise that dying of boredom is not as implausible as it may sound. But living with boredom is worse.

Shut Up, I'm Watching

One of the problems of imprisonment or the bush is, of course, solitude. Had I had companions, we could have talked into the night, providing we could think of anything to say.

And we have recreated compulsory solitude with a horrible recklessness in this infantilised age. Donne may have famously declared that 'No man is an island', but he was persuading his congregation against the lure of solipsism, not cheerfully con-firming a common view. And since then, we have got worse. Social structures have been broken down, in collusion with the very tricks of distraction which ease the effects of their breakdown. It is a strange synergy that the more we *can* be distracted, the more we arrange our lives so that we *need* to be distracted. Television was initially identified as the new centre of family life, replacing the coal fire as the focus of attention, with the difference that, with the coal fire, people looked at each other; with the television, attention was on the screen. Randy Newman, perhaps the greatest living satirist (certainly the most concise), drew the picture of the TV as family friend in *My Country*. There they sat, bathed in its gentle radiance, speaking, not to each other, but bouncing their remarks off the screen. 'We were watching, and we couldn't look away . . .'

If we want an epitaph for the Age of Distraction, that must surely be it. And watching what? Newman's (tele)vision is apocalyptic in its deadly stupor, the soul-sucking revenge of the fifth horseman of the apocalypse, Entertainment. We don't live; we watch living being done. We don't play; we see others playing; even our minds are filled, not with our own inner narrative, but with 'other people's voices'. And the response of Newman's ventriloquial Family Average? 'Thank you, Jesus . . .'

Watching. If the adult is defined by his freedom to act autonomously in the world, then the Big Baby is characterised by being deprived of that freedom. Reduced to docile spectators, we watch others acting (in both senses of the word) in fictitious lives and believe that by observing their phony autonomy, we somehow acquire it ourselves; perhaps by the same sort of osmosis that leads the deluded followers of 'kabalah' to think that, by holding a 'sacred' text, they can absorb its virtues without the effort of reading. A raft of Talmudic writings in the shape of TV magazines and 'celebrity' magazines – not to mention what to our forebears would have been an inconceivable and shameless obsession with actors and performers in the daily and Sunday newspapers – confirms us in this crazed and infantilising belief: that the lives of people who pretend to be other people, in carefully constructed fictional illusions, are more

114

important and more real than our own; and that, by watching them (we couldn't look away), they are somehow living our lives for us, on our behalf.

Just like a child looks upon Daddy, going out into the world while she remains at home: passive, contingent, distracted.

Something for Everyone

But even the open-mouthed distraction of Randy Newman's TV family can now seem like a golden era of communication and togetherness, everyone talking about the same programme the next morning – which in itself is desperate enough, though now we look back on it fondly. The proliferation of media devices and the increasing narrow-casting of special-interest distractions have reduced our lives to such a degree of elective solipsism (how we long to be alone, with the imaginary friends who can distract us from our solitude) that the real world is becoming increasingly irrelevant. A television in every room, in front of which sits a single person, watching something of no interest to anyone else, not participating in any sort of communal life, least of all the ancient commensality of the family table. If not a television, then a computer. Here's one person in a chat room, abjuring reality for a false persona moving in virtuality among other false personae. Here's another, playing Second Life,* if 'playing' is the right word for this participation in a made-to-order alternative universe where the lonely middle-aged man can be a gorgeous young woman, hot as butter, and where real money is used to buy imaginary things, to such an extent that the American Internal Revenue Service is now looking to see whether it can tax Second Life income in the same way it

---

* An online 'game' in which the Steinberg cartoon 'On the Internet, nobody knows you're a dog' is carried to its ultimate conclusion.

taxes income in reality: a development which calls reality itself into question.

In another room, here is someone else, watching sport: once a young man's game, something to be played, it too has become something to watch, as the defining paradigm of the Age of Distraction becomes not participation, but voyeurism. Wandering from room to room is someone with an iPod; music no longer requires going out, being with other people, or even sitting in a room on your own, listening. Now it is a permanent distraction, a matter of right, a way of affirming your identity without having to be identified by other members of your chosen tribe; even when we interact with the outside world, reluctantly, our ears are plugged with the iPod buds, trickling music into our minds. Our grandparents would have thought it an appalling rudeness; after all, what does it say but 'I do not acknowledge your existence. You are superfluous to me. I may be moving in the same physical space as you, but don't expect me to acknowledge it.'

And what music it is, too: stripped steadily of all the attributes which make music music – complexity, structure, modulation, ambiguity, dynamic, tonal colour, tempo – much, perhaps the majority, of music in the Age of Distraction has become a coarser, harsher simulacrum of the womb, a matter of repetition at a steady beat, tap-foot oof oof tap-foot oof oof, of repetition, of repetition, of a bit of a bore a bore a bore who pokes you in the chest in the chest and says the same thing over again pokes you in the chest and says the same thing over again pokes you in the chest tap-foot oof same tap thing chest tap oof oof . . .

. . . because the Big Baby cannot bear ambiguity, is unhappy with subtlety, seeks not engagement but a curious oceanic oblivion. *De gustibus non est disputandum*: there's no arguing about taste, but what we can say is that the level of complexity and ambiguity in popular music has been steadily declining for decades, while art music has largely lost its ability to engage; Romantic music is boring, the Baroque is dry, and if there is an engagement with 'world music' then it is on the level of the Orientalism which Edward Said so condemned: the perception of foreign cultures as 'exotic', as the 'Other' on which we can project those qualities we lack, feel ambivalent about, appropriate, or envy: North Indian classical music (the other great musical language of humanity) is by this token 'sensual' and 'spiritual', Latin-American is 'vibrant', Afro-Cuban is 'colourful' and 'seductive' and, those judgements having been made, the intellect and the critical faculties can be safely put into neutral and we can fall back on purest distraction. Which is appropriate for a form which largely devotes itself to the adolescent distractions of thwarted erotic love and unspecified grievance. My baby doesn't love me. The world's all wrong. Nobody understands me. I don't belong in this world.

Start the 'World', I Want to Get On

The culmination of the instruments of distraction, their apotheosis if you like, is when life itself becomes a distraction from . . . life itself. The more sophisticated Big Babies can cheerfully mock the horrible but captivating idiocies of 'reality TV' but they might well find themselves on very shaky ground, much like the older generation of 'housewives' would rail against prostitutes for offering sex for money while failing to notice that their trade (before romantic love became the *sine qua non* for marriage) was not entirely dissimilar except that they had fewer clients, worse payment terms and no right to refuse.

Reality TV is, in many ways, just playing at Wendy House, or rather, watching people playing at Wendy House; in any case, it is entirely disengaged from anything to do with the real world, except through an almost impenetrable net of let's-pretend. Taking the iconic reality TV show as *Big Brother*, we can say that

- The contestants are pretending to be ordinary people, though of course
- They cannot be ordinary people because they are now on TV but
- They were ordinary people before they went on TV which means that
- They are even more extraordinary than they would be if they weren't ordinary people but actors, because, after all,
- It's a really, really extraordinary thing for ordinary people to be on TV, which is why
- They then get invited to host their own chat shows or write their own books, because
- They are extraordinary, having been on TV, but unfortunately
- They have now become TV people, so
- It is now no longer extraordinary for them to be on TV, so
- We have to pretend it is extraordinary for them to be on TV, when all along we know that
- Although it was extraordinary for ordinary people to be on TV, which made them extraordinary enough to be on TV without its being extraordinary for them to be there, it is still extraordinary to be on TV at all, whether or not they themselves are still extraordinary or whether they are just ordinarily extraordinary, but in any case they are on TV and we are not, which is good enough for them and so it should be good enough for us.

We are pretending to believe the things that we need to believe in order to believe the things in the list above, and, in particular, we are pretending to believe that

- There is no need to pretend to believe anything in the list above because
- We know it's only a television show because
- It's on the television and so
- The people in it are in a television show so
- They are by definition television people, so
- There is nothing extraordinary about them, so
- If it's not extraordinary, then it's sort of, you know, like, real, and so
- It is interesting.

The press are going to write about it at length, despite saying that they aren't going to write about it because it's a flop, which they are saying because nothing will make people watch a reality TV show more assiduously than being told it's a flop, so it won't be a flop after all, which means that they can pretend that

- They really did think it was going to be a flop, but simultaneously
- They knew it wasn't going to be a flop, so
- They knew that we are going to be interested, because
- We can't tell that everyone else is pretending to be interested.

So much for the first level of nested let's-pretend. Shall we go further into this terrible web? Let's not. Let's instead consider that, for many, if not most, Big Babies, something very similar operates in their own lives. Or, rather, lifestyles.

We Don't Need a Life, We've Got a Lifestyle

My grandfather (may his name be a blessing) was born in 1888 and he didn't have a lifestyle. He had a hat and a car and a wife and two sons and a housekeeper and a maid and a nanny for the children, and the housekeeper had a dog and the dog had a canker and lived in a kennel and there was an odd-job man who had had a spot of trouble (small boys). And later on he got Rediffusion, which was like cable radio so that you didn't have to tune in, and it could be played all over the house if you wanted. And later on from that, he got television, which was also Rediffusion and you didn't have to tune that in, either, not least because my grandfather (may his name be a blessing) only had the one channel, initially because there only *was* one channel, subsequently because the other channels were either commercial (common) or BBC2 (arty). My grandfather read Charles Dickens mostly. Sometimes they went on holiday. His house was furnished with furniture. There were some exotic things in it which people had brought back from exotic places. The most exotic things were African carvings and Benares brassware. The African carving had been brought back from a war, possibly the Boer one. The Benares brassware was brought back from Benares by my grandfather's friend Dr Chand who lived next door but was a Brahmin from Benares. Dr Chand didn't have a lifestyle either. He looked as though he had a lifestyle, but that was because he was from India. Dr Chand probably thought my grandfather had a lifestyle, not realising it was just because my grandfather was from Lancashire.

By now, it was the Fifties, and nobody had a lifestyle then because there was nobody to tell them to, and anyway they were too busy having lives.

They were grown-ups. They went about their business. In my grandfather's case, it was seeing patients and making them better, where possible. In Dr Chand's case, it was the same, because he was a doctor too. It was also the same for my grandfather's other friends, because they were doctors as well. For my father, it was much the same, because he was a doctor too. Doctors stuck together. That was how it was. And they didn't have a lifestyle because they didn't know they were meant to.

I suspect that my grandfather's life was real in a sense that my father's life hasn't quite been, and my life is not at all. The crucial difference is the lack of self-consciousness, and that self-consciousness is yet another hallmark of the perpetual, infantilised adolescents we have all become, monsters of introspection hovering twitchily on the edge of self-obsession, peering into the abyss of our own inner disconnection, occasionally aware that while the unexamined life may not be worth living, the life which only exists to be examined is barely manageable; barely, indeed, a life. It is (as is appropriate for the real baby, the real adolescent, but not appropriate for the Big Baby) a preparation for a life. The consistently introspective life of the Big Baby is as much a simulacrum as life on *Big Brother*.

To keep the simulacrum going – to stop it flickering and fading, with an Epilogue *pling*, to a small white spot in the centre of the screen – we need help. And we need that help because that help is available. It's the old paradox again, of the infantilised life being somehow malevolently self-sustaining. We need distraction from our fragmented and solitary lives because the distractions available to us have rendered our lives fragmented and solitary. And we need lifestyle advice from magazines and websites and newspaper supplements and health advisers and personal trainers precisely because we are being nagged about our lifestyle all the time by magazines and websites and newspaper supplements and health advisers and personal trainers . . .

If one of the markers of adulthood is autonomy, then one of the preconditions of autonomy is being left the fuck alone. My grandfather wasn't nagged. Once he turned twenty-one, he was a man, and a grown-up, and nobody battered him round the clock with opportunities he was missing, miseries he didn't know he had, aspirations ditto, inadequacies doubly so. Nobody told him about being good in bed, grooming tips, what his car said about him, what he should have to eat, how much he should drink, what his house said about him, how Benares brassware was *so* over, where he should go on holiday, what this season's must-have product would be, how his suits should look.

He knew some of these things, and didn't care about the others because nobody was drawing them to his attention. He knew what his suits should look like: trousers, waistcoat, jacket, all made out of the same material. He knew about grooming: you shaved. He knew what he should eat: breakfast, lunch, dinner. He probably had no idea good-in-bed even existed, or that furniture did anything except furnish, or that where he went on holiday was of any significance, or that his car said anything about him at all, except 'Oh, here comes Dr Bywater, I recognise his car.'

The idea of life-as-a-text (because in the world of postmodern Modernity, everything is a text) did not occur to him, unless it was in a vague hybrid Enlightenment sense of the world as God's book, glossed and footnoted by mankind. That his own body was a text, to be written and read and re-inscribed, would have struck him as nonsense unless it had struck him as utterly incomprehensible first. That a man – a man – should go to the gym in order to acquire a six-pack because the world was in thrall to a manufactured obsession with the male abdomen: this would have been something for a psychiatrist to deal with. Muscles were for lifting and fighting and hammering-in. Fighting was out of the question, and if he wanted something lifted or hammered-in, he got someone to do it, and they wouldn't need to go to the gym either because they'd have all the musculature they needed as a result of all the lifting and hammering-in.

> ⚠️ The president of the Men's Health Forum, Dr Ian Banks, said men were now experiencing the same pressures as women, with the result that they were increasingly body-obsessed. He said: 'It is often easier to get through to men using image than it is to get through to them on health. But there is a danger with the way that we highlight issues that it can skew perceptions of risk.'
>
> He added that about 10 to 20 per cent of all eating disorders were suffered by men. 'We don't know if it is increasing because of body image issues or just because we are urging men to go to the doctor and report their concerns.' (BBC News, 16 March 2006)

But the Big Babies have no such autonomy, and are harangued to death; nor have they learned the adult trick of simply ignoring the shrieking, nagging, fishwife-and-huckster voices, of disengaging on the very good grounds that such a clamour betokens serious derangement. Instead, Baby tries to comply. Believing it when he is told that he is unhappy, he then believes the cure the same fishwives and hucksters proceed to offer. The house, the furniture, the car, the exotic holidays, the new wines to try, the squid and worms and foreign muck cooked in jam with the gravy underneath the meat, the peculiar vegetables like weeds or tumours, best thrown away; the uncomfortable places to go, the uncomfortable ways to get to them ('Travel the Amazon on anaconda-back'), the uncomfortable and dismaying sex ('Do we have to do buggery?'), the uncomfortable and dismaying life, funded on credit, built on debt, Carol Vorderman smiling as the bailiffs home gloomily in and the Official Receiver prepares for another day's official receiving.

And it is all a world of make-believe, a *Big Brother* house, a set of status symbols notable only for symbolising someone else's status . . . except that when there is nothing but status for the Big

Baby in the Age of Distraction, then our symbols *are* our status. So we become someone else, and there is nothing else. We are viewed as we view ourselves: as media. Imperfect media, but media all the same. And just as all media now exist as functionaries or imitations or avatars of show-business, whose job is to divert, distract and, above all, *deliver* – deliver us to the advertisers selling us the distractions on which our lives depend – so we find ourselves in show-business too. But we are doomed to fail. We live on a diet of shadows, and we can only imitate them, stuck in the playpen, waiting to be distracted. Shadows of shadows, and our lives flickering behind glass.

CHAPTER 6

Where Were You
Last Night?

It was – it remains – the Great Question of adolescence, usually preceded with 'and', to suggest a whole range of questions previously asked, unsatisfactory answers having been given, and now life itself hung in the balance.

It is the ur-question, the one that makes us all quake. Don't pretend you don't feel a chill up your spine just reading the words, even if where you were last night was where you were meant to be. (And where might that be?) It is the precursor of all the other questions which make us shudder, judder our knees nervously, want a wee *now*, get a dry mouth, experience that sense of incipient dissolution which characterises parasympathetic meltdown. It means discovery. We have been found out. We have been found out, curiously, even if we have done nothing wrong. Especially if we have done nothing wrong, because the question is like bankruptcy: all other debts are called in, and our assets are removed from our control. It's curtains.

It tears away the years like damp tissue-paper and leaves us mewling, or wishing we could remember how mewling is done. 'And where were you last night?' 'Where were you on the 23rd of January between seven o'clock and midnight?' 'Is there something you want to tell me?' 'Is this your car, sir?' 'Am I speaking to Mr Thurgatroyd? Mr J. B. S. Thurgatroyd?' 'Are you the account-holder, sir?' 'Do you recognise this photograph, sir?' 'Does this document mean anything to you?' 'Do you remember signing this?' 'Do you realise what day this is?' 'And where were you last night?'

Later in life, whole small civilisations – spouses, families, private jokes, private languages, households, furniture, holidays, money, pasts, futures, hopes, companionships – can crumble at the question, wrongly answered.

'I was with Snelling. From the office. You know Snelling. You met him at the Christmas do. Last year. Bald chap. Wears a hat. A Stetson Stratoliner, like Howard Hughes, though God knows what he thinks he looks like, given that he's only five foot seven and fat as a –'

But it's no good. You weren't where you were supposed to be. You were with *Mrs* Snelling. Show's over. Hire a lawyer, and run. Go on. Hire a lawyer! Run! It's what we do! There's no point in staying somewhere you're not happy, and it's not fair on the children, and a clean break and a fresh start, that's the thing, one day you'll look back on this and . . .

. . . and weep.

That's what it means to be a grown-up Big Baby in the Mummyverse. It means following your instincts, looking back, and weeping. Because when it comes to our instincts, we simply don't know what to do.

I'm Running Away, Please Make Me Some Sandwiches

For the real adolescent, the one who still has a right to behave like a Big Baby, poised sweatily between dependence and autonomy, the dilemma is at least capable of resolution. The purpose of adolescence is to arrive in due course at a point where nobody can ask you who you were with last night. On the one hand, there is the family. They don't understand you. They have never done anything for you. They hate your music and your clothes and your haircut and they remember you when you were little, and they have the cruelty, the intolerable vile vulgarity, to remember that they remember you when you were little. Merciful heavens, the buggers even have *pictures*.

But they also have food. The buggers have food and sofas and laundry and hot water and a car and things are done as they should be done, when they should be done. Breakfast, for example, always happens in the morning. Coffee turns out to be in cups. It is all very nice.

On the other hand, there is the call of the wild. The bad girls who work in the bar. The bad boys from the computer repair shop. The clever ones, gone off to university. The ones with cars and E and the key to the wide world and their intolerable concatenation of flesh and attitude, filling the air with backbeat and pheromones. That's where to be last night, and tonight, and all other nights. And one day, after innumerable tuggings at the rope of domesticity, the adolescent will slip his moorings and be gone, never suspecting for a moment that his parents have been wondering what the hell was taking him so long.

That is how it should be.

But for the Big Babies, it should be different. Slip the moorings and head for other moorings: that's how it should be. That's how Nature (if Nature designed us) designed us: a transition from port of departure to port of destination, and then ring down – Finished with Engines.

⚠ **Birth rates in the UK have been falling for years. Is this a surprise? We are so well entrenched in our infantilised self-obsession that we surely have no room for *real* babies, little ones, *nasty* little ones with demands and requirements who can keep us from finding out who we really want to be and *buying* it?**

It is not our way. Suckled on the notion that the good life is about limitless self-actuation through limitless shopping – egged on by the advertisers, who know exactly how to tickle us under the chin – we have no option but to extend it into our everyday and most intimate lives, so that when we find what we believe to be The One (who will generally be only A One but will do perfectly well nevertheless) we go through the motions of dropping anchor but in reality, we are still shopping. Still looking. Still on the *qui vive* for something better that will make, in its turn, something better of our objectified, commercialised, endlessly fiddled-with lives.

You Think You're Happy? Now Read On

Like everything else in the world of Big Babies, the press and television lead the attack on our slim chance of contentment. The infant, the child, the adolescent, all live under constant exhortation to be different, to measure up, to amend themselves. Responding to these demands is like the venerable comedy sketch where the man is trying to flatten the hump in the newly laid carpet: wherever he presses it down, it pops up somewhere else. Miller was very clever and Murphy was very diligent and Milroy was very good and then there was Fennimore, and Fennimore was neat. Fennimore's socks never bagged and his jacket was always neat and his tie done up and his hair combed and his briefcase latched, and if I got clever, why then could I not be like Murphy and Milroy and Fennimore, and if I made myself diligent, why then could I not be like Miller and Milroy and Fennimore, and if I turned myself into a good boy for the limited period of time that I could sustain being a good boy then why could I not be like Miller and Murphy and Fennimore, and if, by some terrible miracle, I managed to be clever and diligent and good, then why (if I was so clever and diligent and good) could I not *also be like fucking Fennimore?*

You have doubtless had similar experiences.

One day many years later I got on a train and there was Fennimore: neat and combed and his briefcase polished and a white hanky in his pocket and his spectacles just as his spectacles had always been and his hair just as his hair had always been, and I thought: now I can kill him; I will wait for a tunnel. But I did not kill him. Instead, I thought: he looks . . . diminished. He looks very small.

That's what happens if you do everything you are told. You are . . . diminished.

And we are all being told things, all the time. You cannot finish your morning newspaper without feeling that you have survived the most terrible hectoring from people to whom you have done no harm; why do they despise you so much? Why do they want you to be different? Making their assumptions of false matiness, dropping into phony demotic, sugaring their pill (soap, liquorice, cascara, no therapeutic benefit at all), ticking us off. The sex columnists tell us how we could have much better sex and the medical columnists tell us that our impotence or lack of desire are perfectly normal but treatable, and ageing is nature's way of telling us to piss off but we shouldn't let ourselves go, and here are the Family Values pundits and there, just across the way, are the gossips, telling us that it's best if we settle for a quiet home life just like Jesus wanted us to,* and, simultaneously, that Tom Cruise may appear gay but just look! at the hot babe! he's porking! and he's so in love he's bouncing on the sofa, so why can't we bounce on the sofa too (providing it's the family sofa, of course)? Brace up! they shout. Bounce on the sofa! Live a little! Or your husband/wife will leave you/hate you/cheat on you/go into a decline. It will be your fault. Yes it will.

---

* They never mention that Jesus didn't exactly live a quiet family life, of course; never mention that he was one of the biggest spanners in the works of all time. They tell us that he was like Fennimore. It's not true.

The media want us to be everything. Diligent yet adventurous, domesticated yet devil-may-care, chilled yet careful, living wild yet watching our health. Buy this outfit, visit this restaurant, and enjoy mad sex with your spouse; to hell with the credit-card debt, live a little (but use the opportunity to palpate your wife's breasts and check your husband's prostate).

And so a terrible discontent sets in. Nothing that should be thought about is thought about. Here is a man who was funny on the television, and he says the word 'arse' in the newspaper! And here is another man who wasn't actually funny on the television, he just shouted a lot with a big telephone, and he's writing about his life and he doesn't even say 'arse', he just writes about his life; and if he is allowed – no, *paid* – to write about his life because he had a big telephone and shouted on the TV, then how much less significant are our lives, which *nobody* wants to hear about? We are less than a man with a big telephone, less than a woman pretending to be a prostitute, less than the man who tells us our houses won't do, less than the women who tell us our clothes look awful, less than the cooks who cook better than we do . . . *less*.

We may enjoy individual bits of this haranguing. We may nod in agreement. We may resolve to change our ways. But the aggregate result is that we lose our confidence. Our own lives are lesser lives, and we find it hard to measure up. We cannot be Miller and Murphy and Milroy and Fennimore . . . so what *can* we be?

You Gotta Know When to Hold 'Em, Know When to Fold 'Em

The poker player's great maxim is also a lesson for life. But here in the Mummyverse, we are surrounded by so many people commenting – on the hand we've been dealt, advising us how to play it, sucking their teeth when we play it badly – that we can no longer make up our minds. And so we lose our cool, we hedge our bets, and next thing you know, we're out of the game.

The wildcard in the game is sex. Since the time of the Great Infantiliser himself, Sigmund Freud, sex has been uncoupled from its wider context and has become a thing-in-itself – not just a thing-in-itself, but the *thing*. We must tread carefully here, for, like the Devil in the old monastic office of Compline, the *Daily Mail* and the neo-cons, the family-values squirts (the ones always getting caught with their pants down) and the professional dis-approvers are always circling like a ravening lion, seeking whom they may devour; and we'd rather be dead in a ditch (wouldn't we?) than have them think we are on their side.

⚠️ One mark of the ill-raised child is its parents' end-less making of excuses. He's just tired. He's just curious. He's just going through a phase. He's just hyper-active. He's just very gifted. We don't believe in discipline. The ill-raised and infantilised kidult has to make his own excuses, and one of the best is addiction. Addiction was once, and properly, reserved for drugs. Now it can be anything. Best of all is 'sex addiction', which Dr Thaddeus Birchard & Associates (of www.sex-addiction.co.uk) describe as 'a grass-roots term that has emerged from the experi-ence of ordinary people to describe what it feels like'. ('Just think, darling, there was a time when I was just a sleaze-ball and you were a trollop.')

But no matter how clear one's liberal humanitarian beliefs may be, it remains the truth that we've got ourselves into a dread-ful mess over sex, and a dreadful mess over how families should work, and it's all making a dreadful mess of a lot of other things, and we sit here in the middle of it all feeling powerless and harassed and bad and not sure what we can do about it, or if we can do anything about it at all. And while the right-wingers and the God-botherers and all those other types cursed with the terrible delusion of certainty swank about the place ticking us off, we Big Babies can only sit here wringing our hands and muttering the old Latin motto of the Greystocks: *Volo non valeo*, One wishes one could, but *no can do*.'

Everything New Is Old Again

In the early part of the fourteenth century, one Arnaud de Verniolles was arrested by the Inquisition in the Pyrenees, the future Pope Benedict XII being anxious to stamp out the Albigensian heresy in south-western France. Arnaud was a former Franciscan monk; he was also a 'homophiliac' and the monastery of which he had been a member was notable for sodomy. By his own account, Arnaud picked up the habit from a boy (also called Arnaud) with whom he shared a bed at school:

> On the fourth or fifth night we spent together . . . when Arnaud thought that I was fast asleep, he began to embrace me and put himself between my thighs . . . and to move about there as if I were a woman . . . he went on sinning thus every night. I was still no more than a child . . . I was so ashamed that I did not dare tell anyone of this sin.

There are, of course, as many ways of reading a text as there are readers, but the difference between our reading now and the reading in the fourteenth century is telling. Then, Arnaud was under inquisition – 'Where were you last night?' – for a sin; a sin into which he had been initially led by another sinner. Now, he would not be under inquisition, nor would he have been considered a sinner himself, but rather a victim, one who was abused, violated, subjected to the most terrible thing – 'inappropriate' sexual contact – that we can imagine.*

Paedophilia is the modern Satan. We see it everywhere. It is the one crime for which we hold the tacit – or often vociferous – belief that rehabilitation is not possible. And in a sense it exemplifies everything that has gone awry in our thinking about sex; everything that is infantilised.

Grown-ups arguably could be defined as people who have integrated the apparently opposing demands of their instincts, so that love, sex and family combine together in a coherent whole. Some years ago I saw on the Paris Métro an advertisement for Dim brand tights which has stayed in my mind: a photograph of a mini-skirted woman's legs, glossy in her elegant hosiery, her feet in stilettos, the whole enough to, in Raymond Chandler's phrase, make a bishop kick a hole in a stained-glass window. And clinging to one of her endless elegant legs: a toddler. A little child.

The image impressed itself on me because it was pretty obvious that it could never play in England or the USA. The combination of sexuality and motherhood was too complex. One or the other for us; we have not emerged from – or have perhaps been pushed back into – the infantile condition where sexuality is focused, transgressive, overpowering, and disaggregated. We view it as a set of binary oppositions: sex/family, mother/whore, innocence/corruption, child/adult, gay/straight. Freud's overt obsession with sex (like a boy with a pornographic magazine under the bed), far from liberating us from sexual

---

* Unless, of course, he lived somewhere like Palm Beach County school district, which, in May 2006, configured its Internet filters to block pro-gay sites but to allow access to, for example, Focus on the Family, the American Family Association, the Traditional Values Coalition and the National Association for Research and Therapy of Homosexuality. Interestingly, the website which publicised the affair, morons.org, is listed by the 'Blue Coat' filter as 'humor and jokes'. Ha ha, especially if you happen to be a gay teenager down in Palm Beach County.

repression, cast us even more under eroticism's thrall; his terribly peculiar idea of the Oedipus complex turned the physical relations between adults and children into a criminal war zone. The strange thing, of course, was just how *inappropriate* the name was. Oedipus didn't want to sleep with his mother. Oedipus wanted to marry a woman he met in the town he'd fled to to escape the curse upon him; to be her husband and the father to her family. There was nothing illicit in Oedipus's desire at all; indeed, when he discovered what he had done, he blinded himself in horror.

But Freud let the imaginary cat out of the fantastical bag and muddied the waters for ever. We cannot cuddle our children now with a clear conscience; like children ourselves, we live in terror of finding out that we are actually bad, or of someone else telling us we are bad. At the same time, the primacy of sex – egged on by the Baby Boomers' two secret sexual weapons, the contraceptive pill and (for a brief glorious window in the Sixties and Seventies) the vanquishing of sexually transmitted disease – uncoupled sex from reproduction and turned what had been a component of the human family into a recreational right.

The media has still not managed to offer any reconciliation, and we have become too childish to tell the media to shut up. Instead, we grope after sex like adolescents, long after dignity and aesthetics should have encouraged us to continence. People well-stricken in years go off to group-sex clubs or advertise themselves on the Internet for what is termed 'adult fun' though it is seldom fun (and good sex shouldn't be fun) and certainly not adult. Women define themselves, despite everything, in terms of their sexuality and even the natural periodicities of life are subjugated to the need for a perennial, almost inconsolable, sexual desire and desirability. The menopause, when discussed at all, is discussed, first, as meaning that women can't get good parts in films or jobs on television (because the exemplar of women is now the actress, the perpetual adolescent perpetually becoming someone else), and, secondly, in terms of its being held at bay with hormone replacement therapy, just as the male equivalent of waning potency and waning interest are now dealt with by Viagra or, in extremis, something called Caverject: a sort of penile stiffener injected into the flabby inert member which has the advantage over Viagra that it can raise something resembling an erection even in the complete absence of sexual desire. Such a triumph.

Who Are These Children and Why Are They Calling Me 'Dad'?

And so the die is cast. The supremacy of sex and the fear of its manifestations; its separation from the social life of the family; the notion that it is a right to have better and more sex, constantly reinforced by the media; the infantile inability to integrate cause and effect. And we become engines of disconnected desire, once again held captive in the solipsism of perpetual adolescence.

The first victim is the conviviality of the family. When our erotic lives become ends, not means, the consequence becomes too easily irksome; and we run away. I did it myself, abandoning a two-year-old daughter because I thought that by doing so I was 'fulfilling' myself and 'being honest' and all the rest of the blather for which, in a sane and adult society, I would have had my face slapped, but which, in the world of Big Babies, meant that I was able to wallow in a sort of terribly smug self-pity, demanding that others feel my pain instead of behaving like a grown-up and not causing pain to anyone, including myself, but particularly the child for whom I was responsible. It was, naturally, for erotic enthralment. Like a teenager wriggling under the Question – 'Where were you last night?' – I made all sorts of excuses to myself, but in the end I was a grown man of thirty-two behaving like a thirteen-year-old. It was, of course, unforgivable.

135

⚠️ 'I accidentally had unusually lengthy sex with my husband on Wednesday.[1] Not to be recommended. It's not the sex with my husband that is the bad idea – others are not an option – but the duration of the event to which I refer. Bloody hell. Why? What exactly is the point of long, drawn out intercourse?[2] I know that in crappy novels and bawdy jokes the popular theory is that pleasure for all is increased incrementally to[3] protraction but . . . in terms of time, it's just not cost-effective.' – Arabella Weir, *Guardian*, 26 May 2006.

1 'unseemly access' (Thomas de Zengotita, *Mediated*; referring to the universal collusive voyeurism of the media age).

2 'Long-drawn-out,' presumably.

3 'proportionally to'? 'exponentially against'?

And, having infantilised ourselves in this way, we end up infantilising each other. We seem to find it almost impossible to establish adult relationships between men and women without dreadful hurdles, idiotic posturings and unimaginably naff intermediaries. We have speed-dating and self-styled 'pick-up artists', both of which are perhaps appropriate for the pathologically incompetent teenager but (with their approach to human affection being as a marketing project on the one hand and an exercise in PsyOps on the other) a lamentable admission of witlessness in 'adults'. Men run from woman to woman, seeking the elusive transcendent orgasm which will make us finally seem whole to ourselves, and women respond with a bitter impersonality, commodifying themselves and marginalising men as irrelevant in a daily outpouring of public contempt which most of them privately consider demeaning and unhappy. We hunt down imaginary avatars in chatrooms, knowing full well that most – some estimate up to 85 per cent – of online 'women' are

136

in fact men. We place too many eggs in the basket of our relationships, regarding our spouses or partners in the way an infant regards its mother: as a cornucopia, guardian, protector and fount of all gratification.

Our erotic disaffection bursts out not only in ourselves but in our children. Adults' children have some hope, but the children of other children have a harder row to hoe. When Daddy runs off and holes up with a popsie in a mobile home, when Mummy is upstairs shagging her latest man, how can trust be built? Couple that with the disintegration of commensality – perhaps the most crucial of human virtues, and one of the most ancient: the breaking of bread with others – and the stage is set for discord and disintegration.

We have had to make it up as we go along, we Big Babies. And we have not done a terribly good job. Absent fathers, harassed mothers, the endless shortage of money when a single income has to be split between two households. An inappropriate eroticism and a profound distrust of motive, so that affection is suspect and the sexual enemy – inappropriateness – is forever at the gate. A sexual politics based on division rather than harmony. And, as an insistent ostinato to our perplexity, the infantile shrieks of the body-fascists, the anorexic girls, the 'bigorexic' boys, the implants, the anxiety, the fellatio tips in teen magazines, the endless terror of paedophilia, the women-only hotel floors ('Security staff will be women, creating privacy and security for guests who will be able to walk along corridors without encountering businessmen' – but there are plenty of men who would like to be able to walk along corridors without encountering businessmen, too), the phoney war between men and women, the Child Support Agency, the welfare mothers, the families that never sit down to a meal together but graze like animals, the website devoted to students having sex, the dreary implausibility of Internet porn (Brazilian waxes, scrawny women with huge sudden breasts, the neoteny of their faces – Big Babies watching big babies), the artificial hatred got up . . .

137

Here's a story from the *Independent* newspaper of 8 April 2006, headlined 'All the Money and Power Won't Help a Man if He Hasn't Got a Pert Bottom':

> Big news from the sexual front line. Women like handsome men. They like them so much, in fact, that they're determined to get one. Forget those boring old male attributes of money and power. What women want now, according to a survey published in *New Scientist* this week, is a real stunner to go with that Mulberry handbag.

It's all there. To deconstruct it would be otiose. We've been making it up, and doing very badly. Perhaps we thought we were arriving at a new, grown-up attitude to sex and all it entails. But all we did was drift backwards into perpetual adolescence: sex as a right, with no balancing duties.

All we can hope for is that the kids do better at making it up . . . Where are they? Where are the kids? Where have they been all night?

CHAPTER 7

What on Earth Are You Thinking Of?

Oh, oh, for the Golden Age, that ancient and ignoble notion that humanity was born wonderful (so close to the gods, how could it be otherwise?) and has ever since been falling away. It would be at least comforting to believe it. 'It is not our fault,' we could murmur to each other as civilisation declined, 'we have declined; it is our nature; it would be folly to resist.' And then we could giggle winningly, and cast about for something to regret (shamanism, voodoo, Chinese medicine, fortune-telling, ghosts, old ladies cycling to Holy Communion in the morning mists, proper typewriters, pipe-smoking, minstrels, dryads, phoenicopters, Aramaic, tweed, mandragora, Eldorado, fealty, paregoric, umbrellas, wizards, fog, cherubim, necromancy, hieroglyphics, venison, scholasticism, revenants, mead) and tell ourselves how things have got so much worse, and once there was a time of loveliness when we were in touch with Nature and ectoplasm and those selfsame gods, and there were sybils and respect and people Knew Their Place and tipped their hats (home-made from rancid leather) and lived by firelight and wisdom was valued and everything was, like, organic, right? and we lived in, like, harmony and what a lot of nonsense.

We have never lived in harmony, not with anything: not with our neighbours, not with Nature, not – in particular – with the world of the supernatural, because there is no world of the supernatural, only the world of things, and we haven't got a clue how those work or why they work, given that a lot of our baseline 'understanding' of the world is on much the same level as poultry. That is to say, we confuse correlation with causation, the abiding error of humanity and one which poultry clearly share. Why do cocks crow, starting before dawn? As Kingsley Amis wondered, who do they think they are helping? The answer is, they don't think they are helping anyone. They think they are actually making the sun rise. After all, it's worked every day so far; you make enough racket and eventually the sun comes up. Hey, they think, we did it! We made the sun rise! Again! Woo-hoo! Let's go fuck some hens!

And we do just the same.

How Did We Get in This Pickle?

The problem is that we have forgotten something the poultry never knew. It is a little thing, but vital; and we have forgotten it because it has been both educated and ridiculed out of us. It is something we all knew once. It is something even toddlers know; the one thing about them which is not babyish. It is the great question: the one which will, if followed rigorously, lead to an answer which may or may not turn out to be '42' (though there are some postmodern literary theorists who would argue that it might as well be '42' as anything else). And the question is this:

'Why?'

When we hit the age of around three, we discover the immense power of the word 'Why?' We learn that it will hold the attention of adults for much longer than words like 'Waaa' and 'Gimme' and even 'Going be SICK'.

'Why?' gets noticed. 'Why?' gets engagement. And if 'Why?' doesn't get answers – or, at least, the answer – it is simply because we stop asking it too soon; or it stops being answered too soon.

– Why have you taken your coat off, Daddy?

– Because it's hot.

– Why?

– Because the sun's out.

– Why?

– Because it's summer.

– Why?

– Because that's the season.

– Why?

– Because the earth rotates about its own axis and about the sun.

– Why?

– Because it is governed by the laws of gravity.

– Why?

– Because everything is governed by the laws of gravity.

– Why?

– Because physics is based on the proposition that there are no purely local exceptions to general conditions; for example, it is so unlikely as to be zero probability that, just to the left of where I am standing, there is an adventitious gravity well which, were I to step into it, would suck me beneath this elegant York stone pavement and into the bowels of the earth.

– Why?

– Shut up and ask your mother.

– Why?

– Because otherwise you'll get a smack.

Curiosity will only get us so far, and the limits of knowledge are defined by *force majeure*. Later on, in school, our 'Why?' is pre-empted. Having done nobody any harm at all, we are made to sit down and hear about potassium permanganate, the Pilgrim Fathers, the class arachnida (kids playing chicken on freeways get smooshed),* Cuban bat guano and Pythagoras. Did they wait until we asked? No. Here is how it could have gone:

---

* A mnemonic for biological taxonomy. Kingdom, Phylum, Class, Order, Family, Genus, Species. Funny how it never leaves you.

– Why are the crops so lush, sir?

– Fertiliser, boy.

– What sort of fertiliser, sir?

– Bat guano, laddie.

– What's that, sir?

– Bat shit.

– Gosh, where do they get that from?

– Cuba.

– Why?

– Cuba has millions and millions of bats.

– Cor, sir, that's wizard.

Instead, it went like this:

– Cuba drone drone island drone planned economy blah Caribbean blah agribusiness yadda USA yadda bat guano blah caves blah export yadda blah.

– Sir, sir, what's bat guano, Sir?

– You know perfectly well what bat guano is, Bywater.

– No I don't, sir, honestly, what is it, sir?

– Shut up, boy.

And so curiosity is sat upon, due to the twin demands of (a) the syllabus and (b) schoolmasters' natural urge not to be forced to say 'bat shit' by twelve-year-old boys.

Which is a pity. If an essential part of adulthood is not so much control of the world (only infants and Big Babies yearn for control, lacking the intellectual or emotional maturity to cope with ambiguity) as understanding of the world, most of us are condemned never to quite grow up, because we condemn ourselves never to quite get the picture.

The picture can be got by using a simple but infallible method* which is unfortunately only widely used by scientists and by incident investigators. Put briefly, it falls into two stages:

---

* Yes, really, 'infallible', providing that you accept that getting the answer 'Don't know' is only a *failure* if you haven't really asked the question; otherwise it is a clear statement that you need to look harder for some missing information.

1. Gather all the available information but do not attempt to make logical connections. Just lay it out like a story, in rough chronological order.
2. Analyse the information using the word 'Why?' and only the word 'Why?' And keep on asking 'Why?' until you get no further useful information.

The results can be extraordinary, illuminating even the most basic and apparently mysterious of phenomena. Take that old saw, delivered with a weary sigh: 'Bloody marvellous, isn't it, how the keys are always in the very last place you look?' Sod's law, eh? Just one of those damn things about the universe. Just goes to show. And you want to tell me there's no God? Ha. There is so a God, and he's got a malicious streak . . .

Except let's interrogate the statement. 'The keys are always in the very last place you look.' Split it up: 'I have found my keys. They were in my desk drawer. It was the last place I looked.'

Now question the components.

(1) I have found my keys. Why? I looked in the place where they turned out to be. Why? Someone had put them there.

(2) They were in the desk drawer. Why? See (1) above.

(3) It was the last place I looked. Why? Because obviously once I had found them, I didn't carry on looking, you fool.

Lo and behold. The problem is not the quirkiness of the Universe at all. Everything lost is always going to be in the last place you look, because after that it ceases to be lost. The problem isn't in the finding; it's in the losing. And so things flip through 180 degrees and we have to make the best of it.

It's Lovely Down Here in the Playpen

The problem is, though, that being a Big Baby is easier, more comfortable, often better for our fragile self-esteem. The Key

Question turns out to be about our behaviour, not the Universe's. Accidents turn out to be not so accidental at all, but events with causes, some of them perhaps going back years, and requiring a change in our behaviour if they're not to happen again; and we know how little even grown-ups, let alone Big Babies, like changing their behaviour.

Sometimes our most closely held beliefs turn out to disintegrate when subjected to an intelligent questioning. Road-safety markings encourage dangerous driving. The computerised 'paperless office' leads to vastly increased paper consumption. Constant washing makes us more susceptible to bacteria. We get more allergies because we don't have worms any more. More helicopter pilots have been killed *practising* emergency landings than have been killed *making* emergency landings.

But do we want to know these things? Are we prepared to know the truth – or as near as we can get to the truth – or would we rather live within our assumptions, putting our fingers in our ears and – hummmmmm hummmmmm NOT LISTENING hummmmmmm CAN'T HEAR YOU hummmmmmm – smile in our self-serving ignorance.

⚠ CBeebies – *such* a witty little pun on 'BBC', don't you so agree? – has been broadcasting a new version of *Little Red Riding Hood* in which the Wolf doesn't want to eat anyone up at all. Oh no, what the Wolf wants is a *snack*. (RidingHood Brand ® Pubesc-O-Chipz™, anyone?) And when the Wolf gets his snack, he is *very happy* and *nobody need be upset* and, most of all, there is no risk of anyone bringing charges that CBeebies is wolfist.

The answer, all too often, seems to be, no, we don't want to know the answers. We would rather swim in the comfortable lukewarm bath of stupidity. It's the democratic solution, if we are to believe Walter Pitkin, who puts the proportion of stupid people at 80 per cent of the population and, unhappily, goes on to point out that the 20 per cent who aren't stupid stupidly underestimate the threat posed by the stupid majority. And here, perhaps, lies the root, and the irony, at the heart of so much of the nit-picking, niggling, you'll-have-someone's-eye-out-with-that legislation which in turn lies at the core of our current infantilisation. We'll look at that in more detail in the next chapter; enough to say, for the moment, that great swathes of legislation issue from the running mouths of politicians, and even greater swathes – whole forests, whole prairies, whole dank peat-bogs (beneath the brown surface lie the brackish bones of dead laws, unrepealed) – burst from the collective maw of the sticky-beaks, the nosy parkers, the quangoids and lexophiles, the ones with funny ways of speaking or tics or boogers or their legs on sideways like cheap lizards, the ones with tiny heads so that their necks seem to just carry straight on until terminated by improbable hair, the ones with big heads, inflated with marsh-gas or ballooned with squodge, the whining ones, the ranting ones, the ones with dandruff in their eyebrows and faithless wives, the lay preachers and the gold-rimmed-spectacles set, the caring and the careful and the sensible and the prudent, the ones who are a pederasty charge waiting to happen, the grimacingly continent ('Just the one') with a cupboard full of rubberwear, the ones with dry flaky beards and the ones with red greasy noses and the ones with those *trousers*, you know, *those* trousers, that's right, *those ones* . . .

. . . those ones, all of them howling for new laws, for cracking down and stamping out and not putting up with, for sending harsh messages and putting a stop to and imposing standards on and curbing the selfish minority and why should decent people? and saving people from themselves . . .

And the problem is that while their entire outlook upon the world (Jesus loves them; Jesus, too, regards the world with suspicion, intolerance and contempt) is based upon the founding notion that, if not all, at least 80 per cent of us are stupid, they fail to spot the fact that at least 80 per cent of *them* are stupid too. And therefore 80 per cent of their *laws* (proposed or enacted) are stupid, and their regulations and their plans and their consultancy documents and their best-practice scenarios and their compliance requirements and their key competencies.

Eighty per cent of *everything* is stupid. Scan through your newspaper. Read everything. Ask 'why?' of everything you read: news stories, political reports, opinion columns – the columnists, more often than not, trying to pretend they are just like you when they aren't (good grief, they are columnists and you are not), the leader writers, young people only a couple of years on from that middling 2:1 at university, the sports balls and the business balls and the, God help us, alternative medicine balls and beauty balls and all the balls.

Eighty per cent of which is stupid. QED.

Which would be fine for toddlers, who haven't been around that long and can't be expected to talk sense; fine, too, for adolescents, who, for reasons of hormones and identity, inhabit a schizotypical universe of delusions, hallucinations and mad ineluctable yearnings. But it is not that fine for grown-ups, and once we get our eye in, it's a bit like coming out of one of those prolonged dissociative states and realising that we have been living a whole life we knew nothing of, and, what is worse, living it among mad people.

Mad people who believe in ghosts and demons and secret conspiracies to plant false evidence in the earth, and who call their collective delusion 'Intelligent Design', and demand that it be taught in schools despite the fact that there is a better explanation, because they believe it and therefore, under the laws of Modernity, it is valid. Mad people who agree, because under the laws of Modernity we may not mock others' beliefs.

Mad people who believe that the ancient Hittites knew more about physiopathology than we do, and that smelling rhubarb in your sleep is a sign of disembalance of aak-k'hmwawa in the blibber, a body part unknown to modern (Western, phallocentric, hegemonic) medicine which needs to be corrected with chanting and urine-baths.

146

⚠️ *Nice little boys don't ask that sort of question*, as Nanny was so fond of saying. And conservative Protestant Christians want, above all, to be nice little boys; and they want everyone else to be nice little boys, too, by force of law if necessary. By *force* if necessary.

'Intelligent Design' is one of the more politically potent, if intellectually dishonest, weapons in their quiver. The doctrine's name is emphatically *not* self-referential; a less intelligent response to evolution by natural selection (*not* Darwinism, a specific subset of the theory) it would be hard to devise.

Science is not a *thing* but a *process*. In particular, it is a *cumulative* process, fiddling with the model until the next bit falls into place, then fiddling with it some more until the *next* next bit falls into place, then ... But 'Intelligent Design' won't have it. There are *gaps* in the scientific model, it correctly points out, and so the model is *no good* and *incomplete* and it's time to *stop fiddling* and factor an Intelligent Designer into the equation. In other words: thus far and no further, scientists; *nice little boys don't ask that sort of question*.

Intelligent Design may be 'little more than creationism in a cheap tuxedo,' writes Geoff Brumfiel in *Nature* (28 April 2005), but under the principles of Modernity it is hard to attack it directly. The situation is not unlike the one in which the comedian Lenny Henry found himself in during a late-night interview on Irish TV. At the back of the audience sat Van Morrison, and the great bluesmeister took it into his head that he wanted Mr Henry to imitate Norman Wisdom. 'Do Norman Wisdom,' he called repeatedly; '*Do Norman bloody WISDOM.*' In vain did Mr Henry explain that he didn't do imitations; in vain, that he had only ever seen Norman Wisdom once, when he was little; in vain, that he, Mr Henry, was a tall, imposing black man

147

while Norman Wisdom was a small, scrawny white man. In the end, Mr Henry succumbed. He did Norman Wisdom. There was a round of applause, then one disgruntled voice from the back. 'Nothing like him,' announced Van Morrison.

Science doesn't *do* Not Asking That Sort of Question any more than Lenny Henry does Norman Wisdom. Intelligent Design is not addressing any question of any legitimacy to the scientific method. It is – as one of its most prominent evangelists, Salvador Cordova himself experienced – an attempt to address, not the problem of science, but the problem of God. To pass it off as part of a wider scientific discourse is not only dishonest but infantile; infantilising, too, as in the comment to Brumfiel by Eugenie Scott, director of the US National Center for Science Education: 'The point here is that Americans don't want to be told that God had nothing to do with it ... College professors need to be very aware of how they talk about things such as purpose, chance, cause and design ... You should still be sensitive to the kids in your class.'

And you thought college professors should be sensitive to truth, reason and intellectual honesty? No, no. Nice little boys don't ask that sort of question. Nice little boys don't point out the 'intelligent design' is incompetent theology masquerading as legitimate philosophy of science. Nice little boys just *do Norman Wisdom*.

Mad people who think that leisure-facility administration is something which should be taught in a 'university' rather than learned on the job, and other mad people who think that everyone should go to university even if they don't want to.

Mad people at Microsoft who think that everyone else is six years old and likes having things on their computers called 'My

Documents' and 'My Computer' and a dancing paperclip, and that those same people will waste money on new software if they produce advertisements dressing them up in joke rubber dinosaur heads and poking fun at their stupid jobs.

Mad people who think that if only we have enough laws there will be nothing nasty ever again, and even madder people who think that laws will deter criminals, even though the definition of a criminal is someone who is not deterred by laws.

Mad people who think that reality is a matter of opinion, that children know better than adults, that there can be rights without responsibilities, that unkindness and mockery are grown-up responses to anything, that all men are brothers under the skin, that saying 'like' a lot will, like, soften the like blow of like unpalatable truths.

Mad people who possess the solipsism of the truly insane, believing that others see themselves as they are seen, so that terrorists think they are terrorists and perverts think they are perverts and homosexuals think they are bad, and mad people who show their legs and show their tits and go on television and think there is no incompatibility between being a major political leader and wearing jeans and a cowboy hat.

Mad people who . . .

No. Look for yourself. Look hard, and ask 'why?' and before long you will wake up and rub your eyes and say to yourself: *What on earth was I thinking of?*

CHAPTER 8

Read the Notices Or You Will
Get the Runs

Picture a great European capital city in the twenty-first century. Look down. What do you see? Not holes, I imagine: unguarded holes, holes with men in them, men not wearing any protective clothing (no hard hats, no Kevlar-toed work boots, no luminous high-visibility jackets, no ear defenders, no safety glasses), holes not properly demarcated with proper exclusion zones and proper cones and barriers and signs and tapes; holes which pedestrians – the general public, untrained – can cross via thin planks, unguarded planks no thicker than a plank from which the untrained general public (who have carried out no risk assessment, received no site induction briefing or toolbox talk, signed no access permit) could fall, if jostled by another member of the general public, into the unguarded hole and on top of one of the men-not-wearing-any-protective-clothing.

Look up, too; and I bet, in your mind's eye, there are no projecting girders, loosely dangling high-voltage cables held together with duct tape; no curling, razor-sharp pieces of corrugated iron, no filed-down-pointed-brackets poised at you'll-have-someone's-eye-out-with-that height. You won't be thinking of the sparks flying from the angle grinders grinding metal on the pavement, of the hammering and welding and flying dust and brick-grit, the motorcycles on the pavement, the broken paving stones, the pavement itself suddenly stopping and decanting you into the street of not one- or two- but apparently three-way traffic, defeating the laws of space-time.

Welcome to Athens, 2004. Whether or not people get hurt more in Athens than in London or Minneapolis, Nottingham or San Diego or Stockholm, is not immediately discoverable. But what seems to happen is an odd kind of vigilance; an autonomous regard for self and others kicks in. People's eyes are constantly in motion, like fighter pilots'. Instead of being cocooned in iPoddage, bumbling through their protected environment like carefree children wrapped in auditory cotton wool, people in Athens are alert, watching the city above their eyeline for things about to drop on them, watching the ground beneath them for things to avoid tripping over or falling into. When nothing can be taken for granted (the quiet back street may at any moment swing round a corner, past an unguarded crane hoisting insecure pianos, and become an urban motorway, a precipitous gully, or just stop altogether) the primary skill of the citizen is expecting the unexpected.

It is not what we expect of cities, now. We expect them to look after us, to hold our hand, to pluck at our sleeve at every potential threat ('Careful! Mars bar wrapper at ten o'clock!'), to tell us when we can cross the road and when we can't, to show us where things are coming from, to wrap all its Terrible Men (hammering, drilling, digging, steamrolling, sawing, welding, angle-grinding men) in the bright orange jackets of servitude, to tuck away or pad or seal or file down the corners of anything which might hurt us; to warn us of anything we might bang into.

The city was once an animal. London was depicted as a cross between a Piranesi prison and a wild voracious beast, a furry sabre-toothed Moloch which ate its children and excreted money; but that was in the nineteenth century when a pall of smog lay atop the city and a slather of mud beneath, when Little Jo died in a slum, a rookery beyond our worst nightmares today, when men spontaneously combusted as if they could no longer sustain the interior scorching of the Great Wen. The city consumed, ground down, maimed, infected, crushed and ran us over. It had a monstrous force before which we were helpless.

> ⚠ **The Campo dei Fiori in Rome on New Year's Eve is a roaring affable tumult of voices and bodies, some of whom will fall over. London's Trafalgar Square on New Year's Eve is sullen, policed within an inch of its life, fountains boarded up, underground stations closed, messages telling people to Stay at Home broadcast throughout the season, police, firemen and politicians announcing that it is For People's Own Good (while trying not to laugh hysterically at the exercise of petty power). Rock concerts are banned because of lavatory worries. A section of the M25 was coned off to stop people watching the (unnecessarily) grounded Concorde make its last flight into London Heathrow, which airport also deliberately made it impossible for spectators to watch the new Airbus 380 arrive on its maiden flight. 'There's nothing to see,' we cry deliriously. 'Go home! Go to bed! With your hands *outside* the covers!'**

Not now. Now, the city, like everything else, conspires to contract our autonomy, to hedge us about with signs and procedures and instructions and cameras (the price of safety is eternal vigilance, and we pay for it with our freedom and privacy); with wardens and cones and lights and, above all, with notices. Our streets now, in our safe modern cities, are so riven with notices that we no longer notice them. They tell us we can park here or we can't park here or if we do park here we will be ticketed, clamped, towed away, killed; they tell us to keep to the right or to keep to the left, to walk this way, to cross over and walk that way, to watch out for traffic from the left, the right or the centre. They announce headrooms and hydrants, warn of bicycles and old people (bent double like cartoon witches on knotty sticks) and hot tar and loose stones; they beep at us and tell us about buses and trains and taxis ('Queue here!' 'No! Queue *here*!').

And every sign, every notice, requires its own piece of 'street furniture' so that the most likely injury in the modern, safe city is banging into something holding up a notice, and breaking your teeth; and every piece of street furniture holding up one notice (and lightly splattered with nose-blood, its paint chipped with broken teeth) is immediately deployed to hold *more* notices. Parking notices are adorned with clumsy, corrugated kindergarten signs demanding 'Have You Secured Your Home?' and warning you not to leave your dog (animal welfare) or child (the omnipresent paedophile) in the car; street lamps support notices about dog shit (bad; Scoop the Poop is what children call it, of course), anxiety-provoking questions ('Laptop Mobile Handbag Where Are Your's?') and warnings that someone has their eye on you ('For your convenience numberplate recognition technology is deployed at this facility' and '24-hour CCTV surveillance and detection is in operation'), even notices about themselves: when they were last checked by a Designated Trained Light Inspection Person (and when did you last hear of someone being electrocuted by a street lamp? See: it's working) and who to ring if they go out (but not who to ring if you're electrocuted, and you can bet the city's lawyers are ex-directory).

Nor is it just the external street and its external dangers. The Tyranny of the Notice ('Stop it at once or you'll hurt yourself/ have someone's eye out/get a smack') is everywhere. Here on the floor: look! Little yellow easels crying aloud that someone is cleaning the floor, that the floor is wet, that female staff are cleaning the male toilet while male staff are cleaning the female (wouldn't it be easier just to swap them over?). Buses have notices saying 'Give Way to the Bus' (why? Why the hell? When did the bus ever give way to us?), and any public space where anything at all is happening is defaced with notices addressed to the people (presuming them to have the mental and social age of eight) who are doing the happening, while the rest of us, going peaceably about our business, are visually assaulted by colour-coded injunctions: Warning: Do Not Jump over the Pit. Warning: High Voltage. Caution: Narrow Walkway. Fire Action! No Smoking! Return Hook to wall after Use. Remember: You are Responsible for Your Own Health and Safety and Other's. Keep Your Work Area Tidy. Do Not Stack. Caution: Do not Obstruct this Door. Safety Notice: Dispose of your Rubbish Carefully. Wear Safety Harness. No Hats No Boots No JOB. No access WITHOUT PERMIT. Warning: Fork Lift Trucks. Warning: Heavy Plant Crossing. Warning: Pedestrians Use this Area. Entering Worksite. Men Working Overhead. Visitors Report to Site Office Without Exception . . .

> ⚠ A true sign, above a hot tap: **DANGER HOT WATER.**
> Possibly there would be a place for such a sign above an electric socket which had been inadvertently connected to the hot pipe instead of the ring main, but above a *hot tap?*
>
> And only a short step from there to Ann Keen, MP, who wants to pass a new law making it compulsory for us all to fit magic valves to the hot tap to stop us scalding ourselves in the bath. (But why let us take baths at all? Should we not really be cleaned by trained operatives at a properly risk-assessed NHS walk-in Personal Care Centre, where our bellies could be prodded and our ears inspected and our genitalia checked into the bargain?)

And so it goes on. If we weren't exhausted by the endless recitation of the dangers and proscriptions which face us, constant exposure to the hectoring of others, for fear of what may happen to them, would be enough to finish us off. It's a miracle we get out of bed at all.

You Can't Say You Weren't Warned

The initial reading of this vile discourse – minatory, patronising, infantilising – is that the perpetrators don't realise we've already been brought up. Our parents raised us, and they mentioned this stuff along the way, while telling us that they didn't like to say they told us so.

So why are we being told again? By people we don't know, and who don't know us? Are they judging us by their standards (infantile, incompetent, reckless, none the wiser)? Or is something else going on? It is fear – our fear? Someone else's fear, on our behalf? – that drives the Notice Culture?

We collude, as always, in reconstructing for ourselves the parent/child relationship, simultaneously terrified of being hurt and horrified at the prospect of allowing people to hurt themselves. The fear shows in our ready recourse to lawsuits ('Mum! Mum! Look what the man did to me!') and in our belief than nothing untoward should ever happen to us ('Not fair!'). Turned into Big Babies, with our own willing collusion, we experience the postmodern world as a slippery place, built on spooky hauntological contingencies which possess just enough reality to kill us. And when they do, it will be our own fault.

You can't say you haven't been warned. It's a whole industry now, a whole new politics: warning us so we can't say we haven't been. Think of it: when you fall into the pit or slide between the gap which you have been told to mind, when you cross the road against the little red man (or, in the USA, until very recently, against the sign saying DON'T WALK, which has now been replaced by a little red man, Americans having decided, along with the rest of the infantilised West, that its people cannot read, or, if they can read, are too stupid or self-absorbed to make any sense of what they read, or that it is inappropriate to assume that they can read English) . . . When the champagne cork puts your eye out or you slip backwards on the newly washed floor, when your coffee burns you or your packet of peanuts turns out ('May contain nuts') to contain nuts; when the passing train creates an air current or when, in the unlikely event of an emergency, you have forgotten that your lifejacket is under your seat and so you sink into the depths without even a whistle to blow 'to attract attention' (why, bless my soul, I thought the whistle was there to cheer us up) . . . When you unexpectedly encounter female staff cleaning the male toilets and your last thought as you pass into the palpable obscure is 'Why, they might at least have apologised for any inconvenience this may cause' . . . When you stick your fingers in the toaster and Jesus fucking Christ it *toasts* them, yet (as Barry Humphries pointed out) it can't toast a *crumpet*, you can stick a crumpet in a toaster for hours on end and it still glides to the surface white as a lily, but a *finger* . . . you didn't learn the first time, did you? When the champagne cork puts your other eye out (you didn't learn, did you?), when you didn't do up your shoelaces despite your mother saying 'Do your shoelaces up, sonny jim, or you'll trip over and kill yourself' because you knew – didn't you? – that nobody ever killed themselves tripping over their shoelaces, and then you trip over your shoelaces and kill yourself . . . When you lean out of the window or strangle yourself on your pyjama-cord, when your cellphone fries your brains or you run through the plate-glass window or cut yourself! on a knife! or in the Magimix! . . .When your watch tells the wrong time so you leave the house too soon and slip on some leaves and fall in dogshit and catch *Toxacara canis* and go blind and die . . . When any of these things happen, do not say you were not warned, because you were. Repeatedly, stridently, annoyingly and incessantly enough that the warnings now carry no weight at all, merging into one great hysterical proto-maternal shout of 'I told you so!'

And the only practical difference between the modern, ass-covering, lawyer-driven world of the Big Babies and the cosy world of Mummy is that Mummy at least had the decency to lie. Mummy at least prefaced the phrase with '*I don't like to say* I told you so . . .'

⚠ A proliferating notice in the English-speaking world: the one telling you not to insult or be violent towards staff in stations, airports, government offices or anywhere else. The assumption must be that we are all inclined, potentially, towards that uncontrolled and indeed uncontrollable solipsistic anger that is one defining attribute of the infantile. Road rage, we have seen; recently, I witnessed pavement rage: a red-faced, sixty-ish, moustachioed, crop-headed ex-NCO type who burst into such a frenzied hypertensive foul-mouthed toddler tantrum because three people were talking on the pavement that I feared he would have a massive coronary and fall screaming and writhing to the ground before voiding his bowels in his trousers and expiring. No. I lie. I *hoped*, not feared. Alas, he lived. But *Post Office queue rage*? Have we come down to this?

Nonsense, of course. Saying 'I told you so' is, women assure me, one of the great redeeming consolations of motherhood. Mothers sit poised like pythons waiting for the moment when their offspring fall off the swing and KILL THEMSELVES, trip over their shoelaces and KILL THEMSELVES, go under a bus and KILL THEMSELVES, or, at the very least, HAVE SOMEONE'S EYE OUT WITH THAT so that, as blindness descends or the last breath fades, they can bend over the ruined fruit of their womb and cry 'I don't like to say I told you so, but . . .'

But the real world doesn't need to make that mental reservation. The real world *loves* to say it told us so. Whole industries have arisen to tell us so; careers have been devoted to it; there are conferences on telling us so, where delegates try to sleep together but by the time they have finished telling each other about the potential problems (beginning with the dangers of excessive

157

alcohol consumption above the recommended three units a day – though they never tell us what a unit is, you can get a good idea from watching what doctors do: a unit is a bottle – and ending with dire threats about the consequences of removing the tag from the mattress which says 'It is a federal offence to remove this tag from this mattress') . . . by the time they have finished, it's morning again and time to part.

The two spookiest assertions about the nature of this world are to be found, naturally enough, while driving your automobile in the United States of America, a country which has made the idea of the journey its primary foundation myth. To experience the moment for yourself, you must drive to a certain bridge in New Mexico and, at a particular moment, glance first in your wing mirror, and then out of the window. And you will see two things.

The first, on the wing mirror, is an etched notice which says 'Warning: Objects in the Mirror are Closer than They Appear.' And, a second later (if you have timed it right) a notice by the roadside will announce 'Gusty Winds May Exist.'

Jacques Derrida, the great philosopher of deconstruction, would have gone mad if he had encountered these two eerie propositions. So how on earth are we supposed to cope?

What's the Matter? Can't You Read?

We can cope by being presented with ever more notices, of course. How else?

Those who fell in the Great Dotcom Crash would have done far better to abjure the siren call of technology and instead go into notices. Notices are the future. Notices are the Great Mummy made visible, the reins and the threat of the slap which keeps us on the right lines. Next time you are out, keep your eyes open and see how many times you are shouted at without good cause. Most fruitful are, not surprisingly, the transitional spaces where we are in flux, moving, troublesome, under our own steam, our infantilism in full flood as we stumble from ticket barrier to platform, from check-in to duty-free to departure gate, lulled with our possessions, insulated by our fizzing, twitching iPods, impulse control turned to zero, credit cards itching and pulsing like a hard-on in a whorehouse.

The marginal men who work in those liminal spaces – airports, shopping centres, stations, hospitals, motorway services, anywhere that people are under the illusion of freedom – are scared witless of our potential, not just for mayhem, but for disobedience. The mayhem itself is not the problem. Mayhem is fine. You can deal with mayhem. Mayhem you can shoot. You can squirt it with water-cannon, tear-gas it, arrest it, hit it over the head with truncheons which are now called night-sticks though they work in the daytime, too. If the worst comes to the worst, you can invade mayhem and impose freedom and democracy on it by force.

The problem is what mayhem represents. Just as gluttony, covetousness, fornication, sloth and all other contingent sins are feared not for themselves (gluttony, covetousness, fornication and sloth are, after all, essential components of the archetypal Good Night Out) but because they announce the presence of the Devil himself, al-Sha'itan, The Tempter, in the world; so mayhem is feared because it is disobedience made manifest. Obedient mayhem is fine. Obedient mayhem is called Making the World a Safer Place.

It is disobedience They fear; and, like moral theologians chopping sins to a finer and finer granularity, the marginal men invent more and more forms of potential disobedience in their fiefdoms. And tell us about them. Insistently. Whether we've thought of them or not.

Welcome Aboard. Now Shut Up and Listen.

The authority of notices is as baroque, as convoluted and as pervasive as any fundamentalist theocracy. Take, for example, a single railway carriage – now called 'saloon', a word which nobody uses except train operators, because, presumably, unlike 'carriage' it lacks the implication that, in it, we may legitimately expect to be taken somewhere. A 'passenger' in a 'carriage' might cut up rough if deprived of motion. A 'customer' in a 'saloon' knows where he stands. Or, if lucky, sits.

Look! Here comes an anthropologist. But he is no ordinary anthropologist. He is an anthropologist from Mars. He is here to see what he makes of us. He has chosen (being badly advised) Swindon, Wiltshire, as his base of operation, and is going there on a First Great Western train so as not to attract attention. And, thanks to the Great Mummy and the Authority of Notices, he has plenty of reading material:

1. A complicated safety-instructions notice complete with pictograms designed presumably for those who cannot read the accompanying text, but which are entirely meaningless unless you can read the accompanying text.

2. An exhortation to visit Wessex Trains on the Web. 'Log on to www.wessextrains.co.uk,' it instructs us, 'and join over ¼ million people who visit our website every year.' One of the quarter-of-a-million people – presumably they strayed there by typing 'sex' into Google – is illustrated to show us how we should see ourselves: a carefully non-threatening, non-sexist, thin, almost certainly vegetarian man in an open-necked shirt sitting at a Melamine office table with a coffee mug and small sheaf of papers and scruffy, non-threatening hair, prodding away at a laptop. The text continues, with the obligatory bullet-points so beloved of the illiterate and bossy: 'For all these . . . •Ideas for days out •Plan your

journey •Download timetables & publicity •Buy tickets online •Check out station facilities and locations •View LIVE departure screens •Sign up for e-newsletters •Competitions & sales items •Staff vacancies •Find out more about Wessex Trains . . . and much much more.' It then, of course, throws us the MISSION STATEMENT: 'Connecting People, Connecting Places'.

3. 'Welcome to the Quiet Carriage. Please refrain from using mobile phones and personal stereos in this carriage.' And a photograph of a woman who, though apparently asleep, is experiencing some odd combination of anger and erotic pleasure.

4. On the antimacassar: 'Standard Class Quiet Carriage' and a picture of a mobile phone with a red line through it. And the inevitable logo (this one looks like a train track drawn through an unprotected level crossing) and (you can run but you can't hide) the Mission Statement: 'transforming travel', though *from* what and *into* what is never revealed (but, as mission statements go, 'transforming travel into a living hell, with notices' doesn't quite cut it).

5. Above the door: 'Emergency Alarm. Pull the red handle to stop the train. Penalty for improper use.' ('Improper'? While naked, with an erection, perhaps?) This notice is called Cat No. 56/057182 which seems an awfully big number but perhaps they have a huge catalogue of notices for every foreseeable contingency. (Cat. No. 35/199382: Danger: A person from Jupiter has vomited on the antimaccasar. Cat. No. 82/937488: Phil Collins decided, while sitting in this carriage, that while the new carbon fibre drumsticks were pretty good, there was still nothing to beat old-fashioned hickory.)

6. A notice on the window: 'Shhhhhh quiet zone' with the 'o' of 'zone' being the little mobile phone in a red circle with a line through it.

7. Another ticking off: a picture of a door handle with a notice on it. The text says 'Shhhhhhhh You are in the Quiet Carriage, please be considerate of others by refraining from using mobile phones and by keeping your noise levels to a minimum.' Nothing about personal stereos, though.

8. On the door: (a) 'First Aid Box and Emergency Equipment Located through Emergency Exit.' (b) 'Emergency Exit. 1. Break glass 2. Operate handle 3. Slide door to open. Penalty for improper use.' (Again, pictograms which would be meaningless if you couldn't read.)

9. On the door to the engine: 'Train Manager' and a picture of a peaked cap.

10. Above a window: 'Emergency Exit Hammer. 1. Smash panel to obtain hammer. 2. Strike windows HARD in CORNER to break glass.' More pictograms. What do they mean? The words explain what they mean, but what do the pictograms themselves mean? Anything?

11. On the dividing half-frame: 'Tempting treats Fill the gap All Day Breakfast Bap only £2.95 Super Sandwich Meal Deal Your choice of a fresh sandwich, soft drink and a packet of Walkers crisps only £3.99. Available on every service from the buffet (Coach F) First transforming travel Fresh thinking – Good food on the move.'

12. Above the door: 'EXIT' and a little man running away. Note how he is carefully drawn with rounded limbs, unthreatening.

13. Below the luggage rack and above a tempting socket into which people may recklessly be contemplating sticking things (coathangers, biros, laptops, fingers): (a) 'Socket not for public use.' (b) 'Warning Variable voltage supply may damage electrical and electronic equipment.'

14. Above the door: little running man and a Socialist International fist. 'To open door in an emergency Strike this panel to break seal.' Yes . . . and then what?

15. Above the same door: a pictogram of a keyhole, or possibly a little fat woman, and 'Central Door Locking' (Is it? Or are they boasting?) and Cat. No. 56/057153.

16. By the door: (a) 'To open door 1. Wait for "Door Unlocked" sign above door. 2. Lower window. 3. Open door using outside handle.' (b) 'Danger. Do not lean on the door or attempt to open the door when the train is moving If the door is not properly closed and the train is moving, do not attempt to close it – use the emergency alarm located in saloon' ('Saloon'? That's the first we've heard about 'saloon'.) (c) 'Caution. The train may be longer than the platform. Before alighting ensure this door is alongside platform.' (How do you ensure that?)

17. Above the door: 'Caution. Do not lean out of window when train is moving.'

18. Near the door: (a) 'First Aid and Emergency Equipment. Tools and appliances for use in an emergency are located in the train manager's office at the end of the train. First Aid boxes are located at the buffet and in the train manager's office.' (b) 'Fire Extinguisher'.

19. On the litter bin: litter and a pictogram of what appears to be a miniature T-shirt flying upwards into a woman's hand.

20. Near the door: 'Danger 415 volts. Before using fire extinguisher break glass and turn switch to off.' (A really incomprehensible pictogram here, of a fist punching something and what looks like a small pile of leaves.)*

21. On the fire extinguisher itself: more notices than you could possibly read in the time available before you burned to death.

---

* This is the best one I have seen since the Aerospatiale T-series (Tobago, Trinidad, Tampico, you get the point) which had a new! exciting! pictogram-festooned cockpit. The first time I flew one I sat there for a bit staring at the pictogrammed knobs, levers, buttons and switches with my captain, a man of that mandarin calm and detachment which only the Pakistani upper classes can manage. Presently he said 'Well, I don't know about the rest, but this one definitely operates a bassoon.'

22. In the lavatory: (a) 'To flush press lever downwards. Do not use in stations.' (b) 'Shavers only' (above shavers-only socket) (c) 'Shavers only' (on shavers-only socket) (d) 'For water press floor pad. Turn control to adjust temperature. Please leave wash basin clean after use. Not drinking water.'

23. On soap dispenser: Silly logo. Inexplicable word 'Hypo'. Oddly scrawled logo and inexplicable words 'Deb – naturally'.

24. On broken towel dispenser: sunburst logo and word 'Initial'.

25. On toilet-paper dispenser, logo and name Kimberly-Clark, something you would think they might take pains to cover up, given the tendency of Kimberly-Clark to wad its paper so tightly in its dispensers that, in getting it out, you end up with toilet-paper confetti all over the floor, as though you have been engaged in some frantic bowel crisis.

⚠ 'Kindly remember to take all your personal belongings with you when leaving the train.' But what if you don't *have* all your personal belongings? What if you have left many of them at home?

Yes, Yes, So What Does It All Mean?

The picture which emerges (and it doesn't matter whether it's First Great Western* or Amtrak, Ryanair or British Airways, Greyhound or Stagecoach) is of us. A picture of us as irresponsi-

---

* One does wonder what the function of the word 'First' in their corporate name actually *implies*. That of all the companies called Great Western they are indubitably the best?

ble, stupid toddlers, needing constant admonition, needing every-thing explained, needing an eye kept upon us at all times, needing regular feeding (crisps! burgers! fizzy pop! The in-flight 'meal suggestion' on EasyJet in the summer of 2005 was: a Mars bar, a tube of Pringles and the fizzy drink of your choice) in case our blood sugar falls and we go mad: break the Kimberly-Clark lava-tory-paper dispenser, or drink the water or use the fire extinguisher before we have broken the glass and turned the switch to off. This nonsense is not directed to the pre-infantilised; the escapees from *When Genetics Goes Wrong* with their baseball caps on sideways and their trousers falling down, their absence of impulse control and their peculiar lack not only of a (perhaps nor-mative) socialised sensibility but of any sensibility at all. They do not need to be told. They are beyond any hope of amendment (or perhaps not yet arrived at the possibility of redemption). The water, the Kimberly-Clark lavatory paper, the broken glass and the switch are grist to their mill; their blood-sugar is already at rampage-point; neither notices nor any other sort of social exhor-tation will impinge upon their anthropoid desires.

This parade of urging and snapping and ticking-off is not for them.

No; it is for us. For me and you.

But, beyond that, there is a worse, and more serious assump-tion, which is that we are as yet unformed. That we don't know what to do, haven't worked out what is dangerous, cannot assess risks, will hurt ourselves or kill ourselves, because actually all we are fit for is staying in bed (hands outside the covers, if you please) and anything else is tempting fate.

The Terrified Traveller

When I was a child, we used to go on holiday abroad every other year. (In the intervening years, we would go to Canford Cliffs, partly so that my father's chequebook could recuperate, but also, I suspect, so that we could re-ground ourselves in the English seaside of tar and wind, mad boarding-house landladies and methylated-spirit kettles in the beach hut; of drifting out into the cold sea on a dank rubberised-cotton LiLo, of sand in the toes and the smell of drains and wholesome nasty English things that were slimy and bit down hard; of the dinner gong and children's supper and the Major, just like in Fawlty Towers.)*

Abroad was fun, but serious fun. Things could happen there. It was capitalised in speech, to denote its seriousness: We are going Abroad this year. It was a very grown-up thing to do, to go Abroad. Abroad was also known as The Continent or, if you were feeling Continental, The Continong, like the French said it. The Continent was badly named, since it was characterised by incontinence of every variety, particularly culinary and sexual. On The Continent they ate jam for breakfast (not proper marmalade; *actual* jam, which was properly reserved for teatime) and went downhill from there. They drank wine at lunch and ate anything, particularly when it came to fish, which everyone knew were (a) haddock and (b) plaice. On The Continent they ravened, fishwise, indiscriminately. No stopping them. Faced with the ocean, they became all maw, and everything went in: things with spines and eyes and teeth, glutinous things and gelatinous things, things with green bones and no bones at all, with beaks and suckers and tentacles. Down the red lane it went, and sometimes horse went down the red lane, and the cheese wasn't like cheese at all but more so, like something scraped off something else, and they had 'yogurt' which was milk gone bad, and there was no stopping them and no wonder that there was diarrhoea.

For diarrhoea, the treatment was: it would get better on its own and stop making a fuss because you were on holiday and

---

* There was always a Major, in every seaside hotel. Perhaps there was an office somewhere in the Ministry of Defence. Perhaps they parcelled them out, with orders, and warrants for the train.

there were things to see, because The Continent had nudists too, which my father wanted to see; so we went to see the nudists and my mother kept her bikini on (the only woman not entirely naked) so that all the men took tremendous detours to stroll casually past her – drawn, so they tried to demonstrate, by an interesting patch of sand they had noticed from half a mile away, but really so that they could imagine what she looked like with nothing on, a speculation otherwise denied to them. And my father watched the naked people, happy as a sandbag. 'Look,' he would hiss gleefully, 'that chap's got a congenital hip! That woman's got inverted nipples! Look at that scoliosis! My God, you don't see a scar like that often. Oh dear, that chap's got a basal cell carcinoma; I'll have a word with him.' And so on.

Being nude was all right on The Continent. It was part of Sex, which they did there, on lumpy beds in shuttered rooms in the daytime and the women didn't shave their armpits and they probably smelt of – poo! – garlic, and that's how it was on The Continent, sex sex sex. And drinking. And car crashes and forest fires. The Continent.

It was reasonably tame; about as tame as the Other can get. But all the same we took precautions. The ferry tickets from Dover to Boulogne were booked the previous September. My father had a special briefcase for his Documents, because The Continent required special Documents. There was a Green Card for the car, which was international insurance (Drink! Car crashes!), and travellers' cheques and a lavatory roll with banknotes rolled into it because of something called Currency Restrictions, and passports, and . . . documents. There was also warm orange Fanta, because you couldn't drink the water, and, as soon as we disembarked, there was Evian water too, because not only couldn't you drink the water, but you couldn't even clean your teeth with the water; and if you were foolish enough to do so, diarrhoea would rapidly follow, and then it would be but a short step to VD and tentacle-eating and armpit-hair and sex in the afternoon, on lumpy beds with the shutters closed.

And that was it. Documents and Evian. The risk assessment had been carried out, and all could proceed as normal providing we had Documents and Evian.

> ⚠ Oslo Airport has banned a perfume called Flower-bomb, which comes in a bottle shaped very, very vaguely like a hand grenade. A hand grenade made of glass. A *pink* hand grenade made of glass. The perfume was banned after a Norwegian passenger was found carrying a bottle of the stuff at Beauvais Airport, near Paris. (Source: *Vogue*)

Since then, the world has shrunk but so have we; or, at least, enough of us have shrunk to make fine profits for those businesses which cater to the thesis that the world beyond our tiny shores (whether the English Channel or the city limits of Pasadena, CA) is monstrously dangerous, a generic badland full of pitfalls and bugs and cheats, murderers and thieves and Spics and Dagos and Frogs and Krauts.

> . . . Once upon a time les wogs commenceaient à Calais. Maintenant il est le twentieth century et les wogs commencent à Morocco, but ils restent toutes-le-même les 'wogs' while nous sont White Men et avons quelque-chose à thank God pour.

– wrote the distinguished barrister and editor of *Damages*, Simon Levene, as an undergraduate in the Cambridge Footlights; but his macaronic satire on English insularity has remained as apposite as ever. More so, perhaps, since as travel has ceased to be an activity and become instead an industry (we no longer travel, but consume travel products), the scope for selling elaborate comfort-blankets (which is to say, inflaming neuroses then selling the 'cure') has expanded to a degree which would have astonished our forebears.

Here Be Dragons, Also Bugs and Foreigners

> And now they brought to them the weapons, then put in
> their hands the great swords in their golden scabbards,
> and the bow and the quiver. Gilgamesh took the axes, he
> slung the quiver from his shoulder, and the bow of
> Anshan, and buckled the sword to his belt; and so they
> were armed and ready for the journey.
>   – *The Epic of Gilgamesh* (Third millennium BC)

'Ready for the journey.' And five thousand years later, it is still going on. Consult, for example, the oracular Magellan catalogue.[*] Offering its products for people who are travelling, on the whole, on careful package tours to civilised parts of the world, it nevertheless trades on a terrible fear of being parted from Nurse. The picture its product range summons up is of Big Babies with credit cards, for whom the world is so unimaginably hostile that they can barely contemplate their own survival. They are worried about the electricity supply, the toilets, the toilet seats, the food, the air quality, the rain, the sun, the wrinkles in their clothing, the bacteria and nematodes in the water, the plumbing, burglars, their feet, their toothbrushes, noise, jet lag, motion sickness, vitamin deficiency, skin cancer, heat, cold, insects, deep vein thrombosis, losing their luggage, having their luggage stolen, pickpockets, laundry, packing, and reading. Reading lenses (illuminated or not) await them; as do UV toothbrush sterilisers, wallet notes, underwater ballpoints, earplugs, sanitary wipes, flight sprays, wind-up radios, ID bracelets, a 'mini air supply', pill organisers, mosquito

---

[*] <http://www.magellans.com>

hats ('On our last trip to Mexico I suffered over 45 mosquito bites'), Adventurer Relief-Band gel anti-nausea pressure pads, disposable nasal filters, travel blankets ('We've all read about unsanitary airplane blankets, but who wants to carry along a bulky blanket?' – their customers, clearly), Disposable Urinelles ('Make it easy to answer nature's call'), the I-Can-Breathe-Mask, the ViraMask, miniature flashlights, money belts, Komfort Kollars, travel vests, and a special watch which pops open and shines a bright light through a magnifying glass onto the menu so that you can see just how the foreigners are trying to cheat and poison you.

⚠️ Observe the new first-time parents at the airport, carrying everything with them for baby in case something happens, *anything* happens, something goes *wrong*, something *runs out* . . .

Now observe the sophisticated high-tech business traveller (perhaps preferring to call himself 'road warrior') at the airport. He, too, carries everything with him, for much the same reason. Adrift from more stable ties, unsure of his identity or his prospects, he totes around a huge 'messenger bag' (once a sign of lowly status, the poor shlub who can only get a job *riding his bike* for God's sake, but now a marker of the busy, wired man) containing . . . *everything*. Laptop mobile PDA iPod mouse backup drive pendrive digicam mineral water digital recorder chargers adaptors transformers contact lenses spare contact lenses spectacles sunglasses noise-cancelling headphones GPS cables . . . everything. Like a hobo. *Everything*, in case something happens, *anything* happens . . .

Further deconstruction would be otiose, except to say that one of the more potent tools of infantilisation is persuading those whom you would diminish that the greater world is an impossibly dangerous place in which, without the constant vigilance of those who Know Better, you would be unlikely to survive. Our fears have been commodified. Being a cissy and a scaredy-cat used to be contemptible; now, in an age which regards any mishap as someone's fault, illness as a sign of weakness, and death as a cruel and unusual punishment for which someone should be sued, being a cissy and a scaredy-cat is an opportunity. Our anxieties have been commodified just like our dreams. The magical isle of Bali Ha'i is now a travel product; our fairy-tale romance on the warm sands of some tropical beach is now an expensive commodity; and our matching anxieties (what might be lurking in that sand? What might it have in mind for us?) serve to get a bit more money out of us.

And one wonders here whether the men of the Club Obi Wan, posing for pictures in their complete and accurate Indiana Jones outfits, would not be the first in line with their credit cards for their SteriPEN ('harnesses the power of ultraviolet light to purify your drinking water') and Marsona Sound Machine ('helps muffle unfamiliar hotel noises with regular, soothing sound').

CHAPTER 9

Someone Is Going
To Get Hurt

Oh right said Fred
Climbing up a ladder
With his crowbar gave a mighty blow

Was he in trouble
Half a ton of rubble
Landed on the top of his dome!
So Charlie and me had another cup of tea
And then we
Went home

– 'Right Said Fred' (Dicks/Rudge, 1962)

Work – what remains of work, as opposed to ticking off and walking around and generating paper and emails and spying on each other and sneaking and making up ways to infantilise each other; not McJobs, but work lookalikes, what we might call 'workalike' – is becoming harder and harder. Not to do (technology has, in the English-speaking world at least, seen to it that work has become ever easier) but to be allowed to do.

A scoutmaster (in America, but, by 2006, it could equally well have been in Britain; the British have lost their right to a haughty condemnation of American excesses, and without even the excuse of an overlawyered, greedy culture of litigation) once took his charges camping. One of the most ancient and enduring traditions of humankind, when far from home in the dark wilderness, is to competitively try to scare the wits out of each other with ghost stories. Natural selection purists might argue that it serves the fine purpose of promoting hyper-vigilance and wakefulness; others might argue that we all have a bit of the Fat Boy from *The Pickwick Papers* ('I wants to make your flesh creep') and are none the worse for that.

So the scoutmaster told ghost stories.

They went down well. Very well, in fact. So well that two of the young scouts had nightmares. Nightmares! For several days afterwards!

So the parents sued.

Well of course they did; but why? The obvious answer – or at least the obvious speculation – might be that they saw a chance of damages money. A more charitable speculation might be that they really, really didn't want their little darlings upset in any way at all, because it is a hard world out there, full of nastiness, and there will be time enough for weeping in due course.

But we might prefer a more generic reasoning, which is that the parents fell into a class of people first named in Star Trek: the Grups. In this particular episode, Captain Kirk and his implausible team discovered a planet (an oddly familiar planet) which was entirely run by children who, on seeing the Enterprise crew, referred to them as 'Grups': short for 'grown-ups'. Their own adults had been killed by a virus which protracted the growing-up phase, and, when you did grow up, you died. And yet here were Kirk and his men. Grown-ups, but still living. Grups.

The idea that growing up is a process to be prolonged as long as possible, and that achieving adulthood is the immediate precursor of death, may strike us as horribly apposite. Adam Sternbergh, writing in *New York* magazine, attempts to nail an archetypical Grup:

He owns eleven pairs of sneakers, hasn't worn anything but jeans in a year, and won't shut up about the latest Death Cab for Cutie CD. But he is no kid. He is among the ascendant breed of grown-up who has redefined adulthood as we once knew it and killed off the generation gap.

Mr Sternbergh seems quite happy to believe that his 'Grup' – an adult who has the attributes of a kid – is actually a grown-up. I would disagree; the creature Mr Sternbergh describes is no grown-up, but a cocky and well-to-do Big Baby. But a Grup he is. The 'latest Death Cab for Cutie CD' is as much a marker of his infantilised status as the sneakers, the jeans, the refusal to shut up. And it gets worse. He 'walks around with an iPod plugged into his ears at all times', 'stays out till 4 a.m. because he just can't miss the latest New Pornographers show', 'makes his 2-year-old wear a Misfits T-shirt', 'never shaves', spends '$200 on a bedhead haircut and $600 on a messenger bag' . . . 'This is . . . a story about 40-year-old men and women who talk, act and dress like people who are 22 years old,' writes Sternbergh, who quotes St Paul, before adding:

> This cohort is not interested in putting away childish things. They are a generation or two of affluent, urban adults who are now happily sailing through their thirties and forties, and even fifties, clad in beat-up sneakers and cashmere hoodies, content that they can enjoy all the good parts of being a grown-up (a real paycheck, a family, the warm touch of cashmere) with none of the bad parts (Dockers, management seminars, indentured servitude at the local Gymboree). It's about a brave new world whose citizens are radically rethinking what it means to be a grown-up and whether being a grown-up still requires, you know, actually growing up.

The people Sternbergh interviews are truly terrifying: middle-aged and self-deluding artificial-hipsters who not only believe that they 'connect' with the young, but share common values and tastes, and that this is a good thing. 'I spoke to an undergrad class at NYU recently,' says one, 'and it was terrifying how much we had in common. I'm looking at these kids who look about 12, and we're all going to the same movies and watching the same TV shows and listening to the same music. I don't know if it's scarier for them or scarier for me.'

We should take 'scarier' with a pinch of elixir vitae. Of course this man doesn't think it's scary; his use of the (childish: what man would find a twelve-year-old's taste in television and pop music scary?) word is a pre-emptive rhetorical trope: he calls it 'scary' to stop us calling it ridiculous, lamentable, pathetic, contemptible, sad and, above all, unfair. If the Grups' taste and interests are congruent with your own, how are you ever to become yourself? How are you ever to separate from them and become yourself?

And here, perhaps, is the true explanation of the ghost stories lawsuit: the more infantilised the parents become, the more they have to infantilise their children in their turn, just to maintain the differential. Or perhaps, to be less charitable, the parents are so infantilised themselves that there is no possibility of their presiding over the growing-up of their children, of raising them to the adult world – only of shielding them from it.

In either case, there is only so far you can go by claiming absolute congruity with your children. The mothers who say 'I'm not her mother; I am more like her friend' are only a millimetre away from the empty boast that 'people take us for sisters'. (Only, one wants to reply, those who cannot see the effects of time and gravity.) The fathers who regard themselves as their sons' best pals find themselves closer than a gnat's whisker to the Big Bumptious Boy, a self-deluding wet-lip who joshes senescently with his sons' teenage friends, getting the demotic slightly wrong (what the hell do they think demotic is for? Why do they think it keeps on changing?) and eventually ending up making a lurching repugnant grope at a young woman and being properly demolished by her response. 'Piss off, Grandpa.'

And the children invariably hate it. Ask some. 'Do you want your parents to be your friends?' will do to begin with; and 'What do you think of grown-ups?' The answers will be, 95 per cent of the time, 'No, I want them to be my parents' and 'Nothing.' Grown-ups, to the young, are fossils or dinosaurs, and should stay in their lairs. They are not part of the world of the young, and to see them desperately striving to stave off death by learning the names of new bands is dreadfully sad.

Anyone who regularly encounters the young knows that this is the case; and the legacy of the Big Babies – our legacy – is a cohort of charming, affable but terribly serious and oddly elderly young people. In the university where I am writing these words, it is one o'clock in the morning and all is quiet; the majority of the under-graduates are soberly in their rooms, working for their exams. Many of them have steady relationships, moving decorously through their university careers as, effectively, married couples. They go to dinner in Hall, not (as we did, when it wasn't an 'occasion' but simply where you went to get your dinner) with their stained gowns disguising their wild and heterodox dress beneath, but, dressed as for a dinner party, in dark suits, collars and ties, elegant dresses, high heels. They stand for grace, which is in Latin; they drink their wine moderately; their conversation is a civilised hum. They themselves are civilised.

It is not because they are the forced shoots of a new aristocracy; they have as varied a mixture of backgrounds as you could imagine, though all are fearsomely clever. It is not because they are cowed, nor because they are forced to be there (formal Hall is no longer compulsory). Above all, it is not that we can congratulate ourselves on the wonderful job we have done bringing them up, because we have not. It seems to me more likely that, having seen us masquerading as children, they in their turn are masquerading as adults; and so they announce solemnly that they want to become solicitors, to go into marketing, to study for an MBA, are hoping for a job in finance or retail or the civil service. Our minds were on fame, drugs and venery, on self-actuation and self-indulgence, on gratification and instrumentality and all the shibboleths of Modernity. Theirs are on mortgages and pension plans, on savings and financial projections. Where we once quoted Beckett or Derrida, they quote return-on-investment. What a glamorous world we have handed them.

And these are the clever ones; the good ones who have worked hard and got their exams and are still working hard, while all around them the Entitlement Society yowls in its cradle and struggles under its Asbos, seeks flattened oblivion in drugs, roars in the street, hurtles, howling, towards pointlessness. How is it going with our Martian anthropologist? Is he beginning to think that we are all just making it up?

Danger Man

Just as the scoutmaster may no longer frighten his charges, so Fred (in the song lyric at the head of this chapter) would be in terrible trouble today. Health-and-safety inspectorates would be after him; employer liability insurance would tangle him in its web; someone would have to be found who understood the Latent Damage Act (1986). There would be lawsuits for damages, depredations, trauma, loss of earnings, mental and emotional distress. Root Cause Analysis investigators would be called in, witnesses interviewed, the endless cups of tea analysed (were the builders rushing the job because of bladder urgency?).

Above all, why (it would be asked) had there been no risk assessment?

Risk assessment is the new religion, the Big Babies' equivalent of the apotropaic ritual, the haruspices, the chicken entrails and the goat on the altar. Where our ancestors looked up at the stars, and spoke with the gods, and went off upon the great and dangerous adventures which would return them to their communities as adults, we, adorned not with swords and quivers but with all the tentative apparatus of our intelligence and our carefulness, look upwards and see, not gods, but improperly secured overhead lighting, untrimmed branches, loose cables, inadequately fastened false ceiling partitions; and we decide not, after all, to go. It is, after all, too dangerous.

> ⚠ The Local Government Ombudsman for England and Wales has published a report saying that leaning gravestones are dangerous and should be subject to risk assessments, temporary supports and warning notices. The *Edinburgh Evening News* reported on 23 January 2003 that the 'risk assessment' appeared to consist of council workers pushing gravestones until they fell over.

This modern appeasing of our ancient gods is all we've got. The liver upon which the seer gazed no longer harbours the future in its bumps and gristle, but hepatitis C; the chicken entrails may carry bird flu; when you sacrifice a goat, smoke gets in your eyes. We have no choice, particularly not where smoke – restored once again to its ancient demonic role – is concerned. At George Washington University, the professor of 'public interest law' (surely an oxymoron?) threatened the director of the campus risk-management office with personal liability unless he moved smokers even further away from the buildings than before. Personal liability, that is, for discriminating against non-smokers.

This is not to elicit the usual cries of 'oppression' against the phony tolerance of America, which is in reality an immensely intolerant polity, enjoying nothing more than throwing its weight around, individually and collectively – a quality it shares with

Britain. Iraq is nothing more than a large version of the sort of nonsense that goes on in every condominium in Manhattan and every village in England (and the less said about the Scots and the Welsh, the better). Nor is it my intention to dredge up the hoary concern as to what they will find to shriek about, like toddlers who've seen a spider, when the last smoker has coughed up his last lung (although one can't in truth help wondering what they will find to shriek about when the last smoker has coughed up his last lung).

No. Look carefully, again. Did you spot it? Nor did I, when I first read about the incident, but there it is: 'the campus risk-management office'. Not someone, on a campus, doing a risk assessment of something which needed to be dealt with, but a whole, dedicated, campus risk management office.

Safety Kills

Risk assessment and incident investigation can be remarkable tools, particularly when things go wrong. And, of course, things always *do* go wrong. Someone once observed that there was no point in trying to make something that could never go wrong, because it would go wrong, except it would go wrong somewhere you couldn't get at to fix it. The computer game *Starship Titanic*[*] was based on a variant of this premise.

The premise was simple. Travel in deep space is fine except for the problem of flying space debris, which – this is not a fictional construct, but a real and pressing concern for NASA – can cause catastrophic damage. So our fictional spaceship was equipped with a very sophisticated detection system which would immediately detect flying space debris, and determine precisely any flying-space-debris-damage caused and the best way of fixing it.

---

[*] Of which, to declare a minor interest, I was one of the writers.

In due course (our scenario went), the ship was indeed struck by flying space debris. Big flying space debris, packing quite a punch.

And guess where the debris hit our spaceship?

Exactly.

Right in the flying-space-debris detection system.

Nothing. Not a peep. As far as the crew were concerned, there had been no flying-space-debris incident whatsoever, for the simple reason that there was no longer a flying-space-debris monitoring system to tell them about it. And so the ship in due course blew up.

And one more example, this time from real life. In the Australian bush, aeroplanes are a vital means of transport, but most of the airfields they use are small and unregulated, and so do not have a control tower. Instead, when a pilot is approaching or departing, he will give an 'All stations' call on a pre-assigned radio frequency, telling anyone who's listening that he is lining up to take off, or five miles south descending through two thousand feet, or whatever. If there's someone else in the vicinity, they will reply, and everyone works it out to their satisfaction.

'All stations Meekatharra, November Alpha five miles south descending to circuit height.'

'G'day November Alpha, this is Bravo Delta Zulu, five miles north descending to circuit height.'

'Roger, Delta Zulu. Say your type.'

'Delta Zulu's a King Air.'

'Right. November Alpha's a Cessna 180. You're faster. You go ahead, I'll orbit and wait for you.'

'Good on you, November Alpha.'

It all works itself out.

And one day a pilot is approaching Broome, on the northern coast. It has been a long flight but here is the Indian Ocean like a glittering trophy off his port wing as he tracks along Eighty Mile Beach. He is happy, pleasantly tired and eager to be on the ground for a beer and a piss. The day is coming to an end; the setting sun behind him floods the sands and the scrubland with gold. The bay ahead of him sweeps round in a horseshoe. He clicks on his microphone.

'All stations Broome. Sierra November Alpha is ten miles south-east, three thousand feet, wide left base for the westerly runway.'

Silence. He knows the radio is working; he has been calling airfields on 126.7 all day as he stops for fuel, lunch, coffee, bladder.

So he begins a long lazy descending curve towards the runway.

Nobody out there, but the formalities should be observed.

'All stations Broome: Sierra November Alpha turning long final runway 28.'

Then suddenly a voice.

'Sierra November Alpha, this is Papa Juliet India, just heard your call. Be advised Broome is 126.0, one-two-six decimal zero, not 126.7. I say again, 126.0 is the frequency for Broome, acknowledge.'

The world is suddenly a much more dangerous place.

'Juliet India, roger, bloody hell, thanks, changing frequency 126.0.'

A click of the rotary dial. Before he can speak, the headphones crackle into life.

'All stations Broome, Ansett six six six rolling runway one-zero, departing to the east.'

A commercial flight. A commercial *jet*. Taking off on the reciprocal runway. Coming straight at him. He turns rapidly through 180 degrees.

'Ansett six six six, Sierra November Alpha, Cessna 182 at' – he peers at the altimeter. Jesus – 'fifteen hundred feet, range five miles, orbiting south of the extended centreline, please call when clear.'

If that other pilot hadn't . . . if he'd just kept going . . .

A fail-dangerous system. No news is good news. But no news is also bad news. How can you tell the difference between

181

nobody there to hear you, and somebody there who can't hear you because you've not tuned the right frequency? In both cases, the result is silence. In one case, though, the result could be: dead.

Worrying? Tell me about it. I was the pilot.

There's Nobody Here but Us Chickens

The bigger problem is that fail-dangerous systems are Nature's way. Silence in the night forest does not mean nobody's there; it means everybody's keeping quiet, waiting, on the qui vive to kill or be killed. Evolve better hearing and the other guy evolves better silent-lurking skills. Evolve a powerful sense of smell and the other guy evolves to smell like something else. Only move under cover of darkness and the other guy evolves to being nocturnal. Develop a distinctive identifying call and the other guy will evolve the power to mimic it. The one thing Nature insists upon is that only a fool trusts the evidence of his senses.

But we believe ourselves bigger than Nature. *Semper vigilans*, we tell ourselves, and believe that what we can detect, we can control; and we believe that we can (given training and resources) detect anything. Why, then, should we endure risks? How can it be that, with our extravagant skills, any harm should come to us at all? How can there be 'accidents'? Someone must be at fault. How can we get ill? Someone must be at fault. How can we . . . (whisper it) . . . die? What we need is more information, more care, more risk assessment.

And so the world becomes an endless sequence of threats and dangers, and our job becomes increasingly restricted to negotiating this hostile world – this hostile business of being alive, really – and we adopt a blissful unawareness that it can never be entirely tamed, and the only way to be safe is not to interact with the world at all.

Investigators and safety professionals have a neat categorization:

- A hazard is something that has the potential to harm you.
- A risk is what you run when you interact with a hazard.
- A gamble is what you take when you can't (or don't) manage or control the interaction.

So a road is a hazard. Crossing the road is a risk. Running out into the road with your eyes shut is a gamble.

In the new, caring Mummyverse, we confuse the three dreadfully. Our instincts (accurately enough, Nature being a fail-dangerous system) tell us that everything is a gamble. Our instincts also tell us to engage with risk and to learn to control it. Anyone who has had a child, and watched in horror as that child first swims, or climbs, or drives, knows that the urge to confront and control risks is utterly primal in our species, and, perhaps, accounts for our present triumph in the macroscopic world.

But that is not enough for the behavioural infantilisers – the ones who want to make big babies of us so that nothing ever befalls us. They see everything as hazardous (potentially at least), and they cannot live with the knowledge. Instead of controlling risks, they want us never to engage with hazards at all. They are the equivalent of elderly parents gifted with children (often to their bewilderment) late in life when they had given up hope, and now unable to rid themselves of the belief that their offspring are not only miraculous but indescribably fragile. We have all seen them, laden with baby equipment, gazing fearfully at their young as if the capricious Universe would at any moment extend some hitherto-unthought-of component of itself and simply obliterate their golden hopes.

We instinctively know, when we see these parents, that their obsessional care, their indefatigable micro-management, is not about their offspring at all, but about themselves. And this, too, is why so many of us feel so uneasy about the madder strictures of the health-and-safety collective: it isn't about us; it's about *them*.

One counter-argument is that, no, it's about money. When the government wants us to stop smoking, to drive more slowly, not to bring the car into town, to eat less salt or butter or eggs or red meat or suet – to dine, in short, on a few dry leaves and a sprig of earth – or to give up coffee or drink less or have safe sex or have no sex at all, it is because the harm caused by all the things they want us to stop costs the government money.

But if that were the primary interest, there are (says the libertarian philosophy) plenty of better ways to save government money. Waste less of it on themselves, for a start. Stop interfering with people. Allow private interest to triumph, as triumph it will; look at the so-called 'sub-prime' lenders who batten nicely onto the poor, getting them into debt, then charging them every time the poor bastards can't meet the debt they got them into in the first place. Why wait? Why not have what you want at once? Don't scream and drum your heels and hold your breath until you turn blue; just get into debt and ruin your life once and for all!

Private interests are a great thing. But nobody would call them humane or ethical, when libertarianism, that purest of all gospels of private ownership, would, if it had its way, leave no space at all where someone without property and without permission could even *be*, let alone sleep or urinate in privacy. As Britain and the United States drift slowly and inexorably towards libertarianism, it's worth reflecting that it is the most infantilising of all political cults, not because it is inherently violent or repressive (it simply arrogates all rights and liberties to financial interest) but because it has no underlying ideology – no model of what people are like, or what they need – except the hunger for advantage, and sees no need to explain itself save in the most despotic terms of the nursery: *because I am bigger than you, and it's my house.*

So: if governments' interest in the safety of the electorate is not financially driven (if it were, government would trim itself almost to invisibility and stop confiscating our money) nor ethically motivated (ethical government faces a dilemma, but would certainly choose to maximise either liberty or justice, rather than, in the cases of Britain and America, carefully eroding each by increments), what is it that drives government to fiddle endlessly with the right of citizens to get themselves in a mess? Why do schoolteachers have to conduct risk assessments every time they take children out of school? Why do armies of little men have to stick labels on every lightbulb or plug to reassure us that we won't get a shock when we turn it on? Why are pipe organs facing extinction because they have lead in, and are blown by electricity, and therefore (says the British civil service, eager as camp guards to implement everything to the hilt, regardless of sense) they are electrical devices just like cellphones, computers and televisions, and must not contain more than 0.1 per cent lead?*

> ⚠ An 'outbreak' of three cases of tummyache in Scotland was featured on the BBC News on 30 May 2006, complete with warnings from public health consultants and the establishing of an NHS helpline. Coming up: Man Stubs Toe.

---

* The old principle of *reductio ad absurdam* would suggest that *everything* should be banned from containing lead, since everything is in some way or other electric. The old principle of wanting to have EU bureaucrats put down like dogs is buoyed up by the fact that, while this legislation is designed to protect against landfill disposal of lead, landfill disposal of lead is pretty harmless, since the lead oxidises and becomes inert. The old principle of not being allowed to put bureaucrats down like dogs so having to laugh at them instead is fulfilled by pointing out that the legislation is known as 'WEEE', which about sums it up. And now would be a good time to restate the Darling Principle, which is that anyone can do what they like providing they are happy to go home in the evening and say, 'Darling, guess what *I* did today . . .'

This is nothing to do with wanting us to have better, safer lives, and everything to do with the fundamental principle ruling the Mummyverse, which is that interference, nannying, ticking off, bossing about and whining are fundamental urges of government, and far from being for our own good, it is for theirs. And why? It has never been better put than by the British parliamentary sketch-writer Matthew Parris. Parris, a former MP himself, observed that, when he left Parliament, he started noticing his former colleagues in a new light. Anyone who has ever seen politicians in the flesh would recognise what Parris meant. They were funny shapes. They had peculiar postures. They dressed in an odd way. They talked peculiarly, had odd tics and mannerisms, strange hair, lisps, stutters, dodgy vowels, bad skin, bad breath, bad manners and very, very little insight. Pondering this, Parris had a moment of blazing insight: they were, he wrote, the unpopular ones at school, and now they were getting their own back.

Sosumi

When Apple Computer introduced the Macintosh, they were under threat from the largely dormant Apple Corp., which exists to own the rights to Beatles songs. It wasn't fair (said Apple Corp.) that Apple Computer should be called Apple, because people would confuse the two. (Years of dealing with Beatle fans had clearly left them with a low estimate of human intelligence.)

A deal was struck. Apple Computer wouldn't sell music.

So when the Macintosh exploited its rudimentary musical capabilities to produce a more engaging beep than the IBM PC, Apple Corp. went ape; and, like the spoilt and petulant child that corporations are obliged to imitate (being, as Joel Bakan writes in *The Corporation*, legally constituted psychopaths), started threatening lawsuits.

Apple Computer's response was to introduce a new, brief, but blatantly polyphonic beep called 'Sosumi'. People at first thought it was some Japanese sample; but then they pronounced it carefully, and realized what it was really saying.

So Sue Me.

There's a popular belief that the raft of 'safety initiatives' produced by governments and their agencies are designed to thwart lawsuits. But people seldom sue their government; instead, they sue private companies, measuring their targets' pockets carefully before filing an action. Might it not be nearer the truth to say that the litigation culture and governmental safety paranoia come from the same root: the inability of us Big Babies to accept any responsibility for our actions, and the sad truth that things go wrong? We smoke a hundred cigarettes a day for forty years, get cancer and sue. We open a champagne bottle, cop a cork in the eye and sue. We eat and eat and eat and get fat and diabetic and we sue. We spill hot coffee on ourselves and get scalded and sue. We go up in an aeroplane and crash it and are hurt or killed and we sue. And, as a result, everything now carries warnings. Cigarettes kill. Caution! This cork may hit you! In the EYE! Or someone else's! And then they could SUE YOU! This food contains FAT! It's got a RED LABEL on the FAT part! That means you can only have it as an occasional TREAT, and never at all if you play with yourself like that, don't think we haven't seen you because we HAVE!

As for the aeroplane . . . if you want an idea of how laden aircraft have become with warnings, just look in the handbook of your car. See all the warning triangles with exclamation marks beside them, telling you things like if you drive your car over a precipice gravity will take over and it will do what we call demonstrating falling-over-a-cliff-type-behaviour. Aeroplanes are like that, only more so, because although we can be trusted (after a lot of training and a lot of exams) to get into an aeroplane and start it up (watch out for the PROPELLORS!) and (Wait! It might be a jet! Jets don't have propellors! But watch out in case you get

SUCKED IN!) taxi it to the runway, and take off (DANGEROUS! Taking-off goes into the AIR, which is DANGEROUS!) . . . even though we can be trusted to do those things, we aren't trusted to assess the risk ourselves and act accordingly. And so we might sue.

Here's a proposition: grown-ups don't sue for tort. There is something monstrously infantile about running squeaking to a judge when the world demonstrates that it is not necessarily on your side, and something contemptible about needing someone to blame for whatever-it-was that happened which we didn't like. Children who shriek and shout 'I'll tell! I'll tell on you!' are properly disliked. Big Babies who do the same should be similarly shunned.

Agh! It's One of Those!

For those of us living in the West, the world has never been a safer place. And yet our attitude to life – or, rather, the attitude to life imposed upon us – is best summed up by a road sign, common in Britain. It sits in a red triangle, denoting an awful warning, and it displays one character only:

That is to say, it is no more than an indiscriminate shriek of fear, the hypervigilance of a rodent in a world full of snakes. Is this how we want to memorialise our culture?

Look at the bogeymen we surround ourselves with, some of

which are occasionally real but, even so, not enough to make our entire lives contingent upon them. We have made a world infested with paedophiles and rapists,* so that fathers worry about bathing with their toddlers (in the world of Big Babies, men are dangerous wild creatures, given to badness, while women possess unassailably the moral high ground, just like Mummy did) and children are told that the world is a phallopathy holding its breath with eagerness to rape and despoil.

We have made a world where the National Consumer Council can express itself 'disappointed' that candy manufacturers sell big chocolate bars, because people will eat them and get fat. A world of obsessional, ruinously expensive and almost entirely ineffectual 'airline security' where old men have their walking sticks confiscated while healthy young men are allowed aboard with eyeglasses, ballpoint pens, bottles of whisky, cologne sprays and a host of other things which can be very easily converted into lethal weapons, and where nobody called John Thomas (including a seventy-year-old black American woman) is allowed to fly because one John Thomas was once thought to be a bit iffy.

A world where people sue because listening to their iPods has made them a bit deaf, where governments ban hamburgers from school meals while selling fizzy drink concessions to companies like Coca-Cola, a can of which a day can make you put on a stone every year. Where even the ludicrous Lord Chancellor of Great Britain can complain that people won't work for the Scouts for fear of being sued, won't run school trips for fear of being sued, won't open up public spaces for fear of being sued. Where a can of fly spray announces 'Fly & Wasp Killer. Kills Bugs Dead. Only for use as an insecticide' (as if someone is

---

* Actually, paedophiles are completely harmless, driven by φιλια, the asexual brotherly love which motivates some of our finest teachers. It's *pederasts* we should watch out for; theirs is εραςθαι, the desire to possess and consume.

189

going to think 'Aha: fly spray. I wonder if . . .'). Where a sign out-side the bus station in Bath Spa says 'Warning: Extreme Danger!'. 'Extreme'? If a bus station presents extreme danger, what do you get if you stand beneath the epicentre of a nuclear test site?

A world of dangerous food – eggs, butter, then not butter any more but margarine, poultry, red meat, sugar, sugar substitutes, tea, coffee, then not tea and not coffee, now coffee again unless you have cancer and put it up your arse when it becomes good for you; sweets and chocolate, raisins, nuts . . . is there anything which does *not* harm diddums?

A world where cruise-ship passengers are told that they should not expect to shake hands with the Captain when dining at his table, 'as a precaution against infection', yet one in which we are surprised to catch 'superbugs' (is this the sort of word to be used to grown-ups? To describe a horrible, multiply resistant pathogen? 'Superbug'?) in hospital, when a hospital is precisely where you would expect to find bugs. A world where pills which can kill you – paracetamol – are described on the packet as 'easy to swallow'. Where silly policemen want to hide speed cameras in cat's eyes despite the fact that speed, according to the British Department for Transport, is *not* a factor in more than 80 per cent of accidents, and indeed isn't even in the top six contributory factors (while policemen, rushing about like crazed teenagers in their cars, showing off, seem to be responsible for a hell of a lot of accidents; perhaps they should hide the policemen in cat's eyes instead, beneath the surface of the road where they can do no harm).*

A world in which the highways are so cluttered with signs as to present a steady distraction to motorists, as well as lulling

---

* Speed is another shibboleth of the age ('Walk, don't run!') although Durham chief constable Paul Garvin, who opposed speed cameras and had just one mobile speed unit on his patch, produced casualty figures 40 per cent lower than comparable forces, and only 3 per cent of road accidents in his area involved vehicles exceeding the legal speed limit.

them into a sense of security so that they end up having crashes because either all the warnings make them think they are safe, or they are so busy trying to read or decipher them all that they get distracted and crash.* A world of station announcements ('May I have your attention:† please do not leave personal items unattended as they will be removed by the security forces and may be destroyed' blaring out on a deserted platform into the cold midnight air). A world where the *Sunday Times* can on the one hand regularly rant about shortages in the NHS and, on the other hand, complain that 'experts' think prescription drugs are killing 30,000 people a year. (They just want to make your flesh creep.) Where trick-and-treaters are 'clamped down on' by police 'using powers available to us', and Londoners are warned not to come into Trafalgar Square on New Year's Eve because there will be lots of people there and the fountains have been boarded up and there won't be any trains and so they should stay home in bed. Where smokers are banned from lighting up at home in case a council cleaning person should come. Where a cleaning product describes itself as 'tested on onions and lemons', perhaps so that we don't burn their premises down for testing it on rabbits, but how long can it be before there's an Onion and Lemon Liberation front?

Where schoolchildren have to wear goggles to play conkers. Where a man had a sword-and-sorcery book confiscated by some security goon on a ferry because it was 'inappropriate', even though it was in his bag (suggesting that there are adult human beings who will be alarmed by a book with a swordswoman on the cover; if there are, they should be beheaded).

---

* Which is why there have been experiments in Holland and England to remove all such signs and road markings, to make motorists realise they need to grow up and exercise their own judgement. The results are good, so far.

† There is no 'I' of course; this is a computer. But we are supposed to believe there *is* an eye, just as we were supposed to believe that when our mother suddenly called out 'I know what you're doing,' she knew what we were doing.

> ⚠ A study in the journal *Injury Prevention* has found a 'worrying trend' in the number of childhood fractures linked to trampoline use in the home. The team found one hospital, the Royal Berkshire in Reading, treated eight children for trampolining-related fractures in two summer months in 2003. They said metalwork should be padded and complex moves discouraged.
>
> Gillian Taylor, 37, from Livingston, is calling for pubs to issue smokers with plastic cups and lids in a bid to prevent their drinks from being spiked. She is 'angry' that bars are forcing smokers to leave their drink glasses unattended while they go outside for a fag. Anti-smoking campaigners welcomed the idea of plastic cups for smokers.

Where the New York subway wanted to ban people from taking pictures of their vile trains and stations 'to prevent terrorism' (you might have thought that the more people taking pictures, the better). Where the average Londoner is filmed on CCTV around three hundred times a day, but where a man who wanted to take a picture of his daughter in a swimming pool after she had swum her first width was told that he had to get written permission from every other parent in the place.

Where staff in the BBC are given instruction in how to use revolving doors, and where television cook Nigella Lawson can't allow her studio audience to taste the food in case one of them gets diarrhoea and sues (sues? For diarrhoea?). Where the English Faculty of one of our great universities has a Safety Policy website which maunders on about kettles, for heaven's sake,* and another safety website in that same university advises readers,

---

* 'No personal portable electrical equipment (e.g. kettles, fires etc) may be brought into the Faculty without permission of the Faculty Safety Officer who must be consulted in every instance.' Gosh. Faculty Safety Officer. If only I had my time again . . .

who one may assume are among the more intelligent people on the planet, that 'laptops should not be used when driving'.

Where Scott's Porage Oats Old Fashioned Thick Scottish Milled Oats describes in great detail how to make lovely hot porridge then, in its 'Tasty Tips' exhorts us to 'Please be careful with hot product' and warns that 'BOWL MAY BE HOT', presumably addressing these remarks to Old Fashioned Thick Scots who, remembering Wallace and Scotland the Brave, may be less than pleased.

A world, in short, of Big Babies, nagged, ticked off, exhorted, scared, bullied and corralled into docility by the endless reiteration, with grotesque variations, of a single leitmotif: the world is a terrible place, and we aren't grown-up enough to deal with it on our own.

Envoi: A Walk in the Park

Once upon a time there were cities, which were bad. Bad men lived in cities, and hid round corners, and tapped on the window when you sat in the car, and they offered you sweets or a look at some puppies which they had in a shed, just around the corner, and you weren't to go with them, not ever.

And there were buildings in cities which were unspeakable. Unspeakable people lived in them, and did unspeakable things. Sometimes there would be noises, and sometimes shouting, and these were some of the bad things about cities, and other bad things about cities were (1) cars and (2) alleys and (3) rough boys with accents and (4) Brylcreem, which went with accents, and there were (5) skinheads and they were rough too and had (6) motor scooters and there were (7) prozzies who had (8) fishnet stockings and VD and (8) Chinese people had VD too and (9) Black Men listened to music all day and weren't very friendly although their (9a) mothers were very friendly and they would look after you as would

(10) Indians because they were just like us except more so, although you shouldn't eat their (10a) curry because you would get diarrhoea and there were also (11) workmen and (12) cigarettes and you should leave them alone and also not hang around near the (13) Flying Horse or the (14) Black Boy and you shouldn't go to (15) The Meadows because that was entirely (3) rough boys with accents and (5) skinheads and that was just the (16) start of it, there was a lot more including (1) cars driven by (17) drunk people who had been in the (13) Flying Horse or the (14) Black Boy and would (18) run you over and not even realise it . . .

. . . but . . .

. . . there was also the Arboretum. Which was a big park with trees and a parrot and the parrot used (19) Bad Language but it was only a parrot so it didn't understand what it was saying, so it was all right for the parrot to say it but you weren't to listen to it saying it because you were *not* a parrot and could understand what it was saying, but apart from that the Arboretum was lovely and it was safe and kind except for (20) bullies who pushed each other over and threw your cap in the duckpond, but it was only horseplay so (20) that didn't count. And it was safe in the park, which didn't count as the city at all, and you could go there whenever you wanted.

And once upon a time (but a bit later upon it) you moved out of town and then you could go on bicycle rides for hours and hours, leaving after breakfast but you had to be back before dark and if you went back to Roger Harrison's house or Lindsay Gray's house or in fact *anyone's* house you had to ring up and say so because otherwise your parents would pretend to be Worried Sick although you knew they weren't because what could happen to a couple of thirteen-year-old boys on bicycles cycling twenty miles or more to look at some crumbling organ in a musty, soothing old church in the cool green underwater depths of the woods?

Nothing could happen then that could not happen now. We have been fooled. Just as children are fooled. Fooled by the Bogeyman.

CHAPTER 10

Why Can't You Do
Something Useful?

For me, it was creosote. I can smell it; I can see the can; I can feel, under my fingers, the special creosote flex of the brush, see the wood darkening, sense preservation being done. Good things. Constructive things. Things that men do, to make it all right, so that then they can do the other things that men do, including pushing their hat back on their head (you could always tell a man because he had creosote on his hat) and mopping their brow and saying 'Phew' and 'I'm about all in, what with creosoting that wood' and 'I'll just go out and check that that creosote is drying okay' and 'Damn lucky we had that creosote lying about, that wood wouldn't have lasted another day in this weather.'

There were other things, too, some of which we have touched on in passing. There was being a demolitioneer or demolitionist or whatever it was called when you stood on top of a building and knocked it down under your own feet and nobody told you off. There was being the man who did the gates on the Sandbanks ferry, a mighty business involving chains and sea-weed and the smell of the jetty, salt and iodine and fish and oil and hot steam. There was being a telegraph-pole man: you climbed the telegraph pole, first by a ladder, then, further up, by spikes, but you couldn't get to the spikes unless you had the ladder first, and you had a big leather safety belt which you leant back against, perched on the telegraph pole doing telegraph-pole things in a casual and masterful way, smoking a Boyard Papier Maïs caporal cigarette, which didn't happen in East Circus Street, Nottingham, behind my grandfather's house where I first saw the telegraph-pole men, but was a later retrojection after I first saw French telegraph-pole men.

There was being the man who drove the steam roller which wasn't actually steam, but had been designed to look as if it could have been steam if it wanted, and had simply chosen, on a caprice, to be the depressingly unromantic, workaday diesel. (Not yellow, either, but a decent, steamrollerly green, and the man who drove it wasn't reduced to a luminous unit in a high-vis jacket, just like every other man on the site, but wore his own clothes, including a flat cap. Mother of God, how I yearned for a flat cap.)

But all these things were out of reach, as were:

- Helicopter driver
- Surgeon (leg chopping off)
- Steel mill man (molten)
- Organ player (huge creepy organ, played to Anne Morrell so that she would love me)
- Road crash rescue person (rescuing Anne Morrell so that she would love me)
- Pope (so that Anne Morrell would realise she loved me but it was too late because I was Pope)
- New special kind of through-the-night express train driver which you could do lying down so that it was very like being in bed.
- Engine-room man on a paddle steamer with an oil can to oil the big piston and crank which would kill anyone else except I knew how to do it so that Anne Morrell would love me.
- Ragworm man, who sold ragworms which he dug up for free

- Husband of Cyd Charisse, who was on the cover of a magazine and had legs and bosoms, which would teach Anne Morrell a lesson

These were who I wanted to be, but on the whole (being reasonably pragmatic) creosote led the field. So when they said 'Why can't you do something useful?' I would say 'I could creosote the gate' and they would say 'The gate doesn't need creosoting, you've already creosoted it and a right old mess you made, not to mention the brush, stiff as a board, and creosote all over the deep freeze' and I would lose hope a bit because if they wouldn't let me even creosote, none of the other possibilities for doing something useful would even be considered.

'Well, you can't sit around all day gawping,' they would say. 'Nobody ever got anything done by sitting around all day gawping, you are beginning to get on our nerves, what's the matter with you and close your mouth, have you got adenoids or something? Just for Pete's sake do something useful.'

I was eight, maybe nine years old. How was it for you, then? Were you, too, simultaneously desperate to be allowed to do something useful but only offered a range of 'useful' things that fell widely outside your own parameters of what 'useful' was? Things neither involving chemicals nor machinery, neither danger nor adventure, things quite to the contrary, involving the dog or tidying? We were all in the same boat, and the boat was firmly tethered so that all you could do, even when they said 'Why can't you do something useful?', was sit there, gawping. But when we grew up, it would all be different.

Tempora Mutantur, Plus C'est La Même Chose

Walk round any great city towards dusk on a winter's afternoon – the lights coming on in the offices, people at their desks, unaware of being watched, or possibly all too aware of being watched, glad of it, happy to be observed being ratified, vouched for, significant, employed. Ignore the signs on the big glass doors boasting of telecommunications or corporate law, services to the food industry, public transport consortia, web consultancies, outsourcing consultancies, debt management consultancies . . . ignore them. Just look at the people.

Two things spring to mind:

(1) What on earth are they actually doing?

(2) Whatever it is, they are all doing the same thing.

And what they are doing – when we grew up, it would all be different – is gawping.

Right now, as I write these words, I am doing the same as them. We are, most of us white-collar workers, whether our trade is (as in my case) writing or (in theirs) insurance broking or banking or risk management or oil exploration onshore support services or health service procurement or strategic analysis or human resources or management information or network support services or customer liaison operations or . . . whatever it may be, we are, mostly, gawping. We gawp at the same thing: our computer screens. Every now and then we press a few keys. From time to time (far more often than we would like) there is a bing! or a little window flashes up or the menu-bar blinks at us and there is an email or an 'instant message' and we gawp at that for a moment and then press some more keys and then we gawp a bit more, wondering what we were thinking of before we were interrupted.

Life has dwindled to gawp-and-type: 'knowledge working', it is called, but doesn't it have a strange aura of insubstantiality, as make-work, as not quite doing something useful, not like creosoting or leg-chopping-off or something to do with submarines? Don't we actually feel that we ourselves have become contingent, provisional, temporary? That, far from leading grown-up working lives, we are still in some sense at kindergarten, under the eye of the teacher, working on some hand/eye co-ordination game while gossiping, illicitly?

198

> ⚠ They hated each other at the beginning of the day but at the end of the day they *really* hated each other, and it got worse as the week wore on, with the paintball and the 'real life' dungeons-and-dragons and the yomping and the cook-out and the sing-song and the hide-and-seek ... executives. Business executives, on a team bonding week. Some were sick. One went home. There was a fight. One cried. One of them exposed himself. Four of them went to bed together. It was just another week, same as all weeks. I was taking them for aeroplane rides. We weren't allowed to smack them. We should have been allowed to smack them.

Everything is on the computer screen, and, like Nietzsche's famous abyss, as we gaze into the computer, it gazes back into us. In modern times, our work watches us working. Every keystroke is logged; every URL we type in, every email we send: all are logged and examined by unseen operatives working for unknown companies, or by people in the back rooms whom nobody ever sees.

Baby needs an eye kept on him at all times:

> Any@Mail is a professional email surveillance software specifically designed to capture, monitor and record users emails received or sent through any computers on the LAN. It captures email-related packages on the LAN and decodes the packages into emails exactly as the original ones. Through the interface similar to Outlook Express, Emails captured can be previewed and sorted according to IP address or computer names resolved. It can be used to backup or archive e-mails, monitor and record entry and exit of e-mails and detect sensitive emails on the LAN

advertises a company called Network Monitoring Solutions, because employees are bad and are not to be trusted and so need the equivalent of a baby alarm, switched on all the time.

Find Out What Baby Is Doing and Tell Him to Stop

It goes far beyond the baby-alarms of online monitoring, though. There is hardly an occupation left that is not now monitored, usually on the most spurious and fatuous grounds, to the extent that the monitoring seriously interferes with the time and ability of people to do the job they are meant to be doing. Doctors have to spend less time with patients because they have to spend more time filling in forms designed to measure how much time they are spending with patients. University teachers do something very hard to measure, now that we can't simply measure by results, because failing a student or assigning a poor grade is bad for business – education, like everything else, is now a 'business' – and invades students' human rights. But all the same, it must be measured, because training people to do a job and then letting them get on with it would be treating them too much like grown-ups; so a spurious set of measurements, which have nothing to do with what is supposed to be being measured, are established, laboriously monitored, collected, collated, published, and . . .

And . . . ?

And then they curiously disappear. Nothing much is done apart from using them as a justification for 'management', which usually means sacking people and cutting budgets. The idea that they can be used for any substantive purpose is, of course, anathema; because in the world of Big Babies, appearance is all and actuality, nothing. Just as baby has his security blankie, so Big Baby has statistics, Best Practice guidelines and all the other apparatus of professional infantilising. It's the perfect example of the vicious circle of infantilism: childish politicians who have never grown up enough to accept that not everything is controllable by rules and diktat, instructing civil servants and more or less fatuous 'agencies' to do something, even if only for the sake of the appearance of control; they, in their turn, invent pointless 'metrics' so that they have something to wave to prove they have Been Good, and then treating the people who are actually trying to do something like naughty children who have to account for every moment of their time.

The result is predictable. Because much of what people do is not itself measurable, things which *can* be measured are pushed into false prominence, like the hospital trust which demanded that its nurses count and evaluate boxes of chocolates given by grateful patients. In time, these spurious measurements overtake the purpose of the job itself. Doctors spend more time filling in forms which fail to reveal how much doctoring they are doing, and less time actually doing doctoring, with the paradoxical result that the more we try to measure their effectiveness, the less effective they become.

The idea that the investigator changes what he is investigating merely by the act of looking comes as no surprise to anyone familiar with the famous thought-experiment of Schrödinger's Cat; that it has become the primary principle of public services is, however, more alarming. In this peculiar world, the primary quality required of an academic hoping for preferment is skill in writing grant applications; to which, if he or she becomes a head of department, is added the skills of fudging the research assessments and cooking the publication books. We now make much of our living watching each other like hawks, drawing up implementation tables and designing lists of 'key competencies' and 'quality assurance methodologies' which, having been designed, can then be implemented, tracked and measured *et in saeculo saeculorum* and used instead of work.

The question which occurs to us when we look into those

lighted office windows – 'What the hell are they all actually doing?' – becomes monstrously relevant when we realise that, much of the time, the answer is 'Nothing of any significance', a trend spotted early on by the writer Keith Waterhouse in his 1978 novel, *Office Life*. Set in the fictitious British Albion Ltd, it describes an apparently thriving corporate headquarters which, while superficially indistinguishable from any other business and complete with promotions and reorganisations, staff associations and promotion battles and all the paraphernalia and politics and management bullshit one would expect, consists solely of internal departments. British Albion has no connection with the outside world because it does not actually do anything. It makes nothing, sells nothing, brokers nothing, performs no service. In fact, it exists solely to provide employment for the people who work there: a government scheme to disguise the true level of national unemployment.

Dissent is rare in British Albion. The staff jockey for position, worry about their desks, perform their rituals of biscuits and coffee machine, canteen and sports-and-social club; they fill in their chitties, balance their books, send inter-departmental memos, complain about stationery, steal ballpoints and, all in all, immerse themselves in the cosy predictable certainties of office life. It is like a big kindergarten, a comfortable playpen complete with role play and dressing up.

It may (if we are honest) sound eerily familiar. But one thing has vanished between Waterhouse's fictional world of work and today's proliferation of carefully specified but spookily insubstantial jobs: security.

The manager now, carefully hired from a list of 'core competencies' which have replaced judgement and informed intuition as the basis of employment (we prefer tablets of stone now; we are happier following procedures, even if those procedures are inane, constipated, inflated and impersonal), can no longer expect security. His job is as insubstantial a thing as the work he does. At one moment he may be Senior Development

Executive, Strategic Analysis, with special responsibility for implementing a range of innovative MIS-based tactical delivery methodologies in line with international best-practice guidelines; at the next, he may be hustled away from his desk by security men, as though his desk contained anything of interest. Companies demand terrible loyalty but respond with unutterable capriciousness; senior managers – who believe that management is a noun, not a verb; a state, not a process; a purpose, not an adjuvant to purposes – arrive, shriek for a space in the corporate playpen, disgrace themselves and depart, rewarded, to do it again elsewhere. Meanwhile, the middle ranks and below must learn to live with the knowledge that loyalty is a one-way street, and that their job is to comply, to feign enthusiasm at every fatuous new 'initiative', to swallow the latest mission statement, to spout the pre-emptive corporate jargon of the 'ever-changing world' and 'cutting-edge technology' and 'scalable solutions' and 'fast-paced business environment' and everything else imaginable (and much that is not).

The corporation is a giant bully, frantic and selfish, and, just like the bully in the schoolyard, has no real idea what it wants its underlings to do, except to comply. To comply, and to . . . suck it up when they have to go.

And, like a bully, the corporation trusts nobody. Paranoid in the extreme, it regards its employees as feckless cheats, bent only on discovering when the watchful eye is averted so that they can slack off, steal, cheat and betray. The electronic baby-alarm is set to a hair trigger. Our productivity is monitored, our movements circumscribed, machines count every keystroke we make, our time is accounted for in three-minute increments, we are corralled into meetings to ensure nobody is coming up with any ideas, every action is run through committees and mediated by procedures. The behaviour of employees is controlled in ways which would be excessive even in a prison: despite the fact that over half of us meet our partners at work and over 40 per cent of people admit to having had office affairs, rules governing 'inappropriate' liaisons proliferate, and many companies now make it a sackable offence not to report to 'human resources' even a stolen kiss by Goods Inward. Dress codes are imposed; informal dress rules, too, are promulgated: 'dress-down Friday' mandates, *de facto* if not *de jure*, the terrible uniform of chinos, deck shoes and open-necked button-down shirt, a rig as tightly associated with the work ghetto as the grey suit, blue shirt and red tie mandatory on other days of the week.

⚠ The suicide bomber is regarded as the ultimate manifestation of evil in a whole axis of evil. Leaving aside the simplistic, reductionist idiocy of the current *Weltpolitik*, isn't it nearer the truth that suicide bombers are the biggest babies of all? 'Do what I want! Do it! Do it! Look at me! DO IT!' and they don't even hold their breath until they turn blue; they *blow themselves up*. (But look what lovely prezzies nice Mr God has for you, my chickadee! Sorry? You thought we said 'virgins'? No, dearie, nobody said anything about *virgins*. You must have misunderstood . . .)

Lower down the scale, the infantilisation is even more pronounced. Not just call-centre 'operatives' but sales clerks are handed scripts detailing what they may and may not discuss with customers, and how: even basic human intercourse is commodified and regulated ('Tell Great-Aunt Gerald you love her very much. Tell her as though you mean it') while in the call centres themselves, the poor people answering the telephone, eight hours a day, to angry people made even angrier by the time they've got through, have to stick to a complex tree-structure controlled and delivered through that inescapable, impassive, uniform window on the world, the computer screen, with its utter absence of texture or affect. A person in a call centre is infantilised beyond even the dismal norms of the wider world, denied even the freedom of speech or the exercise of judgement; the calls they handle are logged by machine; frequently, they must seek permission to relieve themselves. If the two great markers of adulthood are, as we have discussed, autonomy and authority, these people have neither. Instead, they represent perhaps the Omega Point, the *ne plus ultra* of man-management, being mere computer-driven mouthpieces for the corporation, but mouthpieces made of meat.

What *Do* You Think You Are Doing?

Ask a child what he thinks he is doing, and, generally, the answer will be twaddle. It may be grandiose twaddle, it may be evasive twaddle, or it may be generic, non-specific twaddle, but twaddle it will be.

Here is a picture of a man. For the sake of precision, he has a squint and cropped hair; he is wearing a grey shirt made of, probably, polyester; his top button is undone, his are cuffs undone, and he is wearing a grey tie like a tie in a Marks & Spencer shirt-and-tie set. This is probably to make him seem unintimidating, someone just like us, an ordinary person. He is wearing a signet ring on the fourth finger of his right hand to show that he is common, so that we need not be afraid. (The ring might be because he is a foreigner, in which case we should be afraid, because foreign is where the BOGEYMAN comes from. But no foreigner would wear his clothes. No; he is common; he is one of us; we need not be afraid, even though he is the Voice of Business, because he is not actually the Voice of Business. He is someone who Gets Things Done. To prove it, he is standing in front of a jet engine, looking upwards and to the left. Here is what he is saying:

BOEING, ROLLS-ROYCE AND THE ENGINE OF CHANGE

To engineer a jet engine that is both quieter and
more efficient, you have to challenge traditional
thinking. And that's exactly what our partnership
with Rolls-Royce allows us to do. Working
together, change is a remarkable thing.

BOEING
Forever New Frontiers

No wonder he has loosened his cheap grey tie and undone the
top button of his cheap grey shirt, because his words are perplexing. Is he saying that, to engineer a jet engine that is *either*
quieter *or* more efficient you don't have to challenge traditional
thinking? Perhaps it's the challenging of traditional thinking
which has made him all hot and sweaty and knackered. Perhaps
it's the realisation that he – or perhaps we – could not challenge
traditional thinking if he (or whoever the 'we' he is part of) were
not in partnership with Rolls-Royce. Whatever the truth, we
appear to be working together: us, him, Boeing, Rolls-Royce,
we're all in this thing together. Working together. But there's a
worm in the bud: if we weren't working together, change, he
appears to be saying, is not a remarkable thing at all. All the
same, he leaves us with a tantalising thought. (Is it a thought?)
'Boeing Forever New Frontiers' Too distraught to punctuate it,
the Voice of Business has left it to us. 'Boeing Forever: New
Frontiers'? 'Boeing: Forever New. Frontiers'? No matter how we
deploy it, punctuation doesn't help. How can this be?

What was it we got when we asked a child what he thinks he
is doing?

Twaddle?

⚠ 'Welcome to the **people ready** business,' says the slogan, over a picture of some people standing around a factory where they are doing something to jet engines. Some of the people have **ready_** superimposed on them. Others don't. There is no indication of what the '_' character means, but we may assume that, in some arcane grammatology (possibly that of the kaballah or Opus Dei) '**ready_**' means more than 'ready'.

The dismal copy continues. '**In a people-ready business, people make it happen. People, ready with software**. When you give your people tools that connect, inform, and empower them, they're ready. Ready to collaborate with partners, suppliers, and customers. Ready to streamline the supply chain, beat impossible deadlines, and develop ideas that can sway the course of industry. Ready to build a successful business: a people-ready business. Microsoft Software for the people-ready business™. To learn more, visit **microsoft.com/peopleready**. *Your potential. Our passion.*™ **Microsoft**.' (Microsoft advertisement, *The New Yorker*, May 2006.)

Never mind what it means. It means nothing. It has achieved what the great Noam Chomsky could not: a syntactically (reasonably) formal utterance which is entirely semantically empty. It is no more meaningful than a toddler shouting 'Look at me! Look at me!' in the belief that the words 'Look at me' are in themselves enough to make him worth looking at.

Is this a way to address grown-ups? Is composing this contemptible, senseless, patronising pap a *job* for grown-ups?

The Martian Anthropologist is Back Among Us

Once upon a time there was a planet, and on this planet was a civilization which was doing very well, except for a sort of odd cultural neoteny in which people who were, by the standards of any other civilization or any other planet, grown-up, had, for a variety of reasons (none of them particularly creditable or even particularly valid), decided they wanted to go on being children. So some of them treated others like children, and, in their turn, the others started behaving like children, and before very long a worrying number of them were, in one way or another, Big Babies.

But the Big Babies knew that there were limits to what they could get away with, and one thing they couldn't get away with was behaving like babies all the time, without any attempt at concealment. They couldn't wear nappies and lie around in huge playpens going 'Waa! Goo! Waa!' because, before long, they would start to get hungry, and anyway behaving like that was a perversion which already had its creepy adherents and the Less Said about That the Better.

So they came up with a clever scheme. They would arrange things so that sometimes they dressed like grown-ups, and went to offices like grown-ups, and had meetings and issued policy statements and had real money paid into real bank accounts, and pretend money called 'credit cards', and because they did all these things they could get away with behaving like babies behind the scenes.

And one day a Martian anthropologist arrived (on a train, late, so nobody thought anything of it), and watched them, and saw what they did, and went back to Mars a bit chastened and a bit perplexed, and when his colleagues said 'So what were they up to, then?' he said:

'Some of them invent things and make them and sell them, and some of these things are quite useful, but others aren't useful at all and people have to be made to buy them, but that's not hard because, after all, they are Big Babies. So if you tell them that something will make them feel better or be bigger or get more sex (sex is something they still do, despite better alternatives), they will buy it, even if it is just something that has a picture of someone on the packaging. But this someone has to be someone who appears on their quaint, low-technology "television". It's no good having someone actually important on the packaging, a physicist or a philosopher or a great poet or a sculptor, because they know that being someone like that involves a lot more than just looking like something. You have to know physics or philosophy or be able to sculpt or write poems, and even the biggest babies know that that's hard. But being on their (quaint, low-technology) television is easy, and so they think it's easy to be like them: all you need to do is buy something with their picture on it.

'And that is where a lot of their money goes – mostly, their pretend money, because a lot of their real money is taken away by the big Big Babies, the ones who boss them around a lot, and mostly wasted on paying lots of people to sit around and boast to each other about how they are bossing the lesser Big Babies around, and on notices telling the lesser Big Babies what to do, and on making sure that they do it, and, most of all, on soothing them whenever they whine that things are unfair or shriek because they've hurt themselves or complain because there are other Big Babies who they don't like the look of or any one of a million other things that the lesser Big Babies don't like, or the big Big Babies don't like, and all these things need special laws, like the law that says they aren't to build organs any more because the organs have lead in their pipes and they get their air from electrical blowers and therefore they are electrical devices containing lead which is very bad because when you bury electrical devices containing lead in the earth what happens is the lead leaks out and poisons everyone, even though nobody buries organs in the earth and if you bury lead in the earth it goes dull and inert and doesn't leak out and doesn't kill anyone, not ever, which isn't the point, nor is the point that if you blow the organ by gas or waterpower or by monks walking up and down on big bellows or even by practuated frission of zebulonium (which they haven't discovered yet) it suddenly stops being an electrical device containing lead and you can bury it anywhere you like because (perhaps) they are so ill-informed that they believe the lead will say to itself, "Did I come from an electrical device . . . ? I don't think I did, so I had better not leak into the earth and kill everybody . . ."

'And that's what they are like, so they need a law, and laws need money and people and so that's what some of the people do, in between telling the lesser Big Babies off for things they haven't done yet. So you can see, fellow anthropologists of Mars, that between telling the lesser Big Babies off and appeasing them, they have their hands full, and also their wallets.

'As for the others, what they do is try to impress each other. They go to special buildings called "offices" which is a word which used to mean the bit of a company where the accounts were kept and someone called Mrs Smee typed out letters to customers and someone else called Mr Baxter told lies to someone called – as far as I can ascertain – Ah I'm Glad I've Caught You I Have Been Wanting to Have a Word, who was the bank manager. And the idea was that in the office were done the things which needed to be done so that the company could do what it really did. Whatever that may have been. Crinolines, patent medicine, dog leads, felt hats: whatever it may have been.

'But the Big Babies didn't like this and thought they would be better off not having to fiddle with eyeglass hinges, vegetable peelers, leatherware or horse restraints and, instead, fiddling with nice clean manageable things like numbers and words, which was called 'white-collar work' until it became called 'knowledge work' and the great thing was that hydraulic rams, toothpaste, lubricants and waxed-paper cartons involved knowing stuff, whereas 'knowledge work' didn't involve knowing anything at all, except what a computer looked like.

'So the office and the business changed places, and the job of the business became to earn enough money for ever bigger, grander, cleaner, brighter offices with ever more people in them, doing office things in an ever more efficient, time-managed, best-practice, total quality assurance way until both building and the people it housed could truly aspire to the status of machines and, what was far more important, until the organisation (which was now almost all office) had matured to the point where everyone could treat someone else like an infant while simultaneously being infantilised themselves.

'And this made the people very happy; so happy that they never had to worry about things that nobody on their (quaint, low-technology) televisions ever worried about either, like what they were actually doing or what it was actually for or whether it was worth it, and, instead, they looked into their "computers" (a computer being something like an unsophisticated Ekk) and moved numbers around and wrote outlines and drew graphs and looked at people having sex and sent each other documents and commented on each other's proposals and devised enormously complicated systems for Getting Things Done which didn't actually Get Anything Done because there wasn't anything to do except stare into the glass gaze of the Ekk, through which all life was mediated until life became increasingly irrelevant and everything became the same thing, virtual, provisional, contingent and free of the horrid texture of the old days, so there was no way of telling what mattered any more and the future blurred and the present blurred and the past was irrelevant and they could be Big Babies happily together and so they were.

'And occasionally one of them thought: "This is all twaddle." But he was soon cheered up with a lovely new toy.'

CHAPTER 11

Mummy Is Everywhere, and Mummy Can See You

> James James
> Morrison Morrison
> Weatherby George Dupree
> Took great
> Care of his Mother,
> Though he was only three.
> James James
> Said to his Mother,
> 'Mother,' he said, said he;
> 'You must never go down to the end of the town,
> if you don't go down with me.'
> – A.A.Milne, 'Disobedience'

James James (believing himself to be an adult) may have taken great care of his Mother; but not half as much as we (realising that we are being infantilised) take of ours. He had no choice; we elected ours, either directly (the government) or by voting with our credit cards (the virtuoso infantilisers of the commercial Mummyverse) or simply by not punching them in the eye and running them out of town like mad cows or flu-ridden ducks.

Our tolerance is almost limitless, and that may yet be our

downfall. But we mustn't blame ourselves. We learnt it early on, when Mummy said 'Don't' and 'Put it down' and 'Leave it alone' and 'It won't get better if you pick at it' and 'I saw that' and 'Go to your room' and 'It'll drop off' and 'Don't blame me when your head caves in' and 'I want doesn't get' and 'You'll have someone's eye out with that' and 'One of these days you'll trip over your shoelace and kill yourself' and 'Go and see what the hell he's doing in there' and 'I told you so' and, of course, the Great Performative, the ultimate statement of power which all politicians, pundits, polemicists, health nazis, blue-sky brother-hood-of-man merchants and, of course, businessmen of all shades of moral improbity wish they, too, could deploy to the same effect:

'Because I say so.'

⚠ Recorded, computerised, insincere announcements are forever apologising for the inconvenience. But they never define it. What *is* this inconvenience we are being caused? Missing our next feed? Getting fractious? And why don't they stop causing it, if it's so awful?

It's the ultimate statement of power. As we've already mentioned, in early 2006, the British Government, under the very peculiar Tony Blair, attempted to shovel something called the Legislative and Regulatory Reform Bill through Parliament which would, if unchecked, have given them the power to pass laws without the frightful inconvenience of consulting Parliament, that shabby and disobliging collective of elected representatives.

Had they been more honest they would have simply called it the Because I Say So Bill and we would all have known where we stood. As it was, people were surprised to discover the extraordinary and unabashedly anti-democratic provisions buried in a Bill that the Government did all it could to present as a model of plodding dullness; which, history indicates, is generally the method by which dictators come into power; and so they knobbled it while they still had the chance.

Mr Blair was, of course, being a bad Mother: simultaneously treating the lot of us like Big Babies, and behaving like an even bigger one himself. But rather than thinking that egregious and peculiar, we might consider it as the root of the problem: that the people who wish to infantilise us are, if anything, even less grown-up than we are, and so their version of Mummy is an insecure, tyrannical, manipulative fishwife, a sort of older sibling imitating Mummy in order to be able to boss the younger ones around, and whose response to any problem is to lash out, shrieking – and not just in the political arena.

Big Babies like nothing more than throwing their weight around, and, in politics, the best way to do that is to ban things: junk food and fizzy drinks (though only in schools, where it looks good), end-of-exam parties at university, car advertisements which show people driving fast, knives, smoking, mobile-phone pornography, Australian wood which might have Australian bugs in, consensual sadomasochistic sex, seeds, unlicensed church fetes, beef, cloning, euthanasia . . . like a dog licking its privates, they do it because they can; and the same mechanism applies to the increasing web of surveillance inflicted on citizens on both sides of the Atlantic.

Surveillance – data collection, phone tapping, monitoring and any other, preferably undetectable and high-tech, method for invading people's privacy – is the absolute highest good that governments can imagine. Mummy wants to keep an eye on Baby all the time, and, while the innocent (as they always say) have nothing to fear, we should all fear the rapidity with which a government (even without the Because I Say So Act) can redefine the word 'guilty'. As Cardinal Richelieu said, 'Give me six lines written by the most honest man, and I will find something in them to hang him.' As Cardinal Richelieu might have added: 'But I won't tell him what it is he is being hanged for.' The

214

infantilised, after all, do not have enough rights to participate in their own governance. Their duty is merely to comply, and who has not been told by an irate parent: 'If you don't know what you've done, then I'm not telling you'?

Once, getting the knock on the door at 4 a.m., being pulled out of the line for questioning, being turned away at the boarding gate, having your documents demanded – *Papiere, bitte!* – or just simply disappearing, were marks of the police state. Now they are becoming increasingly common in the English-speaking West, in the form of immigration authorities responding to hysteria about 'the Other' in our midst, or police enforcing a protest-free cordon sanitaire around Parliament, or little old ladies being told they can't bring their knitting onto aeroplanes in case they overpower the pilots, or mysterious unmarked 'rendition' flights touching down in the dark.

You Can't Go Out Looking Like That

Even when those who have somehow upset Mummy are told why, the explanations can be absurd. American John Gilmore was on a British Airways flight taxiing for take-off at San Francisco airport when it was turned back to the gate and he was removed for wearing a one-inch lapel badge saying 'Suspected Terrorist' – a reasonable point to make given the rigours that Americans now have to go through before they can get on an aircraft. The aircraft captain allegedly told Gilmore that unless he removed the badge, he would be 'endangering the aircraft' and committing a federal crime. Gilmore was later told that he could fly only if he put the badge in his checked luggage, and had his carry-on bag searched to make sure that he wasn't carrying any spare badges which he might put on in mid-air, terrifying the passengers ('No! Help! Please God not a civil liberties activist!') and . . . *endangering the aircraft.*

When he attempted to find out from officials what sort of badge would be acceptable, he was told that a badge saying 'Hooray for Tony Blair' would probably be okay, but a badge saying 'Terrorism is evil' would not get onboard. Gilmore's attempts to find the middle ground were eventually stamped out by the station manager, who announced that she 'wasn't interested' in standing there making hypotheses all night, and it would be a harsh man who did not feel some sympathy with her. Gilmore, in his own account of the matter, comes across as what can best be described as a stroppy asshole, and it may be that most grown-ups would have simply taken the badge off rather than piss off three hundred passengers, delay the flight, inconvenience their girlfriend (who was also removed from the aircraft) and completely bugger up their trip.

> ⚠ Imagine that a grown woman who has had a flirtatious relationship with an even more grown man, goes to his room late in the evening for a drink and then presses charges against him for touching her in a sexual way without her consent ('May I have your consent to touch you in a sexual way?'). Not actual bodily harm; not rape or even attempted rape; not assault, so that she was afraid; no, imagine that this was merely *touching her in a sexual way without her consent*. Would you describe a woman who pressed those charges as a grown-up? Would you consider she was performing a service to other women, or, rather, that she is perpetuating the myth that women are timid, vulnerable, helpless victims all too easily scared by the massive phallocentric power of a MAN? *Any* MAN? And what would you think of the legal system which, instead of telling everyone involved to simply bugger off and grow up, proceeded to hear the case? (Theoretical question only. Such a thing could never really happen, could it?)

But a grown-up society should be able to tolerate stroppy assholes. It should be able to handle dissent with grace, and it should accord its members the respect of thinking them grownup enough to hold heterodox opinions without posing a lethal threat to society. To think otherwise is not merely infantile; it borders on Asperger's syndrome.

Don't Use Metaphor, It Confuses Me

In a pub in Cambridge sit two men, possibly, from their demeanour and earlier overheard conversation, chemical engineers. They are on to their third pint and into their stride, sitting diagonally opposite each other across a large table, both gazing fixedly at the floor. Their conversation goes like this:

> MAN 1: 'Of course Dr Beeching was the only Secretary of State for Transport who was in fact a railway enthusiast and was himself opposed to the lamentable destruction of the British branch line network imposed in his name.'

> MAN 2: 'The North German organ design system of Werkprinzip was not only architectural in its disposition of the Werke or departments of the instrument, but in its allocation of a differently pitched foundation to each department.'

> MAN 1: 'He was said to have been particularly interested in the Castle class locomotives.'

> MAN 2: 'The Hauptwerk, equivalent to the modern Great Organ, would have an eight-foot prinzipal as the foundation of its flue chorus.'

. . . And so it went on. They politely took it in turn to deliver their monologues, and the curious thing was that you knew they were having a lovely evening, and that when the pub closed they would go their separate ways, each thinking that the other had been on particularly good form and how nice it was to have a good old chat.

This, as we must all by now know, is a form of Asperger's syndrome, an odd variant wiring of the brain which causes people – it's not accurate to call them 'sufferers', although the rest of us can certainly make them suffer by simply not getting the point – to have trouble reading facial expressions (hence the careful avoidance of eye contact) or to be at ease with linguistic ambiguity. So, for example, they don't like metaphor, but prefer their communications to be strictly literal. Ask the more seriously Asperger's chap to put the kettle on and he will; but it will not occur to him to light the gas. If you had wanted the gas lit, would you not have said so?

Asperger's people make fine computer programmers, engineers, and mathematicians. Many of them learn to simulate social intuition and do very well in life, being indistinguishable from anyone else except for their extraordinary diligence and single-mindedness. Much of the modern world (and almost of all the computer infrastructure which drives it) would not exist were it not for the Asperger's people. But it is not the design you would choose for a brain good at negotiating the ambiguity of human relationships.

Join the Party and Rewire Your Brain

Looking at how politicians behave, we might well conclude they, too, are built on the Asperger's model. All too often their social behaviour seems carefully learnt; they seem curiously like a dog shaking hands – it's not that it doesn't do it quite well, just that it has no idea at all what it's for or why we do it. When we hear a Bush or a Blair make a joke to lighten the atmosphere, we also hear some inner dialogue box opening in their brain: 'Tell . . . Joke . . . Lighten . . . At-mos-phere . . . Click <OK> to con-ti-nue or <CANCEL> to can-cel.' When they play air guitar to show what regular guys they are, what they actually show is a certain semiotic ineptitude, since they usually give the odd effect of having had lessons. Not guitar lessons; *air guitar* lessons.

But they are not Asperger's people. Nobody with Asperger's would even contemplate the world of politics, dependent on schmoozing and dissembling, a world of words where a talent for ambiguity is the prerequisite of success. Yet see them in the mass and they are clearly, in some way, differently wired, and the only plausible explanation is that that have rewired themselves. Overwhelmed with a terrible neediness, these unpopular ones at school now desperate to get their own back, have stopped listening to what they themselves say in case it stops them in their tracks, and so have lost the ability to listen to anyone else, except in the most calculating way, just as some men know that if you listen to a woman until two in the morning, she will go to bed with you.

Politicians – it's a generalisation, but the buggers generalise about us, so serve them right – use 'thoughts' like men in pubs use jokes: as a substitute for thinking, and as a duelling weapon. Just as the man telling a joke is surrounded by other men in a state of barely contained fury, waiting for the punchline so that they can leap in with their joke, so politicians regard others' words as a temporary block on their own. Poised to spring, they cannot hear what others are telling them; locked in the belief that others are just Big Babies, of no consequence, they do not want to; locked into their own desperate infantility, they could not allow themselves to, no more than a real baby can pause to consider whether Mummy might have other things to do.

And so the brain gets rewired in this strange pseudo-Asperger's, and reason goes out of the window and the great question 'Why?' is never asked. 'Why?' means shutting up and waiting for the answer, but to shut up and wait for the answer would mean not talking, and the world would come to an end as the Big Babies – us – go completely to pieces on the instant.

Just as Long as You Are Who You Say You Are

The obsession with identity and security springs, as much as from anywhere, from these two roots: that left to our own devices we will run riot and flood the fragile world of political control with terrible ambiguity (it's not just terrorism; it's dissent), and that identity and action are somehow linked. The first idea is infantilising, and the second is simply absurd. Our formal 'identity' is nothing to do with our actual identity. I may be so-and-so, born on such-and-such a day in such-and-such a place, with this particular National Insurance number and that particular DNA, but none of these affect how I am, how I think or how I behave: those are the products of events and experiences which no database, biometric or not, can ever record or predict. To suggest that having a national network of identity cards will somehow prevent terrorism, crime or antisocial behaviour is absurd, and has been acknowledged as absurd by politicians. Nobody who thinks of blowing himself up is going to refrain from blowing himself up because someone knows who he is.

But still they move inexorably towards a national database of DNA; still they move towards mandatory fingerprinting and biometric identity cards; still they produce their unpersuasive assertions that no private companies will be able to get their hands on our data and mine it for their own purposes. Still 9/11 is cited as the reason: the barbarians are at the gates and we are all doomed. Difficult times lead to hard laws.

A Dead Language, But Not This One

Let's take a bit of Latin: *dictator rei gerendae causa*. It means 'dictator during the matter in hand'.

Being dictator overrode the major principle of collegiality in the Republic of Rome, around two thousand years ago. The principle was this: you didn't have one man in charge of anything. For extraordinary reasons, though, or in extraordinary times, you might suspend that principle for up to six months, or for however long the war lasted, whichever was the shorter.

And the Roman Republic didn't even particularly like that. After the Second Punic War, they outlawed the office of dictator altogether, instead granting extraordinary powers to the two current consuls. Checks and balances. Good thinking. But here comes Sulla, fallen out with Gaius Marius and marching on Rome. Gets himself appointed to a new dictatorship, one he invented for himself: *rei publicae constituendae causa*, 'for the reconstituting of the republic'. Same thing, but no time limit. Times of perpetual emergency, do you see? Can't tell when Johnny Enemy may strike, or where. Johnny Enemy may be within or without. May be moving among us as we speak. May be sneaking across the borders. Action needs to be taken. Normal procedures suspended. Things back to normal as soon as threat dies down. Can't tell when that will be. The innocent have nothing to fear. National security. Intelligence. Briefings. No weapons of mass destruction, but if there had been, Johnny Enemy would have had them.

Powers, you see. That's the answer: special powers.

First it's *rei gerendae*, then it's *rei publicae constituendae*, and, fiddle how you like, powers, once invented, are seldom willingly resigned. You'll not want to be insulted with the old saw about the lessons of history, but this is an old one and perhaps needs dusting off. There was a direct line from Sulla to the raft of emperors which followed, one after another, until Rome both ex- and im-ploded, and hello to the Dark Age.

Special powers.

⚠ 'A retired businesswoman accused of turning an idyllic rural community into a "hamlet of horrors" has been given an anti-social behaviour order.

'Jeanne Wilding, 57, was described as "running a campaign of hatred and pure evil" in Bottomley, West Yorkshire.

'A judge at Calderdale Magistrates' Court granted Calderdale Council the Asbo against the ex-financial manager.

'Her acts of "mental torture" included damaging vehicles, setting booby traps and placing dead animals in the road.

'The case involved more than 250 incidents in under sixteen months.

'Deputy District Judge Sandra Keen said Miss Wilding, who walked out part way through Thursday's hearing, had "little or no appreciation" of the effect her behaviour had on other people. She said: "If her views are challenged she responds in a wholly inappropriate manner. She takes a confrontational stance, causing others harassment or distress. Her view is there's nothing anti-social in how she behaves."

'Her behaviour included loudly playing a choral work "about rape, pillage and the trashing of villages", damaging neighbours' vehicles, booby-trapping pot plants and tipping oil over her neighbour's drive at night.

'Danielle Graham, representing Miss Wilding, said, "Can you really apply an anti-social behaviour order in order to change someone's personality?"' (BBC News, 18 May 2006)

And the thing about special powers is they cease to be special (times of war! constitutional crisis! the enemy at the gates! the enemy within! the Axis of Evil!) but remain as powers. The process, like some grim fractal of imperium, runs at every level. When did the government – any government – last repeal a law, except to replace it with further, more draconian ones? Each of them little laws, pissant laws, laws of no importance except (exceptional circumstances!) they are laws, and they simultaneously require and legitimise the extended application of power.

And it's a short step from laws about no rare hamburgers and no fireworks to laws about identity cards and imprisonment without trial, from being told what we can do to being told what the state can do, which is anything the dictator says it can do.

But the Cart Is Meant to Be Before the Horse

America spies on all its citizens' telephone calls, Britain is building the most invasive database ever (one the Soviets or the Maoists would have killed for, and indeed did kill for, but all the same didn't actually get), there are cameras everywhere, we are tracked and corralled and monitored as surely as any baby in the nursery playpen, and we make the mistake of believing that this is about security.

We are mistaken. Security is about all this. There was a time (was there?) when the law existed to enshrine various rights: for example, the right not to be killed as you went about your business, and the right of rich people to tell everyone else to fuck off. The rest of it – constabularies, watchmen, narks, bailiffs, dossiers, interrogation rooms and so on – was there to support the implementation of the law.

Now, things have subtly changed. More and more, the law exists to ratify surveillance. Governments do not enact laws and then consider how to enforce them; governments begin with the idea of enforcement, and work back to the laws that would legitimise it.

It is almost, though not quite, the Holy Grail.
It is almost: 'Because I say so.'

It's Our Own Fault for Not Bracing Up

But we don't listen, either, otherwise we would surely have risen in the streets before now. I know very few people who do not feel deeply disenfranchised by the current political system. Most of us feel we are not being listened to. But after the fury – whichever side you were on – that Parliament and public demonstrations over the invasion of Iraq were simply ignored, most of us have also retreated into a sullen impotence. We have had our tantrum. We have screamed 'Not fair! LISTEN TO ME! Won't! Shan't! You MUSTN'T!' and have been sent back to the nursery.

> ⚠ **Novelty comedy fun whacky downloadable ringtones. After much discussion late into the night, we have reached the conclusion that the crucial question here is: why?**

What do we do now? Without intelligent discourse we have had it, but politics hardly offers the possibility for discourse, intelligent or not. Politics has learnt its lesson from commerce and its nursery world of made-up names ('Innogy') and grandiose pronouncements and strangulated language. Sometimes they come together, as in this pronouncement from someone called Martin Ball, who is the Head of Public Affairs for something which, he is explaining, is now to be called 'Together: Working for Wellbeing':

To help readers understand the thinking behind our new identity it will be useful for them to know that our chief executive, Gil Hitchon, went on to say 'We chose "together" because it is a modern, inclusive name that says "we are all in this together", whether service users, carers, families, friends, staff or working partners.' So, while we have the experience of 126 years of delivering services to draw upon, we now have a marvellous new mission for the future.'

Is this a company, talking down to us? Is it a charity? Is it government? Who is it, treating us like stupid, gullible babies? One feels dreadfully sorry for Mr Ball, who is undoubtedly a nice, affable chap trying to do his best, but with this sort of thing floating about as an acceptable thing to say in public, we might be forgiven for thinking that political idiocy is just a bigger and more vicious manifestation of a wider flood of stupidity, beneath whose onslaught we might as well give up, suck our thumbs, stroke our blankies and wait quietly for death. Mummy would understand.

CHAPTER 12

Why Don't We All
Just Grow Up?

In the eighteenth and nineteenth centuries, the Viennese had a
curious preoccupation with the *schöne Leiche*: the beautiful corpse.
To be beautiful, elegant, moving, more life-like in the coffin than
in life was a wonder; people would flock to view you; nothing in
your life became you like the leaving of it. The only problem
was, to be a *schöne Leiche*, you first had to die.

We have moved on.

In 2005, plastic surgeons in the USA raked in a little over $2
billion in fees for nose jobs, Botox injections and liposuction.* But
the fashion is moving towards more dramatic interventions:
swathes of superfluity slashed from the living flesh. Once you've
had your stomach stapled off so that you cannot eat as you once
ate, hundreds of pounds may fall away, leaving frills, aprons,
ruches, whole crinolines of loose skin hanging, folded, like the
great rugose cones of the 'Old Ones', humanity's precursors in
H. P. Lovecraft's tormented imagination.

Lovecraft's monstrosities retreated underground. We scuttle,
flapping, to the plastic surgeon, to be reshaped into a beautiful
corpse: we make ourselves fat, someone else makes us thin, inside
we remain unchanged, and in the long run, we find ourselves,

---

* *Wired News*, 15 May 2006.

outraged *in articulo mortis* – how can this be? – dead. And, for the Big Baby generation, the long run is shorter than we think. We have colluded for so long with the infantilisers who, babies themselves, want to make us into bigger, more docile ones, that time is running out. Affronted, nervous, supervised, timid, self-obsessed, disgruntled, ticked off, bossed about and up to our ears in debt, our only hope is to grow up, and to do it fast.

Et in Arcadia ego

It is said that, when the great Frank Zappa was expiring from prostate cancer, he observed to a friend that it was all rather odd. 'You try to be good at your work,' he said, 'and look after your family and do your bit, and then suddenly there you are, dying; and you think . . . you think: *What the fuck was that all about?*'

It is the modern way; it is the ageless, inchoate, animal instinct of the Big Babies. Poussin might as well not have bothered with his tomb-paintings; whether the gnomic inscription *Et in Arcadia ego* meant that the tomb's inhabitant was in Paradise, or that Death was there too, or that the corpse had once romped and tootled in the pastoral Arcadia so central to the deluded Romantic imagination, his message is lost on us. We no longer divert ourselves with such speculations, preferring instead (and having the technology and the money) to go straight from the arrested and indefinitely prolonged infantility of adolescence to the condition of the *schöne Leiche* while still above ground. The tomb concealed the rot, and earlier imaginations could project a transfigured body somehow housed within the marble, whether actual (made lovely by the embalmer's art) or metonymic, poised in its incipient glory, awaiting the General Resurrection. 'In a flash, at a trumpet crash, This Jack, joke, poor potsherd, patch, matchwood, immortal diamond,/Is immortal diamond.'

But we can't wait for that. Why, if we waited for the trumpet to sound, we might be here – or, worse, not be here – for ever. Big Babies that we are, we cannot imagine the world without us, cannot imagine it going on, our places being taken, an indefinite future in which we will only be a memory. What we know is that this corruptible must put on incorruption, and this mortal must put on immortality, and if it's a question of money, why, one can always find the money. Doesn't the American Express Company tell us so? If you can imagine it, we can get you there, it lies, like Daddy (like a bad Daddy, like a sugar-Daddy: *spread 'em for Poppa*) demonstrating his power, peeling off a wad from his bankroll, not mentioning the day of reckoning which will come, not with the sound of trumpets but of threats, phone calls, writs fluttering through the letter box like Manila Furies.

And off we go (*This is a credit agreement. Only sign if you agree to be bound by its terms*) for the magical injections which will stop time, the Botox which immobilises expression, which freezes and embalms while, beneath it, our dissolution continues. Life itself is the *sarcophagus* – literally, the 'flesh-eater' – but we can't be doing with that. Forever young, we pursue the romantic utopia of perpetual potency, living the Advertised Life which holds out an unachievable synthesis of the brainless body-beautiful, high-altitude gourmet canoeing with penguins in the shadow of Table Mountain with a five-star toy-boy waiting in the tropical Ferrari, a sun-bronzed Savile Row professional chef's leather sofa drinking imported Jeep beer in a rural cottage-style apartment in uptown Patek Phillipe to ban arthritis for ever with farm-grown organic Campari for the sportsman who has everything except Sperry Gold Cup Top-Siders with Gold Eyelets and Deerskin Linings . . . Antigua! The Côte d'Azur! Mayfair! Turn left on boarding! Personal banker! And, of course . . .

. . . the nose job and the chemical peel and the breast implants and the knob job and the tummy-tuck and the buttock-lift and the gym and the trainer and the antioxidants and the man-tan and the sound bite and the PR person and the colour consultant and the endless, endless striving to become, even when, by all that's diabolical, we became long ago, and now we're slowly undoing, buried above ground in our locked-in, vap-O-sealed aspirational perfection.

Because Life is for Living.

Et in Arcadia ego . . . NOT.

How Not to Be a Big Baby

Harassed to death, treated like silly greedy kids if we're lucky, and bad naughty kids who need to have an eye kept on us (biometrics, risk assessments, the Innocent Have Nothing to Fear) if we're not, we have all had enough of not being good enough. We long to be grown-up: autonomous, comfortable in our skin, left to our own devices. But how do we do it?

> A paper entitled 'Toward a Feminist Algebra' by Maryanne Campbell and Randall K. Campbell-Wright calls for an end to sexist stereotypes in college algebra textbooks. Problems which used examples of a girl and her boyfriend running towards each other were denounced for portraying heterosexual involvement. On the other hand, they recommended approval of problems about Sue and Debbie, 'a couple financing their $70,000 home'. They wanted algebra problems to present female heroes, to analyse sex differences and to affirm women's experiences. They set out to prove that metaphor plays a central role in the language of mathematics, offering verbal examples culled from textbooks – 'manipulate an algebraic expression', 'attack a problem', 'exploit a theorem' – as evidence that mathematics is a nest of aggression, violence, domination and sexism and that it 'is portrayed as a woman whose nature desires to be the conquered Other'. (Keith Windschuttle, 'Higher Superstition', *The Australian*, January 1995)

Rule number one: stop trusting people who tell us How Not to Be a Big Baby. Stop trusting people who tell us how to do, or not to do, anything. We have all served our time under those who brought us up, telling us how to do, or not to do, things, and we don't have to swallow any more of it.

And note, too, that we have to say 'those who brought us up'. We can't say 'parents' because some people weren't raised by their parents, and might find the word 'parents' homophobic or racist or inegalitarian or, heaven help us all, inappropriate. And we have to say 'heaven help us' because, although what we may want to say is 'God help us', there may be people who do not believe in God, or believe in a different God, or who believe in God so much more than we do that they can't even mention his name. Which is silly. It's as if a man were to say to someone, 'Meet my wife. I can't tell you her name because I love her.' But we can't say it's silly because someone who believes it will be very, very offended if we say it's silly. We can't say anything is silly, really, because it might be inappropriate.

And anything might be inappropriate. A friend (A) got into terrible trouble for asking someone (B) if she believed in witches and demonic possession. This, apparently, was racist. The exchange went on like this:

A: Why is it racist?

B: Because you are suggesting that black people are primitive when you ask me if I believe in witches and possession.

A: But an awful lot of evangelical African churches believe in witches and possession.

B: Yes.

A: And you are a member of an evangelical African church, so it's not unreasonable to ask if you believe in witches and demonic possession.

B: Yes it is. It's making racist assumptions. I find it offensive.

A: But do you believe in witches?

B: Yes.

A: And demonic possession?

B: Yes.

A: Well, I find that offensive. And silly.

B: You're a racist.

So when we say we have to stop listening to people who tell us how and what to do and what not to do, that includes – that particularly includes – people who say things are 'inappropriate' or 'offensive', which are just particularly sneaky and imperious ways of bossing us about.

That having been said, how can we break free from the tyranny of the Mummyverse and its instigators – the puling, yawling generation of self-absorbed, thick, selfish, smug, bullying infants who want to make us into even Bigger Babies than they are? (And anyone who finds any of it inappropriate or offensive gets an automatic fail and is thereby condemned to be a Big Baby for ever.)

How Not to be a Big Baby (II): Fifty Ways to Leave Your Mother

1. Time we all let go of Nurse / There's not a hope of finding worse. The vested interest lies in restricting our autonomy. Autonomy is the primary marker of being grown-up. Babies, children and adolescents don't have any. We don't want to be in their boat.

2. *Cui bono?* The media isn't about us. It's about them: the people who produce it, and the people who fund it. We are merely so much maize, growing in the cash-fields, ripening to be harvested.

3. Don't be affronted. Being affronted (or offended, or complaining about 'inappropriateness') is no response for a grown-up. Only children believe the world should conform to their own view of it: a sort of magical

thinking which can only lead to warfare, terrorism,
unmanageable short-term debt and the Blair/Bush
alliance.

4. Mistrust anything catchy, whether it's the Axis of
Evil, advertising slogans, acronymic legislation ('the
US PATRIOT act') or blatant branding ('New
Labour'). Catchiness exists to prevent thought
and to disguise motive. Grown-ups can think for
themselves.

5. Ignore celebrities, except when they are doing what
they are celebrated for doing: acting, playing football,
singing et cetera. Skill does not confer moral, political
or intellectual discrimination. (Except in the case of
writers. Writers know everything and can lecture
us – lecture you, in this case – with impunity.)

6. If a celebrity is not celebrated for doing anything,
but being a celebrity, smile politely but pay them no
mind.

7. We should not assume that market forces will decide
wisely. The market is rigged by manipulation and
infantilisation.

8. Whenever we read something, we should ask ourselves:
'Who wrote this? And why?' And we should then try to
imagine the circumstances of its composition. American
Airlines' new slogan is 'After all, life is a journey.' Before
we ask ourselves whether it's true, we should imagine
the executives from American Airlines in their offices
and their suits; we should imagine the briefing to the ad
agency, the psychological profiling, the thousands of
very expensive 'creative' hours, and the objectives of the
exercise. We would no longer comply if dodgy Uncle
Peebles said 'Put your hand here,' so why do we nod
sagely when an airline company says 'After all, life is a
journey'?

> ⚠ '[The] modern mind has become more and more calculating. The calculative exactness of practical life which the money economy has brought about corresponds to the ideal of natural science: to transform the world into an arithmetic problem, to fix every part of the world by mathematical formulas. Only money economy has filled the days of so many people with weighing, calculating, with numerical determinations, with a reduction of qualitative values to quantitative ones.' (Georg Simmel, 'The Metropolis and Mental Life' in *Readings in Social Theory*, ed. James Farganis)
>
> Or, rather, only money economy *and infantilism*. ('Mummy, I got three sweety! Mummy, Lucy got more an me! Mummy, I gone up this stair in eleventy goes! Mummy . . .')

9. Only then should we consider the proposition itself. Is life a journey? No. Bollocks. Life is a biological process distinguished by complexity and self-replication. Because of strictly local conditions, some instances of *Homo sapiens* have chosen to choose the journey as a metaphor for a particular view of human life, occurring in *The Epic of Gilgamesh* and made explicit by Dante. But for an airline to tell us life is a journey (and note, particularly, that chummy, we're-all-in-the-same-boat 'After all . . .') is tripe. What they mean is 'Help! Buy tickets! Go somewhere! Anywhere! We need your money.'

10. Whenever we are bossed about, remember Air Traffic Control. In particular, we should remember the pilot who, confronted with a controller who was being grumpily and deliberately unhelpful, asked, with great courtesy: 'Are you down there because we are up here . . . or am I mistaken and it's actually vice versa?'

233

11. Consider our own motivations. We may rail about being treated like children, ordered about, kept from the truth, nannied and exploited . . . but are we complicit in it? Could the reward actually be the infantilisation itself? Waa! Waa! A-goo! Waa!

12. Suspect administration. Its purpose is to free the organisation to do what it's meant to do; but the triumph of the adminstrators – the lawyers, the accountants, the professional managers – means that too many organisations now believe that what they are meant to do is administer themselves. This is a profoundly infantile attitude, although they dress it up as 'the real world'. Only the infantile believe that the world is there for them.

13. Do not love yourself unconditionally. Unconditional love is for babies and comes from their mothers. When we try to love ourselves unconditionally, we go in for self-aggrandising which no normally integrated personality can bear, and the result is something like George W. Bush, Donald Rumsfeld, Paul Wolfowitz, Tony Blair, John Prescott . . . If they had thought a little less of themselves, they might not have ended up with quite such a babyish sense of entitlement.

14. Self-hatred is a problem, too. But rather too much self-hatred than too much self-love.

15. Denounce that sententious *Desiderata* that people have hanging in their lavatories. It was a fake anyway. We may possibly get away with going placidly among the noise and haste (though that will only make us into sitting ducks) but we should not delude ourselves that we are a child of the universe, empiricism alone should persuade us of that: the people of the hippy era (who, whether hippies or not, were defined in relation to hippydom – not least by all those dreadful 'psychedelic' graphics) are now running the show and look what a pig they're making of it.

234

16. Ignore fashion, particularly in music. Even if some of us may be unfortunate enough to be locked into the impoverished discourse of mainstream pop, we should have the grace to stick with the stuff we like when we were young, and not try to keep up with the stuff the young like now. It spoils it for them (what could be worse than a greying parent announcing that they love Eminem too?) and spoils us by forcing us to engage with something which should be beyond (or below) our cultural radar. A middle-aged person Keeping Up with the Trends in Music is as lamentable and as infantile as a middle-aged person in Lycra.

17. Ignore fashion, particularly in clothes. *GQ* is not our friend and it is not on our side. It is there to sell advertising, so it encourages us to buy the stuff it flogs so that, in turn, it can go to its advertisers and say 'Look: our readers buy lots of the clothes you guys are flogging. Yes, they're shlubs, but they're extravagant shlubs, and business is business, so place your advertising with us.'

18. The same applies to women. Only more so. You don't want to look like a teenager forever. When men were all over you like a cheap suit you complained. Now they're not, you complain. Not only do you complain, you eat nothing – a lettuce leaf and a spritz of Badoit is not food, it's a tantrum – and go to the gym and have plastic surgery and end up looking like someone sucked into a black hole, leaving only their ghostly image frozen at the event horizon for ever. This is not dignified; ask any planet.

19. Denounce relativism at every turn. Shouting 'not fair' is childish. Demanding respect without earning it is childish. Believing that other people's religious beliefs should not be mocked is to devalue all religious beliefs; if we believe that our religious beliefs are right, we must by definition believe that people who diverge from those beliefs are wrong and that we should therefore bring

them to the error of their ways by pointing out that, for example, while witches and demonic possession are simply silly, transubstantiation and papal infallibility are not. And if we do not believe that our religious beliefs are right, we have no business holding them anyway, and should just give up and be agnostic.

20. Being agnostic is a very grown-up thing to be. It stops us throwing our weight around ('Our god is WHITE. Your god is a WOG. We are therefore going to impose bicameral legislature on you by force of arms') while allowing us a simulacrum of the comforts of religion ('Actually I rather like the preconciliar Tridentine rite myself, given that it's all much of a muchness in the long run').

21. We should distrust those who believe they have found Jesus. Can they prove it? Otherwise, they're just describing an imaginary friend, of which there is nothing more infantile.

22. We should distrust ourselves if we believe God loves us. At best, God tolerates us, and his self-interest is at the root of it. Our job is to safeguard our souls for God to enjoy being with in due course, much like someone looking after someone else's dog. ('I'm afraid it got humped by a retriever and it's pregnant now.' 'Depart from me, ye accursèd, into everlasting fire.') And anyway the relationship is terribly asymmetric, not to mention explicitly infantilising and, quite possibly, inappropriate.

23. Don't fear seriousness. Babies aren't allowed to be serious, and the infantilised adolescent confuses seriousness with po-faced solemnity. The world of Big Babies is too often earnest about trivia; far better to make jokes about important things, which is as good a way of being serious as any. That we can be thrown into prison for making bomb jokes at airports is as good an indication as any of how bad things have become.

24. Watch our language. Children play with language because so much of it floats delicately above any sort of semiotic correspondence; but is there really much difference between a six-year-old in a fright-wig and a pair of his father's waders shouting 'I'm the Mighty Wurgle-Burgle-Urgley-Goo' and an ostensible grown-up demanding to be called 'Tony Blair's Respect Czar'? If something looks too good and slick to be true, it probably *isn't* true; but unfortunately this is the language in which much of politics and most of twenty-first century business is conducted. If it doesn't mean anything, or if it means something which isn't true, it is an attempt to pull the wool over our eyes and that's something grown-ups don't tolerate.

25. Hide. Grown-ups are not required to be perpetually accountable, while the instincts of government and big business, both of which are, almost by their nature, great infantilisers, are to keep an eye on everyone all the time. They come wrapped in a cosy blanket of excuses and falsehoods – loyalty benefits, air miles, national security, protection against identity theft, safety – but all these things are excuses for surveillance.

26. Eat it up. There is nothing more babyish than having dietary requirements. We can choose what to eat in our own homes; we can select from the menu in a restaurant. But when we are fed by other people, it is not only infantile but the sheerest bad manners to express any opinion on the food whatsoever. Babies can't eat this, hate that, are allergic to the other and suffer from general intolerances. Grown-ups eat what we are given, leave (without a word) what we don't like, and are glad to have been invited. On which subject:

27. Cultivate commensality. The art of dining together is one of the great cornerstones of civilisation. The word 'companion' derives from the Latin for one you share

237

bread with. The Jewish sabbath begins with the sharing of bread, wine and salt; the Christian communion is a sharing of bread and wine; shared food marks us out as grown-ups and walking along the street shoving wads of oily, slick, grey stenchburger into our mouths, lettuce falling, 'special' sauce* squelching, onions reeking, jaws grinding, jumbo Coke clutched in podgy hand, Mine! Mine food! Mine food! Mine! marks us as infantile. The same applies to the dog-faced businessmen on the commuter trains, cramming railway food into their gobs, splattering burger-mulch into their yakking mobiles, delivering the message that they don't care about their fellow passengers; that they are alone and unaware of our shared humanity. Babies have to be fed in public; their needs are urgent; ours are not, and we should wait until we are with friends or family, and eat like civilised men.

28. Never do business with a company offering 'solutions'. It is a pernicious weasel-word, not just because it is pompous and self-aggrandizing (*Private Eye* monitors its use assiduously, identifying such perversions as 'Alternative Sitting provides ergonomic furniture solutions which minimise the postural strain associated with sitting' – chairs; and 'Post Office Mailing Solutions' – brown paper) but also because it is telling us that we have a problem. That, since we are grown-ups, is for us to decide.

29. Never vote for, patronise, do business with or be pleasant to anyone who uses the words 'ordinary people'. The invariable assumptions are (a) that they themselves are, my dear, far from ordinary, and (b) that 'ordinary people' are infants, fools, gulls, fodder. (You may note

---

* 'Special' serves a similar function here to the one it performs in the phrase 'special clinic', where you go when you've got the clap.

that if this rule is followed to its logical conclusion, we would not be able to vote for anyone. Very well. As the late Auberon Waugh observed, the desire to hold political office should of itself be reason enough to disbar one from even running.)

⚠ Go into a McDonald's. Ask for a Big Mac. (You will not have to go through with the purchase, never fear.) The unfortunate behind the counter, emblazoned with the appalling corporate lie 'I'm Lovin' It' (the terminal 'g' on 'loving' might upset us) will automatically say: 'Just the burger?'

Go into any chain coffee shop. Ask for a cup of coffee. 'Do you want any pastries or biscotti with that today?'

Baby doesn't know his own mind. Baby forgets to say, 'And fries! And a milk shake! And onion rings! And one of those horrid ice-cream things with bits of greasy "chocolate" swirled up in it through a gynaecology spoon! And biscotti! And pastries!'

Adults, on the other hand, say: 'Please advise your manager that if I'd wanted it, I'd have asked for it. Thank you for your trouble. I do hope things work out for you.' And leave.

---

30. Demand – and display – good manners. Manners are vital to civilisation and are what distinguish the infantile from the grown-up. How many of our troubles are caused by lack of manners? Probably most of them, the rest being caused by silliness. Bad manners include: shouting, whining, violence, making scenes, telling lies, manipulating the other guy, telling lies when you've been found out manipulating the other guy, seeking power over the other guy, exercising power over the

other guy, sneaking things into the small print, suicide bombing, eating in the street, being an iPod iDiot, assuming false familiarity, invading other people's privacy, invading other people's countries, throwing your weight around, discounting others' humanity, demanding more than your share, swearing, not controlling your anger, pushing in, elbowing aside, smelling bad, appearing ill-dressed in public, smirking, pointing, sneaking, poking your nose in, officiousness, being a bore, being a boor, occupying more than your share of space, putting yourself first and looking down on others.

31. Never trust an estimate. Big Babies are gullible. Only a Big Baby would have believed that this list would really contain fifty items just because I said so. Do you think I have nothing better to do than fulfil my promises? I have a life! I have needs! You are nothing to me! I want food! I want *special* food! I want it now! I want to read the newspaper and find people to hate! I want my prejudices confirmed! I want to go *shopping!* I want more money! I want consumer goods and false reports and secret information! Shut up! *Shut up!* Now! Or I'll . . . I'll . . . I'll hold my breath *until I turn blue!* And that will show you. Fifty I promised, thirty-one you'll get.

It's Really Very Simple

We could at this stage go in for a long and intricate summing-up, citing evidence and summarising our arguments, but we won't. We're tired of Big Babies – even though we are, at least some of the time, implicated ourselves – and we want it to stop. We want (don't we?) to grow up.

Here's the simple answer:

Watch carefully, ask why, and mind our manners.

It's really that simple. How would it be if everyone did it? It would be grown-up. And wouldn't that be better than to slowly sink, a gaggle of Big Babies giggling – a-goo! a-goo! – into the endless sea of infantility?

Thank you for your attention. It's been delightful. Have a nice day.

Selected Bibliography

Abrams, Fran, *Below the Breadline: Living on the Minimum Wage* (London: Profile Books, 2002)

Ackroyd, Peter, *Shakespeare: The Biography* (London: Chatto, 2005)

— *London: The Biography* (London: Chatto, 2000)

— *Albion: The Origins of the English Imagination* (London: Chatto, 2002)

al-Zayyat, Montasser, Sara Nimis, *et al.*, *The Road to Al-Qaeda: The Story of Bin Laden's Right-Hand Man* (Critical Studies on Islam) (London: Pluto Press, 2004)

Arnold, Catharine, *Necropolis: London and Its Dead* (London and New York: Simon & Schuster, 2006)

Auster, Paul, *The Book of Illusions* (London: Faber, 2003)

Bakan, Joel, *The Corporation: The Pathological Pursuit of Profit and Power* (London: Constable, 2004)

Barber, Paul, *Vampires, Burial and Death: Folklore and Reality* (New Haven: Yale University Press, 1988)

Baron, Alexander, *The Computerised Identity Card: Harbinger of the Coming Repression* (London: InfoText Manuscripts, 1997)

Barthes, Roland, *Mythologies* (London: Vintage, 1993)

Bartholomew, Robert E., and Hilary Evans, *Panic Attacks: Media Manipulation and Mass Delusion* (Stroud: Sutton, 2004)

Bayley, Stephen, *A Dictionary of Idiocy* (London: Gibson Square, 2004)

Bhabha, Homi, *The Location of Culture* (London: Routledge, 2004)

Blackburn, Simon, 'Would I Have Gone to Cambridge in Clarke's Brave New World?', *Independent on Sunday*, 26 January 2003

Bly, Robert, *Iron John: Men and Masculinity* (London: Rider, 1990)

Brown, Donald E., *Hierarchy, History, and Human Nature: The Social Origins of Historical Consciousness* (Tucson: University of Arizona Press, 1988)

242

Bunting, Madeleine, *Willing Slaves: How the Overwork Culture is Ruling Our Lives* (London: Harper Perennial, 2005)

Burke, Colin, *Information and Secrecy: Vannevar Bush, Ultra, and the Other Memex* (Metuchen, NJ, and London: Scarecrow Press, 1994)

Burr, Chandler, *The Emperor of Scent: A Story of Perfume, Obsession and the Last Mystery of the Senses* (London: Heinemann, 2003)

Bywater, Michael, *Lost Worlds: What Have We Lost and Where Has it Gone?* (London: Granta, 2004)

Cannadine, David, *In Churchill's Shadow: Confronting the Past in Modern Britain* (London: Allen Lane/Penguin, 2002)

Carr, Simon, *The Hop Quad Dolly* (London: Hutchinson, 1991)

Carroll, Paul, *Big Blues: The Unmaking of IBM* (London: Weidenfeld & Nicolson, 1994)

Carter, Graydon, *What We've Lost* (London and New York: Little, Brown, 2004)

Chen, Milton, 'Television as a Tool', *Talking with Kids* <http://snipurl.com/lrk0> (accessed 3 March 2006)

Christakis, Dimitri A., Frederick J. Zimmerman, *et al.*, 'Early Television Exposure and Subsequent Attentional Problems in Children', *Pediatrics* 113 No. 4 (April 2004)

Chua, Daniel, *Absolute Music and the Construction of Meaning* (Cambridge: Cambridge University Press, 1999)

Classen, Constance, David Honer, *et al.*, *Aroma: The Cultural History of Smell* (London: Routledge, 1994)

Colbert, Dan, *What Would Jesus Eat?* (Nashville: Thomas Nelson, 2002)

Corbin, Jane, *The Base: Al-Qaeda and the Changing Face of Global Terror* (New York: Simon & Schuster, 2003)

Coren, Giles, *Winkler* (London: Jonathan Cape, 2005)

Cornwell, John, 'Don't Stress for Dinner: Eating Together as a Family Could Prevent Crime and Adolescent Depression.' *Sunday Times* (London), 1 September 2002, Magazine 46–50

Craik, Dinah Maria [Miss Mulock], *John Halifax, Gentleman* (New York: Thomas Crowell, 1897)

Crump, Thomas, *A Brief History of Science* (New York: Carroll & Gray, 2001)

'Current Beliefs Among the American Public', <http://www.religious-tolerance.org/aft_bibl2.htm> (accessed 4 April 2004)

Davenport, Thomas H., and John C. Beck, *The Attention Economy: Understanding the New Currency of Business* (Cambridge, MA: Harvard Business School Press, 2001)

Davenport-Hines, Richard, *The Pursuit of Oblivion: A Global History of Narcotics, 1500–2000* (London: Weidenfeld & Nicolson, 2001)

Despres, Charles, and Daniel Chauvel, eds., *Knowledge Horizons: The Present and the Promise of Knowledge Management*, (Boston, MA, and Oxford: Butterworth Heinemann, 2002)

Eamon, William, *Science and the Secrets of Nature: Books of Secrets in Medieval and Early Modern Culture* (Princeton: Princeton University Press, 1994)

Ehrenreich, Barbara, *Nickel and Dimed: Undercover in Low-Wage USA* (London: Granta, 2002)

Finkelstein, Daniel, 'Dozy? No skills? Unavailable? Then the Job's All Yours', *The Times*, 29 September 2004

Frank, Thomas, *What's the Matter With America? The Resistible Rise of the American Right* (London: Secker & Warburg, 2004)

Franken, Al, *Lies and the Lying Liars Who Tell Them: A Fair and Balanced Look at the Right* (London: Penguin, 2004)

Frean, Alexander, 'You Think You Know What's Cool in Britain? Well You Could be in For a Shock', *The Times*, 29 September 2004

Friedman, David M., *A Mind of Its Own: A Cultural History of the Penis* (London: Robert Hale, 2003)

Gelernter, David, *The Aesthetics of Computing* (London: Weidenfeld and Nicolson, 1998)

Giles, Judy, and Tim Middleton, eds., *Writing Englishness, 1900–1950*, (London: Routledge, 1995)

The Epic of Gilgamesh, trans. N. K. Sandars (London: Penguin, 1972)

Gladwell, Malcolm, *The Tipping Point: How Little Things Can Make a Big Difference* (London: Abacus, 2001)

Glor, Eleanor D., 'Innovation Traps: Risks and Challenges in Thinking about Innnovation', <http://www.inovation.cc/peer-reviewed/glor-ethics.pdf> (2002)

Grant, Richard, *Ghost Riders: Travels with American Nomads* (London: Little, Brown, 2003)

Greenfield, Susan, *Tomorrow's People: How 21st-Century Technology is Changing the Way We Think and Feel* (London: Allen Lane/Penguin, 2003)

Guest, Katy, 'Revenge.com: How the Internet Fuels the Battle of the Exes', *Independent on Sunday*, 26 September 2004

Haig, Matt, *Brand Failures: The Truth About the 100 Biggest Branding Mistakes of All Time* (London: Kogan, 2003)

Harris, Sam, *The End of Faith: Religion, Terror and the Future of Reason* (New York: Norton, 2004)

244

Harrison, Robert Pogue, *The Dominion of the Dead* (Chicago and London: Chicago University Press, 2003)

Heath, Michael, *Welcome to America* (London: Heinemann, 1985)

Heckscher, Eli F., *Mercantilism* (London: Routledge, 1994)

Hennessy, Peter, *The Secret State* (London: Penguin, 2003)

Henry, John, *Knowledge is Power: How Magic, the Government and an Apocalyptic Vision Inspired Francis Bacon to Create Modern Science* (Cambridge: Icon Books, 2003)

Henshall, Ian, and Rowland Morgan, *9/11 Revealed: Challenging the Facts Behind the War on Terror* (London: Robinson, 2005)

Hobsbawm, E. J., and T. O Ranger, *The Invention of Tradition* (Cambridge: Cambridge University Press, 1983)

Huntington, Samuel, *Who Are We?* (New York: Simon & Schuster, 2004)

Illouz, Eva, *Consuming the Romantic Utopia: Love and the Cultural Contradictions of Capitalism* (Berkeley: University of California Press, 1997)

Jacobs, A. J., *The Know-it-All: One Man's Humble Quest to Become the Smartest Person in the World* (London: Heinemann, 2005)

Johnson, Steven, *Everything Bad is Good for You: How Popular Culture is Making Us Smarter* (London: Allen Lane, 2005)

Judson, Olivia, *Dr Tatiana's Sex Advice to All Creation* (London: Chatto, 2002)

Kelley, Tom, and Jonathan Littman, *The Art of Innovation* (London: HarperCollins, 2001)

Kramer, Hilton, and Roger Kimball, 'Farewell to the MLA', *New Criterion* 13 (2 February 1995)

Laqueur, Thomas W., *Solitary Sex: A Cultural History of Masturbation* (New York: Zone, 2003)

Lefkowitz, Mary, *Greek Gods, Human Lives: What We Can Learn From Myths* (New Haven: Yale, 2003)

Lençek, Lena, and Gideon Bosker, *The Beach: The History of Paradise on Earth* (London: Secker and Warburg, 1998)

Levitt, Theodore, 'Creativity is not Enough', *Harvard Business Review*, 1963 (republished August 2002)

Lewis, Michael, *The New New Thing: A Silicon Valley Story* (London: Coronet/Hodder & Stoughton, 1999)

Lowe, Steve, and Alan McArthur, *Is it Just Me or Is Everything Shit?* (London: Time Warner, 2005)

Lowenthal, David, *The Heritage Crusade and the Spoils of History* (London: Viking, 1996)

Maltby, Richard, ed., *Dreams for Sale: Popular Culture in the 20th Century* (London: Harrap, 1989)

Mann, Charles C, 'Why Software is So Bad', *Technology Review* (July/August 2002)

Manning, Robert, *Credit Card Nation* (New York: Basic Books, 2004)

Mansfield, Harvey C., *Manliness* (New Haven: Yale University Press, 2006)

Mapping Strategic Knowledge (London: Sage, 2002)

Mauss, Marcel, Mary Douglas, *et al.*, *The Gift* (London: Routledge, 2001)

Micklethwait, John, and Adrian Wooldridge, *The Right Nation: Why America is Different* (London: Penguin, 2004)

Midgeley, Mary, *The Myths We Live By* (London: Routledge, 2004)

Miller, Stephen, *Conversation: A History of a Declining Art* (New Haven and London: Yale University Press, 2006)

Miller, William Ian, *Faking It* (Cambridge: Cambridge University Press, 2003)

Mount, Ferdinand, *Mind the Gap* (London: Short Books, 2004)

Murphy Paul, Annie, *The Cult of Personality* (New York: Free Press, 2004)

A National Identity Card for Canada? Report of the Standing Committee on Citizenship and Immigration (Ottawa, 2003)

Naughton, John, *A Brief History of the Future: The Origins of the Internet* (London: Phoenix/Orion, 2000)

Nuland, Sherwin, *How We Die* (London: Chatto and Windus, 1994)

O'Connor, Joseph, and Ian McDermott, *The Art of Systems Thinking: Essential Skills for Creativity and Problem-Solving* (London: Harper Collins/Thorsons, 1997)

O'Hagan, Andrew, 'Watching Me Watching Them Watching You', *London Review of Books*, 9 October 2003

Oborne, Peter, *The Rise of Political Lying* (London: Free Press and Simon & Schuster, 2005)

Ogilvy, David, *Confessions of an Advertising Man* (London: Pan, 1987)

Orwell, George, 'Politics and the English Language', *Horizon*, April 1946

Paul, Pamela, *Pornified: How Pornography is Transforming Our Lives, Our Relationships and Our Families* (New York: Times Books, 2005)

Perez, Carlos, 'The Navigator: Icons of Wristwatch Design', <http://www.timezone.com/library/cjrml>

Pinker, Steven, *The Blank Slate: The Modern Denial of Human Nature* (London: Allen Lane/Penguin, 2002)

Pipes, Daniel, *Conspiracy: How the Paranoid Style Flourishes and Where it Comes From* (New York: Free Press, 1997)

Pitkin, Walter B., *Short Introduction to the History of Human Stupidity* (London: Allen & Unwin, 1935)

Priestley, J. B., *English Journey* (1934; London: Mandarin, 1994)

Rowlands, Mark, *Everything I Know I Learned From TV* (London: Ebury, 2004)

Rubenhold, Hallie, *The Covent Garden Ladies: Pimp General Jack & the Extraordinary Story of Harris's List* (Stroud: Tempus, 2005)

Rybczynski, Witold, *One Good Turn: A Natural History of the Screwdriver & the Screw* (London: Scribner, 2001)

Schell, Jonathan, *The Fate of the Earth* (New York: Knopf, 1982)

Schlosser, Eric, *Fast Food Nation: What the All-American Meal is Doing to the World* (London: Allen Lane, 2001)

Schopenhauer, Arthur, and A. C. Grayling, *The Art of Always Being Right: Thirty-Eight Ways to Win When You Are Defeated* (London: Gibson Square Books, 2004)

Schor, Juliet B., *Born to Buy: The Commercialised Child and the New Consumer Culture* (New York: Scribner, 2005)

Schultz, Patricia, *1,000 Places to See Before You Die: A Traveler's Life List* (New York: Workman, 2003)

Schwartz, Barry, *The Paradox of Choice: Why More is Less* (New York: Ecco, 2004)

Segal, Alan, *Life After Death: A History of the Afterlife in Western Religions* (New York: Doubleday, 2004)

Sennett, Richard, 'The Age of Anxiety', *Guardian*, 23 October 2004

Shesgreen, Sean, *Images of the Outcast: The Urban Poor in the Cries of London From the Sixteenth to the Nineteenth Century* (Manchester: Manchester University Press, 2002)

Smith, Bruce R., *The Acoustic World of Early Modern England* (Chicago: University of Chicago Press, 1999)

Spang, Rebecca L., *The Invention of the Restaurant: Paris and Modern Gastronomic Culture* (Cambridge, MA, and London: Harvard University Press, 2000)

Steinberg, Neil, *Hatless Jack: The President, the Fedora and the Death of the Hat* (London: Granta, 2005)

Sternbergh, Adam, 'Up With Grups', *New York Magazine*, 3 April 2006

Stoppard, Tom, *Rosencrantz and Guildenstern Are Dead* (London: Faber, 1964)

Sutch, Dom Anthony, and Carol Midgley, 'I Believe all Children are Capable of Evil', *The Times*, 28 September 2004

Taverne, Dick, *The March of Unreason: Science, Democracy and the New Fundamentalism* (Oxford: Oxford University Press, 2005)

Truss, Lynn, *Talk to the Hand: The Utter Bloody Rudeness of Everyday Life, Or Six Good Reasons to Stay Home and Bolt the Door* (London: Profile, 2005)

Twitchell, James B., *Living it Up: Our Love Affair With Luxury* (New York: Columbia University Press, 2002)

van Boxsel, Matthijs, *The Encyclopaedia of Stupidity* (London: Reaktion Books, 2003)

van Gennep, Arnold, *The Rites of Passage*, ed. and trans. Monika B. Vizedom and Gabrielle A. Caffee (London: Routledge, 1960)

Waterhouse, Keith, *Office Life* (London: Michael Joseph, 1978)

Weizenbaum, Joseph, *Computer Power and Human Reason: From Judgement to Calculation* (London: Penguin, 1984)

Wheen, Francis, *How Mumbo-Jumbo Conquered the World* (London: Perennial, 2004)

White, T. H., *The Age of Scandal* (London: Jonathan Cape, 1950)

Wilkes, Roger, *Scandal: A Scurrilous History of Gossip* (London: Atlantic, 2002)

Williams Purcell, Kerry, *Weegee* (London: Phaidon Press, 2004)

Zengotita, Thomas de, *Mediated: How the Media Shape Your World* (London: Bloomsbury, 2005)

Index

as seen by Martian anthropologist, 208ff

sex, distorted thinking about, 130ff

a society of impostors, 50

spectators, not participants, 114

spied on by computer, 199

tendency to envy who they also despise, 50–51

tendency to food intolerance, 237

what do they do all day?, 197ff

what we lack, 47

40-year-old, pretending to be 22, 174

bin-j'Ja'abli, Reborzo, 79–80

biology, evolutionary, effect on sex life *see* poetry, Latin

Blair, Tony, curious insubstantiality of, 23

as compared to Homer Simpson, 56

Blockbuster Video, 100n

boat, God in same as us, 67

body, obsession with, men getting as bad as women, 123

Boeing *see* Rolls-Royce

book, fantasy, confiscated by security guard, 191

books, self-help, imbecilic, 2

bookshop, running away from, 8

Boom Generation *see* Baby Boomers

boomerang generation, 31

Boomers *see* Baby Boomers

boredom, dying of *vs.* living with, 113

bottoms, pert, men's, 138

Boy, the Fat, 173

boys, bad, 127

brain, enhancement of, 27

brand names
terrible justification for, 223
winsome shrivelling of, 108

breasts
cost of showing on television, 15
enlargement competition in *Zoo* magazine, 26
huge, sudden, 137
wife's, media want you to palpate, 130

British Airways, Senior Captain of,

author should have been, 33

brothers, all men are palpably not, 39

buggery, glum, 123

bugs, 12

bukkake, 6

bull accord, racy, 46

Bush, George W., curious insubstantiality of, 23

as compared to Homer Simpson, 56

business
idiocies of
bonding weekends, 6
mission statements, 5, 6
principles of, 30

C

cabin crew, announcements, peculiar syllabic stresses of, 16

calculation, modern obsession with, 233

call centres, 44
infantilisation of 'operatives' in, 205

Cambridge, role of Basque beret in, 84

cameras, hidden by silly policemen, 190

cancer, of housing market *see* *Daily Mail*

Canford Cliffs, mad landladies of, 166

celebrity
ignoring, 232
primary task of, 70

censorship, of elderly rock stars, 27

chavs, 1
see also youths

cherubim *see* necromancy

children, ill-raised, parents' making of excuses for, 131

children, UK government's desire not to punish, 18

chip, little, in this book, 9

Chomsky, Noam, trounced by Microsoft, 207

Christie, Father Joseph, S.J. *see* bin-j'Ja'abli, Reborzo

Cicero, observations on infantilism, 28

cirrhosis, popular accessories, 27
city, modern, riddled with dangers, 150
civil liberties, relentless erosion of, 3
clergymen
    adulterous, 20
    guitar-playing, 24
clothing
    democratisation of, as infantile, 92
    grammatology of, 91
    insane, 89 (*see also* hats; wristwatches)
    subtext-free, 88
Coca-Cola, as home sacrament, 100n
cocks, Kingsley Amis's worries about, 140
coffee
    anal, 190
    frothy, in special beaker, 65
cologne, subtextuality of, 99
combo, groovy hot-beat, Jesus's liking for, 24
comb-overs, revealing of wearers' attitude, 10
come, word offensive to Christians, 27
comedians, prevalence of, 17
commensality, a great virtue, 237
commodification, 2
communality
    bogus, 98
    in Greek tragedy, 100
Communion, Holy *see* typewriters, proper
competencies, key, 201
computer, screen, like Nietzsche's abyss, 199
computer games
    time spent playing, 116
    see also Second Life
conductor, world-renowned, author should have been, 33
conkers, compulsory goggles for, 191
Connolly, Billy, on politicians' comb-overs, 10
contact lenses, role in false reality, 66
Continent, The
    eating habits, peculiar, ravening, 166

    nudists of, author's mother's allure for, 167
contraceptive pill, invention of, 11
cookery, Viking implements used in, 109
coriander, hatred of, 73
corporations
    demand loyalty, offer none, 203
    infantilisation of staff, 200ff
    intolerance of hats, 86
    as psychopaths, 186
    team bonding weeks, 199
corpse, beautiful, Viennese, 226
cots, giant, 25
cow, embossed, 63
crabs, soft-shelled, bibs for, 6
credibility, curious, by contagion *see* Vorderman, Carol
credit cards, charges, potential illegality of, 101
creosote, significance of, 195
cries, ape, inarticulate, 2
Cruise, Tom, very much in love with a woman, 129
crusades, figurative and literal, 12

D
Daily Mail, 11
    devotion to ranting, 19
    like the Devil in Compline, 131
The Darling Principle, 185n
death
    the Deadly Pit of, 81
    as Nature's way of telling you off, 19
debt, consumer, vast, 44
    companies preying upon, 184
decency, defined by its absence, 1
Dell Computer, inability to accept compliments, 106
Derrida, Jacques, transcendental signified, Spice Girls' utterance as example of, 50
Desiderata, phony, sententious, 234
diarrhoea
    litigation, 192
    precursor of VD, 167
dictatorships, historical models for establishing
    Roman, 221

as used by Tony Blair, 214
diegesis, usefulness of word, 17
dinosaur heads, rubber, patronising, 149
discrimen, quality of, 38–39
Distraction, the Age of, 114
divorce, author's shame over, 135
Doctor Faustus, 41
doctors
  generic, addicted, 20
  homicidal, 191
  not having a lifestyle, 121–122
  see also translation
Do-It-Yourself, the proper clothing for, 90
Donne, John, 113
dress
  appropriate, disappearance of concept, 91
  national, 84–85
  public, infantile, 70
  religious, absurdity of concept, 91
dress codes, rigid informality of, 204
dribble, blotting, 41
Dupree, James James Morrison Morrison Weatherby George, 212
duty, social, shopping, 43

E
eating disorders
  'bigorexia', 137
  not just confined to women, 123
egg custard, warning of presence of eggs in, 18
Eldorado *see* fealty
Eliot, George, quote misattributed to, 32
emergency, unlikely, 16
emissions, untoward, 8
emotion, selling nothing except *see* Lottery, National
emperors
  life of, seeping downwards, 21
  similarity of modern population to, 17
enforcers, grit-faced, 19
Epic of Gilgamesh, The, 169, 233
Erinmore Flake, as smoked by school caretaker, 69

erosion, relentless, of civil liberties, 3
escalator, assumptions of people's not knowing what to do on, 14
estimates, authorial, not to be relied on, 240
Et in Arcadia ego, 227
ether, interstellar, 57
ethnicities, Balkanisation of, 12
experience, shared, assumptions of by advertisers, 97

F
family, conviviality of, vanquished by hypersexuality, 135
Family Values, 129
fathers, deluded, 175
fealty *see* paregoric
feather and badge, how to obtain, 29
Fedora Lounge, The, 90
  see also hats
femfresh, as metonym for everything monstrous, 95ff
Fennimore (forename forgotten)
  author urged to be liked, refused to comply, 128
  not like Jesus, 129
  seen on train years later, 129
field reports, on prostitutes *see* Punternet
fingers, fish, diagnostic of infantilisation, 88
firefighters, banned from running, 14
fireworks, laws about, 223
First Great Western, train company, function of word 'First' in name, 164n
Firstplus, loan consolidation company, banal advertising pitch of, 101
Fna'a, the Ark of *see* bin-j'Ja'abli, Reborzo
fog *see* cherubim
food
  dancing, 6
  dangerous, 190
  in-flight, EasyJet, 165
  intolerances, not tolerating them, 237
  squid, worms and foreign muck, 123

pre-post-modern, left alone to get on with it, 121–122

telegraph-pole, 195

mandragora *see* Eldorado

manners, importance of, 239

marine antifreeze protein, allegedly, 26

mayhem, not actually the problem, 159

McDonald's, slogan obviously nonsense, 15

McGegan, Nicholas, 69

McJobs, 172

McNeil, Duncan MSP, 14

McVitie (biscuit manufacturer), the alleged passions of, 110

mead, 139

media
  assumption of borderline psychosis in consumers, 16
  describing back to us what we already know, 3
  what they want us to be, 130

medicine
  alternative, non-existent body parts in, 146
  Chinese (*see* fortune-telling)

meltdown, parasympathetic, 125

men, repo, 2

Men's Health Forum, 123

mensch
  defining qualities of, 23
  vanishing concept of, 22

meteorology, as subject to the will, 86

methadone, adding contraceptives to, 14

methodologies, quality assurance, 201

Microsoft
  infantilising advertisement, 207
  infantilising software, 149

Milne, A A, 212

minstrels *see* phoenicopters

mission statements, 5, 6
  imbecilic, 26 (*see also* slogans)
  see also God

Modern & Mature, (magazine), 6

modern life, apparent insubstantiality of, 6

Modernity, the awful trap of, 32ff

money laundering, 13

monitoring, universal, 200–204

morons, mêlée of *see* escalator

Morrell, author's early passion for, 196

mosquito-bites, Mexican, horrors of, 170

mothers, deluded, 175

Mount Everest, hypoxia holidays, 19

Muji Effect, the, 62

mullahs, not to mention paedophiles, 1

Mummyverse, the, 48, 126, 212ff, 231
  confusion of hazard and risk, 183

murder, number seen by American children, 15

Murdoch, machine, 51

muscles
  abdominal, uselessness of, 92
  in general, uselessness of, 122

music
  attributes of, 116–117
  middle-aged people 'keeping up with', 235

N

name, unnecessary, 105

National Consumer Council, disappointed about big chocolate bars, 189

Nature
  how it designed us, 127
  living in harmony with, not to mention ectoplasm, 139
  the one thing it insists upon, 182

necromancy *see* hieroglyphics

neoteny, of porn stars' faces, 137

New York, subway ban on photography, 192

Newman, Randy, 114

news, good *see* Bell, Martin

newspaper columnists, pompous, vapid, spluttering, hypocritical, 20

newspapers, Sunday, repulsive qualities of their heroes, 50–51

Niebuhr, Reinhold (1892 - 1971), author of the 'Serenity Prayer', 15n

no-fly list, everyone called John
    Thomas is on it, 189
Normal, Mr & Mrs, views on sex
    romp *(q.v.)*, 20
Norton, Graham, 71
notices
    on aeroplanes, 187
    insane proliferation of on First
        Great Western train, 160ff
    porridge, warning, 193
    tyranny of, 153ff
    wing mirror, metaphysical, 158
    see also pictograms
Nottingham
    East Circus Street, 196
    see also Arboretum
nudity, Continental, acceptable, 167
Nuns, Three, and the vicar, 47n
nuts, peanuts may contain, 155–156

O
Oakland, California, what's there, 23
Oedipus Rex, nothing illicit about, 134
offices, what goes on in them?, 198ff
Oliver, Jamie, his qualities, 109
one, going off on, tendency of the
    infantile to, 37
onions, cleaning product tested on,
    191
orange juice, new and improved,
    how?, 25
Orange (telecoms company) *see*
    animals, anthropomorphic
organ, crumbling, 194
organ music, effect on sex life *see*
    poetry, Latin
organs, pipe, facing extinction
    through bureaucracy, 185
orgasms *see* wolves
orientalism, in music, 117
Orwell, George, on advertising, 46
Oryan Tar, author as a Three King
    of, 81
O'Toole, Peter, definition of acting, 17
outcast, oiled, 9

P
paedophiles
    harmlessness of, it's pederasts you
        want to watch out for, 189

not to mention mullahs, 1
paedophilia, the modern Satan, 133
Palm Beach County, homophobia of,
    133
paranoia, catalogue of, 169
paregoric *see* umbrellas
parents
    elderly, transfixed, 183
    infantile, infantilising their
        children, 175
    Worried Sick, 194
parents, UK government's desire to
    punish, 18
parking, death penalty for, 152
Parris, Matthew, explanation of
    politicians, 186
parrot, foul-mouthed, 194
pasta, boiling, what to do while it's,
    108
Patience & Prudence, not virtues but
    singers, 104
pavements, gum-flecked, 2
pension funds, depredation of, 12
peppers, as seen on TV, 102
perfume, banned, 168
petrol station, refuses to sell petrol,
    15
Philadelphia processed cheese,
    smeared on chicken, 108
phoenicopters *see* Aramaic
photographs, digital, no need to look
    at them, 107
pick-up artists, 136
pictograms, incomprehensible, 16,
    160ff
    on aircraft control panel,
        apparently a bassoon, 163
pills, lethal, easy-to-swallow, 190
pilot
    author's inability to accept he is
        one, 76ff
    fictional qualities of, 77–78
    real qualities of, particularly
        fretfulness, 77
pipe-smoking *see* minstrels
Pitkin, Walter, on stupidity, 145
Place, a time when People Knew
    Their, 139
planet, stable, 11
plastic surgery, 226ff

poetry, Latin, effect on sex life, 11n
poker, maxims as lesson for life, 130
police state, tactics of, re-emergence, 215
policemen
    clamping down on trick-or-treat, 191
    hidden, out of harm's way, 190
    invisible, 2
politicians
    and Asperger's Syndrome, 218ff
    generic, corrupt, 20
    mouths, unappealing qualities of, 38
        legislation issuing from, 145
    referring to 'ordinary people', 238
    safety concerns purely financial, 184
    sodomitical, 1
    unsavoury nature explained, 186
Polonius, sententiousness of, 34
Pope Benedict XII (C14), 132
popsters, drug-fried, 1
pornography, online, dreary predictability of, 137
porridge, warning, 193
Post Office queue rage, 157
postmodern world
    the conditional nature of, 49
    spooky hauntological contingencies of, 155
poultry, what they never knew, 140
Poussin, Nicolas, 227
poverty, old people facing see pension funds
power, phallocentric, massive, illegal, 216
powers, special, precursors of dictatorship, 221
Prayer, Serenity see Serenity Prayer
Priestley, J. B., displeased with Britain, 59–60
productivity, endless monitoring of, pointless, 203
promises, never trust, 240
pronouns, gendered, no point in complaining about, 30
prostate see breasts, wife's
prostitutes
    mimetic skills of, 51–53

website for reviewing (*see* Punternet)
psychosis, borderline *see* media
Punternet (prostitute review website), 51
Pythagoras *see* guano
pythons, mothers poised like, 157

Q
questions, tricky, 125

R
rape, date, 6
reader, stern, 97
reality, television as only measure of, 53
Reality Lite, 53
regret, foolish things we tend to, 139
relativism
    denounced, 235
    ethical, 10
    pinioning, 34
religion, three-part cycle of, 3
    invention of new, 79–80
respect, slogans concerning, 61
respect, Czar, 26, 237
revenants *see* mead
rhubarb, a symptom of blibber trouble, 146
rhymes and jingles, silly, 7
Richelieu, Cardinal, on reasons to hang a man, 214
ring-tones, 224
risk
    definition, 183
    primal desire to confront, 183
risk assessment
    the new religion, 177
    pushing over gravestones, 178
rites of passage, 50
rituals, apotropaic, contemporary, 11
    see also safety culture
road signs
    terrifying, meaningless, 188
    distracting, dangerous, 190
'Road Warriors', as synonym for travelling middle-manager, 170
rodents, hypervigilant, 188

Rolls-Royce, meaningless
    advertisement with Boeing, 206
root cause analysis, 177
Rowlands, Mark, philosopher, 32
Royal National Theatre, Artistic
    Director of, author should have
    been, 33
running, dangerous for firemen, 13

262